LAYERS OF TRUTH

Praise for *Layers of Truth*

Rosalie Turner's book takes an inside look at the Mississippi Freedom Summer Project 1964, and focuses on the lives and personal involvement of many of the unsung heroes of the Movement. To learn our true history, this is a must read. I strongly endorse this book.

—Charles McLaurin, a SNCC Field Secretary in the Mississippi Delta and director of Freedom Summer in Sunflower County Mississippi.

Rosalie Turner's riveting novel speaks to the truth of justice, voter's rights, freedom, and a quest to challenge an unfair system that deprived a people equality shared by others. The book explains the essence of a Civil Rights Movement determined not to let anyone turn them around. A must read for anyone seeking to gain knowledge on how a resolute mind can make a difference.

—Dr. LaVelle Hendricks, LCDC, ADC, C-ART, Professor/Department Head of Counseling, Texas A&M University-Commerce

Raw, riveting, racially charged, and revolutionary. Rosalie Turner weaves together a rich tapestry of the historic 1964 Freedom Summer as she recounts the raucous stories of the black and white Northern college students who valiantly risked their lives to register black Mississippians to vote in the upcoming national election. This is a story of bold and daring young men and women who encountered danger and brutality but whose determination and resilience would not allow them to abandon their resolve to focus America's attention on the rampant racial inequality and political degradation in the state of Mississippi. This is a must read for every American who truly wants to understand and embrace a moment in the long and checkered past of Voting Rights for black people in the United States.

—Zoila Airall, PhD, is an Educational Anthropologist and Duke University Adjunct Faculty member in the Program in Education.

LAYERS OF TRUTH

A novel set during the turbulent
1964 Mississippi Freedom Summer Project

ROSALIE T. TURNER

SUNSTONE
PRESS

SANTA FE

Sunstone books may be purchased for educational, business, or sales promotional use.
For information please write: Special Markets Department, Sunstone Press,
P.O. Box 2321, Santa Fe, New Mexico 87504-2321.
Printed on acid-free paper

eBook 978-1-61139-702-4

Library of Congress Cataloging-in-Publication Data

Names: Turner, Rosalie T., 1941- author.
Title: Layers of truth : a novel set during the turbulent 1964 Mississippi
    Freedom Summer Project / Rosalie T. Turner.
Description: Santa Fe : Sunstone Press, [2023] | Includes reader's guide. |
    Summary: "The story of Mississippi's 1964 Freedom Summer through the
    eyes of student Lenore Rogers, when a thousand northern white students
    descended upon the state to work with the Black grassroots organization
    of the Student Nonviolent Coordinating Committee (SNCC) and created a
    crucible of love and hate that reverberates to this day"-- Provided by
    publisher.
Identifiers: LCCN 2023000496 | ISBN 9781632935373 (paperback) | ISBN
    9781632937087 (hardcover) |ISBN 9781611397024 (epub)
Subjects: LCSH: Mississippi Freedom Project--Fiction. | Student Nonviolent
    Coordinating Committee (U.S.)--Fiction. | LCGFT: Novels.
Classification: LCC PS3620.U76595 L39 2023 | DDC 813.6--dc23/
    eng/20230201 LC record available at https://lccn.loc.gov/2023000496

WWW.SUNSTONEPRESS.COM
SUNSTONE PRESS / POST OFFICE BOX 2321 / SANTA FE, NM 87504-2321 /USA
(505) 988-4418

DEDICATION

This book is dedicated to those foot soldiers whose names may never be known, yet without whom there could not have been a Civil Rights Movement. It is in their honor that we must not let our voting rights be compromised.

PREFACE

My mentor once told me that a writer is someone who can't *not* write. For most of us who write, it's not about the dreams of prestige or imagined income. It's about a passion we have, a passion that burns inside us for release, and we can't *not* write about it.

My passion is sharing the background of the Civil Rights Movement; the horrors of slavery, the injustice of the Jim Crow laws, the brutality to keep Blacks as second-class citizens, and the amazing courage of people who dared to hope amidst hopelessness.

Layers of Truth tells the story of some of those people during what has become known as Freedom Summer. At its inception in 1964, it was simply called the Mississippi Summer Project, a visionary attempt to bring a thousand college students, mostly northern whites, to work with a Black grassroots organization to help Black Mississippians register to vote, to set up Freedom Schools, and to establish community centers.

The summer began with the news of three of their number gone missing—and presumed murdered by the Ku Klux Klan. That was only the beginning.

Every person who was working for social justice at that time was putting their life on the line. Every Black who tried to register to vote and every single Black household that provided housing for the thousand who came down was in jeopardy. Every one of them. *Layers of Truth* tells the story of that summer not only for the reader to learn or remember, but as an affirmation of those individuals. There are names in this book that you will never see in history books, but they, along with thousands of unnamed "foot soldiers", were as important to the Movement as were Dr. King and Rosa Parks.

This was the early 1960s. There was a rumble stirring through the country; the cusp of the women's liberation movement, the polarization over the Vietnam War, the changing music and morals, the beginnings of recognizing the rights of gays, the assassination of President Kennedy, and, of course, the Civil Rights Movement.

The federal government was not interested in getting involved in the increasing pressure to intervene in civil rights issues, but when Bull Connor, Birmingham, Alabama's Commissioner of Public Safety, unleashed the fire hoses and the dogs during the Children's March in May 1963, President John Kennedy was compelled to submit civil rights legislation to Capitol Hill in June.

As the summer of 1964 started, the Civil Rights Act that President Kennedy originally proposed was still struggling through the quagmire of government. The state of Mississippi had been a leader in working against the bill by pouring large amounts of money against it, especially in states that had not made up their mind about supporting the legislation.

In the meantime, the Student Nonviolent Coordinating Committee, a predominately southern Black organization was becoming a force to be reckoned with. SNCC (pronounced "Snick") had been formed at Shaw College in Raleigh, North Carolina in 1960. Ella Baker, one of the founders of the SCLC (Southern Christian Leadership Council) was inspired by the sit-ins started by the four young men in Greensboro, North Carolina in 1960, but she felt the NAACP and SCLC weren't reaching the young people. She gathered a group of college students to form a grassroots organization that would be directed not from the top down but run by consensus of the young workers.

SNCC had attracted a few workers from the north, one of whom was Bob Moses. He had been born in Harlem, the son of a janitor. While working on his PhD at Harvard, Moses had to return to the city because of a family crisis and was teaching math there when he learned about SNCC. He headed for Mississippi and in Amite County he met Amzie Moore. "Don't bother with sit-ins," Amzie advised. "We can't afford to eat out anyway. Concentrate on voter registration."

That was good advice for all of Mississippi because the statistics were shocking. Only 6.7% of the eligible Black voters in Mississippi were registered to vote, the lowest percentage in the country. Panola County, for example, had only two people registered representing .02% of the county. Clarke County, with almost 3,000 eligible, had only one registered, and in Lamar County there were none.

Bob Moses had been working for three years with SNCC with little success and no national interest. After a chance meeting with Allard Lowenstein, an educator and activist, the idea of bringing in white students, which Lowenstein could provide with his connections to Yale and Stanford, took shape in 1963. Moses expanded the idea into a three-pronged summer project in 1964: bring down a thousand northern college students to register Black voters; set up Freedom Schools and community centers; and establish the Mississippi Freedom Democratic Party which would go to the National Democratic Convention in Atlantic City in August. With the anticipated national publicity that Bob Moses hoped for, the Summer Project would finally bring America to Mississippi.

It wouldn't be easy, Moses knew. There would be beatings, bombings, harassment and jailings. Maybe even deaths. But, he believed, it was the time and Mississippi was the place. He expected the stories of the beatings and bombings and what really happened that summer to come out, and he wanted the stories known.

I want the stories known, too, and that is why I spent the past two and a half years researching and writing *Layers of Truth*. I used not only all the books and video sources available, but also I went to the archival materials. The most important part of my research, however, was talking with the foot soldiers, spending time with them as they showed me the places and told me the stories.

These are the stories I want to share with you. As you read, I hope your imaginations will put you in that time and place. I believe you will find it not only meaningful, but also very relevant to our world today. I hope you will discuss what you've read with your book clubs, with family and friends as this book could be a steppingstone toward understanding and learning more about racial justice in our country.

Because the term "Negro" was in use as the proper name for Blacks in 1964, and the story is told through the eyes of Lenore in that year, I have usually used "Negro" rather than "Black." The term "Black" was beginning to be used by Blacks at that time so it is also used in this novel. Many older Blacks might also use the term "colored."

Many adapted quotes during the Ohio training session are adapted from the video *Freedom Summer* by PBS American Experience, written, produced, and directed by Stanley Nelson, as well as from other archival sources.

ACKNOWLEDGEMENTS

Just as it takes a village to raise a child, so it is with bringing a book to fruition. *Layers of Truth* would not have been possible without the critiquing, editing and support of Carol Norton. I could not have done it without Marietta Goes, early readers such as my Bridge Buddies, Karen Hearth, Brenda Wolfe, and Gail Ditkof, and part of our "Gang of Six, Giesla Pollock, and Jennifer Klein. I am especially grateful to Charles "Mac" McLaurin, one of the "foot soldiers" of the Movement, for showing me all the places and telling me the stories. The final editing of Jennifer Huston Schaefer was a tremendous help. I am grateful to the team at Sunstone Press for bringing the book forward.

As always, it is the support and love of my husband, Frank Kile Turner, who makes all the difference for me.

1

This summer SNCC, in cooperation with COFO, is launching a massive Peace Corps-type operation in Mississippi. Students, teachers, technicians, nurses, artists, and legal advisors will be recruited to come to Mississippi to staff a large range of programs that include voter registration, Freedom Schools, community centers, and special projects.

—Student Nonviolent Coordinating Committee (SNCC)Recruiting Pamphlet

On that early June morning in 1964, Bob Moses was dressed simply in a white T-shirt and overalls on his slightly built body. Dark-rimmed glasses framed his finely chiseled face, his skin a hardy chestnut hue. At first, he stood before us with his gaze lowered. Even so, his low-key voice calmly reached out and pulled us closer. When he did look around the room and told us the truths about a summer in Mississippi, the conviction in his voice led us into his world.

He drew an outline of Mississippi on the blackboard and explained how the power of cotton had shaped the economy of the state. He told us about the White Citizens' Councils and the Klan. He also informed us of the attempts the Black grassroots organization SNCC, the Student Nonviolent Coordinating Committee, was taking to get Washington involved and how getting the participation of white students might garner the attention needed. Moses talked about nonviolence: how essential it was and what it meant to the Civil Rights Movement. As he spoke, I felt the barriers between the SNCC workers and the students melt away. And

11

in that moment, I began to believe we might become one force working together to change the world.

"Maybe you need to hear about some of the people in Mississippi—the individuals who can no longer speak for themselves. There was a man in Amite County...Herbert Lee was his name, and he wanted to vote. Mr. Lee was a farmer, and he farmed near a white neighbor, a state legislator named E.H. Hurst. Lee and Hurst had managed to coexist for many years; they even helped each other out from time to time. But when Mr. Lee decided he wanted to vote, Mr. Hurst became enraged. On a September day in 1961, Mr. Lee drove to the mill in a town called Liberty. Hurst pulled up next to Lee, waved a gun at him, and yelled at him that he'd had enough. 'I ain't talkin' to you while you got that gun,' Lee shouted as he scooted to the passenger side of his truck and jumped out. Hurst got out of his truck, approached Lee, and shot him dead, right there." Bob Moses stopped speaking, looked down, and shook his head.

"Herbert Lee died on that spot, in plain sight of several men who never would testify that they'd seen anything. Those Black men were afraid to say anything for fear of losing their jobs...or worse. Recently, Louis Allen, one of the men who'd witnessed Mr. Lee's murder, decided to talk to the FBI about what he'd seen that day. When some white folks found out about it, they harassed him so brutally that he planned to leave the state. However, three days before he was scheduled to leave, he too was shot dead."

Bob Moses scanned the room slowly as if he were looking each of us in the eye. "That's life in Mississippi," he said quietly. "Believe it, and be sure you want to join us."

That was our introduction to being part of the Freedom Summer Project. *That was as subtle as a slap in the face,* I thought.

~~~

The truth was that none of my summer plans had been smooth and easy, and it was all Jane's fault.

My adventure with SNCC began back in March 1964. We'd had a few unseasonably warm days in New York City, and the forsythia was already in bloom. Along with the surprise of forgotten warmth on a spring day, the seeds of summer were planted for me at Barnard College when my best friend, Jane Carson, brought a Freedom Summer Project brochure to my dorm room. It explained the goal of setting up Freedom Schools and community centers throughout Mississippi as well as working to get Blacks registered to vote.

I already had a summer job, so I tried to brush Jane off. But then she said, "It's the Peace Corps right here in our own country!"

Jane and I had talked about the possibility of joining the Peace Corps after graduation the following year, so she'd definitely gotten my attention. Even so, I wasn't ready to concede anything just yet.

"Lenore Rogers, don't be so stubborn! I've known you almost all my life, and I know you'd love this experience."

"I'll read it," I muttered. "But after I do my homework."

Jane gave me one of her looks and turned to leave after placing the brochure on my desk. She paused at the door and threw me a final grin. "They're coming to campus next week to interview. I signed us up," she said, closing the door behind her before I had the chance to protest.

I knew I was caught.

And so, Jane and I became two of the hundreds of young students who, figuratively, prepared to pick up the banner of "all men are created equal" and march across Mississippi. However, it wasn't an easy banner to raise. After all, it had been dragged through the mud of the Civil War, through the failure of the Reconstruction period, and more recently, held down by Jim Crow laws. Nevertheless, when SNCC came calling on university campuses with their flyers promising...well, nothing really... many of us were still ready to join the ranks.

~~~

In early June, three months after those spring campus interviews, Jane and I reported for a week's training in Oxford, Ohio. Bedraggled and weary after a long, overnight bus ride, I was already trying to remember why I'd let her talk me into this. Somehow, the idea of working with SNCC to build bridges toward equality and learn about the enigma of the Jim Crow South had held an idealistic appeal back at Barnard in March. But at this point, I was sweaty, grumpy, and unsure of what I had gotten myself into. I cared about desegregation, of course. It was the South—this strange land I'd only read about—that made me uneasy. I just didn't know what to expect.

A SNCC staff member named Marcus met us and stowed our luggage in the back of a tired-looking station wagon. I felt a little uneasy as I wondered if Marcus, with his almost ebony skin, would feel like a chauffeur to a carful of whites.

Jane and I climbed over the station wagon's torn vinyl middle seat and made our way to the back. Two girls, who introduced themselves as Lynn and Sue, and a boy in a Yale T-shirt took the other seats. We all wore the same exhausted expression of travelers who would welcome a bath and a change of clothes, but the Yalie, who finally introduced himself as Phillip, immediately began peppering Marcus with questions.

"When will our first workshop be?"

As he shifted the car into gear, Marcus glanced at Phillip. "Most everyone'll be here by this evening, so we'll gather together at dinner then go into the first session tomorrow morning."

Phillip pressed him further. "And the leaders of these workshops, they're SNCC staff members who've been working down in Mississippi already?"

Marcus's raised eyebrows reflected in the rearview mirror. "Yes, sir, my friend. Our people have already been down there working."

I wondered if everyone caught the sarcasm in Marcus's tone.

He continued, "We'll be sharing all you need to know about getting folks registered to vote in Mississippi and what you'll be teaching in the Freedom Schools."

Lynn, the blonde in the middle seat, leaned forward eagerly and said, "I've been reading up on the situation a lot. I'm really looking forward to helping the older Negroes see how important it is to get registered to vote." With her eagerness overflowing, she beamed at Sue beside her.

Marcus's smile tightened. "Uh-huh," he mumbled.

"How many of us will there be?" Phillip continued.

"About two hundred fifty. By the time we have everyone trained, there'll be about a thousand. Most are college students like y'all, but we also have some teachers, doctors, and such. You'll be placed in towns all over the state. Of course, in the next few weeks, a lot of you will drop out... or we'll suggest you spend your summer someplace else," Marcus added with a chuckle.

"Well, I won't be dropping out," Lynn's ponytail bounced with her confident nod. I was mentally giving that blonde ponytail a yank when Jane placed her hand on my arm. The moment passed in silence.

Marcus used the mirror to glance back at us. "Maybe y'all will think again about staying when you learn what it's like in Mississippi." His face had lost its friendly smile. "Do y'all even know that yesterday was the first anniversary of when Medgar Evers was killed in Jackson? Shot in the back in his own driveway with his family there."

After an awkward moment of silence, Sue chimed in. "I remember hearing about Medgar Evers on the news, and I know he was important in the Civil Rights Movement. Uh, would you tell us a little more about him...about what he did?"

Marcus's hands tensed on the steering wheel. His impatience with us was showing through. He took a deep breath. "He was a World War II vet who fought for his country and came home to the same Jim Crow laws as before. He worked with the NAACP." Marcus glanced around before continuing. "You *do* know what the NAACP is, don't you?"

Lynn started to raise her hand then quickly lowered it. "The National Association for the Advancement of Colored People," she answered with a bright smile.

Jane's hazel eyes met mine. We wordlessly agreed that Lynn would likely be one of those not staying.

"Right," replied Marcus. "Medgar Evers was the first field secretary of the NAACP in Mississippi, and he was working for voter rights and equality in all kinds of ways. You'll learn about him and lots of others this week."

For the rest of the ride, we all remained quiet as an uneasy tension rose and slithered through the vehicle. I wondered what other unexpected feelings might surface during the upcoming week and throughout the summer.

A short time later, the station wagon swung onto an expansive driveway, revealing a view of the sprawling Western College for Women campus. As soon as we entered the registration hall, a wave of excited voices spilled over us and pulled us into the mass of volunteers already there. After the strained silence of the ride, we were ready to let the energy and bustle of the crowd envelop us.

Later, Jane and I made our way across sweeping green lawns and past columned brick buildings toward our dorm. Our room was on the second floor and was connected to another bedroom through a shared bathroom.

"Please don't let Lynn be in that other room," I whispered to Jane.

Jane chuckled. "Careful! She might end up being your new best friend."

Luckily, the girls we shared a bathroom with turned out to be very pleasant. Mary Etta attended Wellesley and Ann the University of Portland in Oregon. We spent the time before dinner getting to know each other and speculating on what the summer would be like.

After a quick shower and dinner, things were looking up. That evening, recruits and trainers gradually wandered outside and gathered under the trees as dusk eased around us, the heat of the day quietly leaving without us really noticing.

There appeared to be two distinct groups: the white college students and the SNCC staff members. The white college students dressed in casual summer dresses with Peter Pan collars or Bermuda shorts and polo shirts. Many of the SNCC trainers dressed like their leader, Bob Moses, in white T-shirts and denim bib overalls. Compared to the recruits with their guitars and easy laughter, the SNCC trainers carried a seriousness about them, an edgy aloofness. They were the Negroes toiling on the front lines. I'd read about the beatings, the burning crosses, the shootings, and the lynchings. *What did it feel like to be the target of such abuse?* I wondered, but I couldn't even begin to imagine. I shivered and rubbed my arms. It was possible that I would soon know what it felt like. *Have I made a mistake in signing up for this?*

Small clusters of young people moved throughout the lawn, shifting, sliding, easing together. I wasn't sure where it had started, but soon the familiar words from my Vacation Bible School days reached my ears:

> "This little light of mine,
> I'm gonna let it shine;
> Let it shine, let it shine, let it shine."

Groups folded in together around a short, stout woman leading the singing.

"Who's that?" I asked the man next to me.

He looked like he might be a SNCC staffer, and his expression indicated that I should know who the woman was. Even so, he politely answered, "That's Mrs. Hamer. Fannie Lou Hamer."

"Oh, yes, of course." I nodded and made a mental note to quickly learn who Fannie Lou Hamer was.

As the singing continued in the darkness, I became caught up in the music and the moment. The leaders from Mississippi revealed the strength and courage of the Civil Rights Movement song by song, while we white recruits picked up their words, making their hope and determination our own. The voice of Fannie Lou Hamer, who was evidently legendary, spiraled over and around us, wrapping us in the warmth and emotion of the music. By the close of the evening, as the entire group swayed with linked arms, singing "We Shall Overcome," Jane and I smiled at each other and, without words, affirmed, for that moment at least, that we had made the right decision.

~~~

On Monday morning, Jane and I entered the cafeteria with its smells of coffee and bacon, the clanking of silverware and plates on trays, and the hum of voices. It wasn't long before we sensed a difference in the group. The easy camaraderie of singing Movement songs was gone. In its place was an unspoken tension, an invisible barrier between the whites and the Negroes, the students and the teachers, the recruits and the staff members.

The SNCC workers ate quickly and quietly at their own tables then left to prepare for the day's activities. We white students continued to eat and get to know each other, but our conversations were less punctuated by the carefree laughter of the day before.

After breakfast, Jane and I migrated toward the building designated for the day's meetings. We entered through double doors to an auditorium filled with rows of wooden seats connected by metal armrests. It had the familiar worn look and stuffy smell that took me back to high school assemblies.

We eased into seats in the middle of the crowded room. I sat down next to a young Negro who could've been a volunteer or a member of SNCC. He was slumped casually in his seat and nodded at me when I sat down.

"Hi, I'm Lenore Rogers," I greeted him with what I hoped was a friendly smile.

"Luke," he replied, holding out his hand. "Luke Guthrie."

I briefly studied his genial, open expression, lips that almost twitched into a smile, high forehead, and closely cropped hair.

In spite of the hubbub from people settling in, I asked as I shook his hand, "Are you a college student or are you with SNCC to train us?"

"What makes you think that no one in SNCC would be a college student?" he growled, his tone ringing with disapproval.

I cringed. "What? That's not what I meant!"

Just as I was ready to kick myself, Luke grinned. "I'm only messin' with you, girl. I'm with SNCC, and part of our trainin' is to help you develop a thick skin. You'll need it when you get to Mississippi. I graduated from Jackson State, by the way."

I rolled my eyes at him and turned forward as the first speaker signaled for attention.

Luke whispered, "Just sayin'. You gotta learn not to react to anything said or done to you, that's all."

I smiled and nodded. I figured that was probably good advice.

The morning passed quickly after Bob Moses gave his introductory talk. SNCC trainers revealed through firsthand stories what life in Mississippi was really like for Negroes. I winced often, appalled to hear reports of being dragged from cars, beaten with sticks or fists, kicked, and spat upon. Sitting beside someone who had probably endured those same things made me very aware of Luke's tall, lean stature. In such close quarters, there was an occasional tickle of our arms touching, mine so safely pale and white in contrast to his.

The SNCC staff members explained what we should expect—that we also might be subjected to the same kind of treatment. I listened, but I simply could not imagine it. One of the strongest warnings was about nighttime. The darkness would be a time of terror and violence, definitely a time to be afraid and be on one's guard. That was not the kind of night I was used to. The trainers explained a system of safety checks they had established, strict rules to be followed. Throughout the morning, I began to abandon the image I had of the South as a beautiful, gentle place filled with magnolias and people who spoke with softly rounded accents. On the contrary, the South I was meeting at this training was definitely a harsh and foreboding place.

Throughout the talks, Luke made little side comments to me, such as a few words about the speaker or emphasizing something that was said. When the alerts about nighttime were given, Luke nudged me and warned, "This is really important. Don't forget it."

Luke was friendly, but so many of the SNCC staffers acted like we volunteers annoyed them. They impatiently answered questions the volunteers brought up during their talks. They weren't rude, exactly; they just made us feel like we didn't quite measure up. But I was hopeful that things would be better by the end of the week.

After dinner that evening, everyone wandered outside again. But this time, there was no joining together and singing freedom songs. Instead, the SNCC workers slipped away to make plans and iron out concerns, while we volunteers scattered into small groups around campus. Some clustered around individuals who had guitars and sang Pete Seeger's "If I Had a Hammer" and "Where Have All the Flowers Gone." Others discussed the day's lectures. As we talked about what we'd heard that day, we asked questions. What are they trying to teach us? How are we supposed to respond? What would our parents do if they heard about how dangerous this is? And, finally, what would it be like to live in a Negro community in Mississippi?

As I observed the dynamics between the SNCC staff members and the volunteers more closely, I began to understand a little more of what was going on. Both groups had felt a connection when Bob Moses spoke and when we sang freedom songs together, but little by little, that feeling ebbed away and an uneasiness began to thrum under the surface. Deep down, neither group was comfortable with the other.

If the SNCC workers from Mississippi didn't like us volunteers, didn't trust us, and didn't want us to work with them, then why did they ask us to join them this summer?

I had expected to be at ease with the Negroes from the Deep South. In my previous summer jobs working with kids from New York's Lower East Side, I'd felt a strong connection with Negroes and Hispanics. The difference I was feeling here puzzled me. I couldn't help but wonder: *Is the stumbling block coming from them...or from me?*

2

We affirm the philosophical or religious ideal of nonviolence as the foundation of our purpose.... Through nonviolence, courage displaces fear; love transforms hate. Acceptance dissipates prejudice; hope ends despair. Peace dominates war; faith reconciles doubt. Mutual regard cancels enmity. Justice for all overcomes injustice.

—SNCC Statement of Purpose

"Love! Mutual regard! That's garbage!" a SNCC trainer hollered and jumped to his feet when Reverend James Lawson recited the SNCC mission statement at the next morning's workshop. "I've been to Parchman Prison, the hellhole of Mississippi, and I've been beaten. And I gotta tell you, that gives me second thoughts about wanting to follow a code of nonviolence."

Reverend Lawson raised a hand to appease him. "Stokely, it's true that a beating can be the price of turning the other cheek, but in the long run, the price is worth it."

Stokely Carmichael shook his head, his hands gripped in fists by his side. "No! Nonviolence was effective when it was new and different, but that time has passed! Now it just looks like we're afraid to stand up to the Man." A few resounding "amens" and many more "not trues" filled the room. Soon the volunteers joined in the debate—a debate that went on throughout the morning session.

We all agreed that the concept of not reacting violently while being abused went against human nature, yet we knew it was an absolute requirement of being part of the Civil Rights Movement. The discussion was powerful on both sides, and those of us hearing it for the first time carried it with us into the week of training. It was an unresolved issue that would never be brought up for a vote.

Until then, I had assumed—like many of the volunteers—that as far as the Movement was concerned, all Negroes spoke with one voice. Dr. Martin Luther King Jr. was the voice of the Civil Rights Movement, and the word he spoke was nonviolence. Bob Moses had made that clear to us on our first day. If we were to be part of the Movement, we must agree to practice nonviolence.

I had expected to learn about differences of opinions between Negroes and whites. That there would be such differences among Negroes was something I hadn't considered.

~~~

We continually heard throughout the training from SNCC speakers who shared their stories—brutal stories that were hard to hear. I understood that they were trying to prepare us for what we might experience, but the repetition left me feeling numb. I was hoping for a change of pace when the next speaker, John Doar, the assistant attorney general for civil rights in the Department of Justice and the first white presenter, took the stage. His dark hair was neatly trimmed, and he was dressed in a black suit, a white shirt, and a narrow, striped tie, as one might expect from a Washington lawyer. I was surprised that he didn't appear much older than some of the SNCC staff members. He carried the same serious demeanor they did but without the edginess. I sensed a kindness, a quietness in his nature. Luke had told me that Mr. Doar had helped avert a riot after Medgar Evers's funeral in Jackson, Mississippi, and he'd even filed lawsuits against a hateful voter registrar, Theron Lynd.

Mr. Doar told us the federal government would watch out for trouble, but the responsibility for protection was up to the local law enforcement agencies. As he spoke, though, his words offered a harsh message. Where was the sense of encouragement we had hoped for? We now faced the real understanding that the federal government could not be counted on, yet something in our upbringings refused to accept that. The questions after the talk became strident.

Lynn jumped to her feet. "I don't see why you can't protect us when you know the local authorities won't help."

John Doar smiled sadly. "I know it's hard to understand, but it's a matter of legal jurisdiction. If there's an incident requiring federal troops to be called in, we will be there for you."

"In other words, you can't do anything until some of us are killed, right?" shouted a boy in the back of the room.

"I thought the government is for the people," said a girl, who stood up then swept her arms around to include all of us. "We *are* the people, aren't we?"

"Yeah!" agreed a boy in a Harvard T-shirt. "How can the government send advisors to look out for the people of Vietnam but not those of us here at home?"

The murmurs rose, rushing together as one combined voice of indignation and anger.

Bob Moses walked up next to John Doar and held up his hand. "We don't need this. Stop and listen to what Mr. Doar has to say."

Mr. Doar took a moment to glance around the room as it quieted down. "Look," he began. "What you're doing is very serious, very important. I admire you for your willingness to take on this job. I wish it weren't necessary. I wish our world was different, but it's not. This is the way things are. No, we on the federal level can't protect you from the violence you might encounter in Mississippi. The only thing we can do today is make you aware. We hope this awareness will be what keeps you careful and attentive to what's going on around you."

"Well, if we're in trouble and we need your help, what *can* you do for us?"

Mr. Doar looked quietly at the questioner for a moment and responded glumly, "Nothing."

~~~

The next morning's workshop continued with another SNCC leader sharing about what we might expect over the summer. The speaker was John Lewis, who had been a Freedom Rider and a founder of SNCC. Although short in stature, his deep voice rolled out over us, tightly gripping our attention as he shared Bob Moses's vision of the Freedom Summer Project. Lewis told us a little about Bob Moses, who had gone down to Mississippi in 1961 to work as a one-man team. Lewis chuckled as he said he didn't know if Bob was brave or crazy to begin working in Amite County, where only one of the over five thousand Negroes was registered to vote.

After hearing some of the statistics about registered Negro voters, Jane told me she definitely wanted to work with the voter registration group that was heading down to Mississippi at the end of the week. I hated for us to split up. After all, she was my reason for volunteering in the first place. But I had signed up to teach at a Freedom School, and that group was scheduled to stay on campus for an additional week of training.

~~~

The schedule for that afternoon showed a speaker I really wanted to hear: Fannie Lou Hamer. As she shared her story, her deep, throaty voice spoke words that were painful to hear. She was one of twenty children born into a family of sharecroppers and toiled in the cotton fields of Mississippi for several years of her childhood. By age eighteen, she had worked her way up to be a timekeeper on the plantation. When she finally went to register to vote, the plantation owner told her to get her name off the voter list or leave the plantation. She decided that she would leave, but her husband and their children would stay and bring in the crop to pay off their debt to the owner. A few months later, the owner fired her husband and took their car, saying they owed him for it. The harassment continued, including shots fired into the Hamer home, but that only made her even more determined to work for voter rights, which she does for SNCC all over the state.

In June 1963, on her way home from a training program in South Carolina, she and several other Negro women were arrested, taken to jail, and severely beaten. As Mrs. Hamer told the brutal details of her beating, I bit my lip, trying to hold back tears. The pain and humiliation of the whipping she received tore at my heart.

Mrs. Hamer said that Andrew Young and James Bevel, two Southern Christian Leadership Conference staff members, finally got her released. She stopped speaking for a moment and took a deep breath. Her whole demeanor changed as she began telling us of the work she was doing now. With the Democratic National Convention in August and the upcoming election in November, she told us that this was the time for political action. She had helped form the Mississippi Freedom Democratic Party to send delegates to the Democratic National Convention in an attempt to unseat the existing Mississippi delegation, which was all white. Negroes made up 42 percent of the state's population, yet they were unrepresented politically. Mrs. Hamer had actually challenged, although unsuccessfully, the Democratic incumbent in the congressional primary.

When Mrs. Hamer related her political action, I was amazed. She wasn't a physically imposing woman, she wore a simple cotton housedress, her words revealed her lack of formal education, and her southern accent was deep. Yet, she spoke with such conviction, such strength and determination, that I couldn't help but think she was a force that could move mountains. I'd never heard a more impressive speaker.

At the end of her presentation, I looked at Jane and said, "Wow!" At last, I knew who this Fannie Lou Hamer was, and I was sure I would never forget her.

~~~

After dinner, we made our way into the auditorium to watch an episode of *CBS Reports* titled "Mississippi and the 15th Amendment." At first, everyone in the room seemed to collectively sigh with an overall sense of fatigue after a long and intense day, yet gradually, we found ourselves leaning forward, riveted to the flickering black-and-white screen as CBS's familiar introductory music and logo appeared.

The episode first showed piece by piece how Mississippi had ignored the Constitution to force Negroes to remain second-class citizens. One scene opened with the serene and stately background of a columned courthouse. The commentator speaks authoritatively:

"Theron C. Lynd, circuit clerk and voting registrar of Forrest County, Mississippi, is one of the most powerful men in America. He and eighty-one other county registrars in Mississippi...have the power under state law to decide who can and who cannot vote." As the obese voter registrar of Hattiesburg, Mississippi, stood possessively in front of the Forrest County Courthouse, his bulk filled the screen as he pivoted as if guarding his territory. He perfectly fit the stereotype of an arrogant, white autocrat with a double chin, a buzz haircut, and dark-framed glasses.

"Where'd they find this clown?" someone mumbled. Laughs rippled throughout our group.

Immediately in the back of the room, several SNCC workers jumped from their seats and stormed toward the exit. "You should be ashamed!" one yelled. He slammed the door behind him, and the news report suddenly became a secondary show. We looked to one another, some with puzzled expressions, others with the raised eyebrows or lips pressed together and glances that wordlessly said, "What was that all about?"

As soon as the episode ended, one of the volunteers stood up and said, "Wait a minute, everybody. I want to know why Frankie and some of the other SNCC guys stomped out of here like that. Why should we be ashamed for laughing at that guy on the screen? The way he looks, he deserves to be laughed at."

A girl in the back added, "Yeah. Ever since I got here, I've felt like you SNCC workers are mad at us. But why? We're giving up our summers to help you."

Luke Guthrie, who was sitting two rows in front of me, swiveled around. "My God, girl, we're not mad at you! We're worried sick about you! You just don't know anythin'! After the last two days of tryin' to tell you, you still don't get it."

Another student jumped to his feet. "You say *we* don't get it, but I think you SNCC guys don't get it. We're trying to learn, and we're open to everything you say and do. But the bottom line is, we're white. We'll always be white. That's who we are. But we're here and we're ready to work with you. So what's your problem?" As a murmur of agreement rose through the crowd, I joined in.

I watched Bob Moses, expecting him to speak up, but he stood along the side wall, his face expressionless and his wife Dona beside him. It was Marcus who stood and held out his hands in a calming gesture.

"Y'all, we can work through this. Listen to me, now. I'm sure we're all just exhausted from the last two days of training, but us SNCC members have been tired and frustrated and angry for years. There's nothing funny about anything we just saw. You laughed at something that is the brutality we live with. That guy, the registrar, he isn't a comic character. He's real. We know him. We know others like him. They jail us. They beat us. They even kill us. So how can you laugh? How *can* you?"

25

Voices both Black and white began pouring out feelings that had been simmering under the surface for days, weeks, years—feelings that built barriers and stunted connections.

One by one Frankie and the other SNCC staffers who had rushed out eased back in and joined in the difficult dialogue. Frankie stepped forward and spoke honestly. "We've lived with the world of hurt that white fools like Theron Lynd have been dishing out our whole lives. But when y'all laughed about him tonight, man," he stretched out his arms as if beseeching us for understanding, "I...I don't even know how to describe it. But, at least for me, it brought on a new kind of pain. It felt like y'all were laughing at us, our suffering, and the way we have to live."

Many of us shook our heads and called out, "No. No way. That's not what we mean at all."

Jane stood and said apologetically, "We would never laugh at what has happened to you! We were laughing *at* that man, at his grossness. I've never been in the kind of situations you live with every day, but we're here to walk with you, to be there with you. Please give us a chance."

A young, thin SNCC staffer I didn't know growled a response. "We *are* giving you a chance. That's what this summer is all about. But you got to learn the truth about the way it is down there. The way you need to keep your head down and always be watchful. It's a *dangerous* place, y'all. That's what we're trying to teach you because if you're not careful, you're going to bring the Man down on us and get us *all* killed!" he shouted as he slammed his fist into the palm of his hand. "But instead of learning, you're laughing. You're laughing at our life and you're going to get us killed!"

Throughout the long evening, the voices continued crying out to each other for understanding, each group speaking from islands separated by the vastness of different experiences and trying to build bridges toward each other. There were angry voices, hurt voices, and calm and caring voices, but everyone—both Black and white—was saying, "This is me. This is who I am. We're supposed to work together. Can you know me? Can you understand what it is to be me?"

Finally, the speaking became listening, the listening became understanding, and the understanding bloomed into something more.

Toward the end of the discussion, Phillip, the Yalie who first rode with us to the campus, said what almost all of us were thinking. "It's almost impossible for us to really imagine what it's like to be Negro in Mississippi— or anywhere. But now we know the stories, and we're so grateful for the real sharing from both sides that went on here tonight. In my opinion, the bottom line is: We care about you. We will stand with you. And we will work with you under your direction. I guess what we hope for on your part is that you don't dismiss us as too stupid to understand your lives. And yes, we wouldn't mind if you appreciated our being with you this summer."

Marcus stood slowly, his body reflecting the fatigue that all of us felt in those after-midnight hours. He smiled in Phillip's direction and said, "We do appreciate y'all. Honest. This...what happened tonight—the angry voices, the honest sharing—it's been good. Tiring but good." He paused as a collective chuckle ran through the group. "I think we all feel a little closer, don't you?" He stopped again momentarily while most everyone murmured affirmatively. "I suggest we go to our rooms and get a little sleep so we have the energy for tomorrow's workshops."

By then, the tension had lifted from Frankie's face. As Marcus finished speaking, Frankie began the SNCC song we'd learned that afternoon. It had been written in memory of Herbert Lee.

"Now we've been 'buked and we've been scorned," he began singing, his smooth, tenor voice making the words come alive.

By the time he got to, "No we'll never turn back, until we walk in peace, "we were all singing in unison. We looked to one another with smiles on our faces as we sang the last line with triumphant enthusiasm, "And we have equality."

It was two in the morning when everyone made their way back to the dorms, our conversations muted, our hearts more at peace.

But while we had been working at building something together, a church outside Philadelphia, Mississippi, lay smoldering.

3

SNCC Safety Rules:

1. When persons leave their project, they must call back to their project person for themselves on arrival at destination point. Should they be missing, project personnel will notify the Jackson office. Care should be taken at all times to avoid, if possible, full names of persons traveling.

2. Travel at night should be avoided unless absolutely necessary.

3. Remove all unnecessary objects from your car which could be construed as weapons. (hammers, files, etc.) Absolutely no liquor bottles, beer cans, etc. should be inside your car.

4. Do not travel with names and addresses of local contacts. Never give anyone any information about your local family.

5. Know all roads in and out of town. Study the county map.

6. Know locations of sanctuaries and homes in the county.

"Call me Mac," began Charles McLaurin, the SNCC staffer in charge of Sunflower County where I hoped to be assigned.

Mr. McLaurin, short and sturdy in jeans and a faded red T-shirt, had our group congregate under the shade of some sycamore trees one afternoon. He appeared as serious as all the SNCC leaders, but a smile peeking out from under his mustache gave away his friendly nature.

"My territory is Sunflower County, right in the heart of the Mississippi Delta," he said. "Indianola, the county seat, is where everyone in Sunflower County has to register to vote. It's also the home of the White Citizens' Council. Do y'all know what the White Citizens' Council is?"

Even though the workshop was meant to be about our own racial understandings, Mac couldn't resist teaching us about the history of his area. With the passage of *Brown v. Board of Education* in 1954, important white community leaders and plantation owners from all over the Delta came to Indianola to discuss what they could do to stop integration. They put economic and political pressure on those who, as Mac said, "were agitatin'." Many agitators had loans called in, their credit denied at stores, or their insurance policies canceled. A lot lost their jobs. The success of that local White Citizens' Council spread over Mississippi and then further around the South.

I learned a lot from Mac that afternoon. He helped us understand that whenever there was progress for Negroes, there would be pushback from whites.

After giving us that background information, Mac cleared his throat and continued. "This workshop, though, is for us to examine your feelings about race. Let's talk about that. You'll be living with Negro families this summer. Most of them are poor, and most of them don't have indoor plumbing.

"So tell me," he directed his question to a girl sitting on the ground in front of him. "How do you feel about living with Black folk? What experience have you had with Blacks?"

The girl's expression became serious. "Well to be honest, I've never been around Negroes. None lived in the little community in California where I grew up, and it was usually Mexicans who were hired to work as maids and stuff. So I guess it would be a little awkward at first, but once we got to know each other, I think that would pass."

Another girl spoke up from the back of the group. "We've had a Black maid all my life. She's just like family."

Mac focused on her. "And by 'just like family' you mean that you all eat meals together?...That you're also close to her children and her husband?...That you spend the holidays together?...That if she needed a kidney transplant, you'd volunteer to see if you were a match?"

The girl flushed and stammered, "Well...uh...no....What I mean is that we don't see her as different simply because of her skin color."

Mac held up his hand in a conciliatory way and smiled. "What I want all of you to realize, to really think about, is the clichés we use and hide behind—without even being aware of it. I believe what you meant in your first statement is that you actually don't see your maid as different because of her skin color. That over time, you've come to know her as a person of worth. Is that right?"

The girl nodded.

"But you don't *really* see her as a member of your family, do you?"

The girl shook her head, embarrassed. "I get what you're saying. I really do. I guess what I wanted to say is that we care about her, you know, like the way you care about a special friend."

Mac shifted his gaze to take in the entire group. "How many of y'all go to school with Negroes?"

I raised my hand along with four or five others.

"And how do you relate to them?"

Our hands dropped quickly. We looked at each other, hoping someone else would respond.

Finally, a redheaded boy spoke up. "The coloreds...um...Negroes kind of stay to themselves. If we have a class with them, we have conversations. And sometimes when we're in the student union building, we hang out together, you know, get a Coke or coffee or something."

"Are there any Blacks rooming with whites?"

Those of us who'd moments earlier raised our hands about having Negro students on campus now shook our heads.

"Is there any interracial dating?" Again, only head shaking. Mac let a silence develop while we shifted and squirmed. It was an uncomfortable silence. I think he wanted it to be that way.

"So," Mac leaned back against a tree and smiled, "let's discuss our feelings about race and the situations y'all will be in when you arrive in Mississippi."

By the end of that afternoon session, we found ourselves beginning to look more closely at our underlying feelings about race. I thought I knew what lie ahead for the summer, but now I was beginning to sense that it would be so much more than what I'd first imagined. The truths I was learning—about myself and about our country—revealed more than I expected. *This is going to be an interesting summer,* I thought to myself.

~~~

For the later afternoon sessions, small groups staked out various areas around campus. Luke Guthrie and Silas McGhee were leading the role-playing group Jane and I were attending. They had situated themselves at a corner of the campus where several large oak trees offered shade. Some of the groups had the press and television reporters recording their sessions. I was glad they weren't filming our group; I felt self-conscious enough as it was.

The role-playing started with some very basic situations. Silas began by saying, "The police are going to harass you. They're going to pull you over for no reason and drag you out of the car. They'll probably take you to jail. But if you're on a deserted country road and they start to beat you there, fall to the ground and cover your head." This reminded me of my elementary school days and the air-raid drills we practiced, which were supposed to protect us from a possible atomic bomb attack.

With the first example, Silas played the role of the police officer and Luke the driver of the car. After a few controlled kicks and punches that didn't actually land on Luke, Silas said, "See how he has assumed the fetal position? He's rolled up, keeping his head as close to his knees as possible. It's very important to keep your legs together! A leg sticking out can be stomped on, and you don't want no broken legs."

Luke stood up and added, "Also, don't wear sandals or expensive jewelry. In fact, don't wear any jewelry at all. And don't have a lot of money in your wallets or purses. Now, I want some of you to get up here and give it a go." He pointed at the boy sitting next to me and said, "Tom, you're up."

As Tom slowly stood and walked forward, Silas immediately grabbed him and threw him to the ground. My hand flew to my mouth at the suddenness of it. Tom lay sprawled in the grass for a moment, gasping for breath.

"No!" Silas yelled at him. "Don't lie there like ya got all day! You're going to be kicked, punched. Get into the fetal position immediately!"

Tom sat up and shook his head. "I didn't know you were ready to start."

Luke stood with his hands on his hips. "Listen, there's a lot of 'em in Mississippi who are ready to start on you now. Believe it. This is why we're training y'all," he said. "You got to be ready...every second."

Tom rubbed his arm. "I'm beginning to understand that," he groaned with a rueful grin. Then he pushed himself up and walked gingerly back to his place. I patted his arm in sympathy and tucked my sandal-clad feet under my legs.

For the rest of the hot afternoon, the trainers took us through several scenarios: being thrown in a jail cell with white segregationists, leading a group of Negroes to the courthouse to be met by a mob of whites, being at the home of Negroes when some whites showed up with shotguns. Those who were assigned the roles of the white opposition got into it by screaming: "Go home, you Commie agitator!" "Nigger lover!" "Get outta here, you damn Yankee!" They simulated weapons like nightsticks, cattle prods, tear gas canisters, and the shoves and punches became more real.

The potency of the simulated violence smoldered in the afternoon heat, leaving us limp and torn between anger and acceptance. Little by little, the reality of the situation in the Deep South seeped into our collective understanding. The emotions brought out by playing the different personas were disquieting, sometimes because they were unfamiliar, but perhaps more so because they already existed somewhere inside each of us.

Dinnertime was subdued as the volunteers shared with each other the experiences of the afternoon, comparing bruises and scrapes. Luke sat down beside me and tapped me on the arm. He looked at me with his compelling brown eyes and said, "There's a group of us from the last workshop going to a bonfire behind the school tonight. Want me to show you where it is?"

Finally, something that sounded like a normal activity for college students. "Sure. Sounds like fun."

After dinner, Luke and I followed others down a path behind the dorms and through some trees to a clearing. We found a log to sit on, and I gazed around at the mostly white assemblage of college students drinking beer, smoking, and just relaxing as we sat around a fire, not for warmth, but for the pure leisure of it. The week's messages had been so intense thus far that they'd thrown us slightly off-kilter.

Luke looked from the fire to me. "So Miss Lenore Rogers with the auburn hair and big brown eyes, what do you think about comin' to Mississippi to teach at the Freedom Schools? Will it prepare for your teachin' career?"

I shook my head. "I don't really want to be a teacher. I plan to go into social work. That's what I'm majoring in, and that's what all my other summer jobs have been about."

"Why social work?"

I shrugged and replied, "It just feels right to me. I grew up passing the windows of tenement houses as I rode the train into New York, seeing

32

the poverty and the expressions on the children's faces. I love working with kids, and I want to do something that will make a difference." I smiled at Luke and inquired, "What about you? Are you going to stay in SNCC?"

Luke shared with me his plan to eventually work in an engineering firm building bridges or dams, things that were strong and lasting. We talked about our disappointments and our dreams and told each other about our families and our sense of place. All of it made me realize what different worlds we'd come from.

"I know you're going to teach at a Freedom School, so I hate to tell you this, but a possible site for a Freedom School got burned by the Klan last night."

My heart sank. "Where?"

"Up from Meridian. Out in the country somewhere near Philadelphia, Mississippi. Mickey Schwerner and James Chaney had met with some people from that church to see if they could use the building as a Freedom School. Klan must've got wind of it and burned it down."

"What kind of person would burn a church?"

Luke just stared at me blankly.

I already knew the answer.

~~~

The next morning going through the breakfast line, volunteers were still talking about the brutality of the role-playing exercises the day before. I set a plate of scrambled eggs on my tray and mentioned to Jane, "At least we won't be doing any more of *that* this week."

Jane looked at me and said, "Is that what Luke told you?"

"As a matter of fact, yes. He did tell me that," I snapped as I plunked my breakfast tray on a table.

Jane put her tray down gently. "I can't help but notice that you and Luke are talking a lot."

I looked at my best friend, hoping she'd see the irritation brewing on my face. "So what? We're in most of the same workshops because we'll be in the same area. It doesn't mean a thing."

"Sure, but a white girl and a Negro?" Jane shook her head.

"Jane! Come on. In the first place, we're getting enough of that message from all the SNCC lectures, and second, it's just not going to happen."

Jane broke off a piece of toast and added some jelly before she spoke. "Uh-huh."

"Enough! Luke and I barely know each other. So let's finish breakfast and go learn some more about this strange place called Mississippi."

~~~

I slept fitfully that night and woke Friday morning before the alarm clock went off. Jane was still sleeping. I was going to miss her, but I was already looking forward to the next week's concentration on Freedom Schools. I stood and padded my way to the bathroom to get the first shower.

This morning, Jess Brown, one of the few Negro lawyers in Mississippi, was discussing legal issues. The message about what we could and couldn't count on legally was discouraging. Mr. Brown gave a most powerful message. Perhaps it was the way he looked at us. For me, it felt like he was looking directly at each of us, warning us. He was a mix of gruff and caring as he told us when—not if—we were stopped by law enforcement not to argue about our rights and not to act as if being white gave us some sort of privilege. We were simply to go to jail and wait for a lawyer or someone from SNCC to come get us released.

His parting warning was really strong: "Don't be thinking you can give some sheriff or deputy a lecture on your constitutional rights. Ain't goin' to happen!"

Some of the students sitting near me shifted uncomfortably in their seats as Mr. Brown painted a disturbing picture of what being a second-class citizen really means.

Although Mr. Brown gave us unsettling news about our legal rights in the Deep South, he also gave us some reassurance. He promised us that he and other attorneys, like Carsie A. Hall, Jack H. Young Sr., and many others would be there to get us out of jail when necessary. Brown's tough manner and bulldog appearance could be intimidating, but it was comforting to know he was on our side.

~~~

After lunch, I found a bench in the shade to wait for the afternoon workshop. Lately, several of the volunteers had admitted to being afraid. I had fears too. The week of training had been exacting, emotionally and physically. Jane would be heading for Mississippi the next day, and I'd be leaving a week later. I couldn't imagine how the summer would unfold for us. I sighed and sat back, letting my thoughts drift as birdsong washed over me. I looked around at this secure, safe place. When the white of a mockingbird's wing caught my eye, I watched as it flitted among some low-hanging branches. *Normalcy. Calm. Why do I want to leave this place?*

Luke ambled up and joined me on the bench. "Whatcha looking so serious about?" he asked, smiling at me. He had such a warm, friendly smile.

"Just thinking about how many of us are still here in spite of you trying to scare us to death with your dire warnings."

Luke chuckled and shook his head. "Yeah. That's been a surprise to us. Very few of y'all have left."

"How many?"

"Oh, I dunno. Maybe eight, ten. 'Course, we didn't really want y'all to come anyway."

I sprang up and retorted, "Well, why in the world did you—" I felt the blush of indignation reach my face and turned away as Luke held out his hand to stop me.

"Hold on there, girl. Let me finish."

I stood stiffly, my eyes still turned away.

"Of course, it was hard for us to plan this, getting you whites involved. It meant that we, as Negroes, needed help, that we couldn't do this on our own and we had to ask the whites for help—and don't forget, white people put us in this position and held us in this position in the first place."

At this point, Luke stood toe to toe with me, his expression bitter. "Yeah, you whites who won't let us vote or hold office, who won't let us eat where y'all eat, who make us always go to the back door, who make us get off the sidewalk when y'all walk by, who call us 'boy' or 'nigger'." Luke's voice was almost a growl, coming from his very core. Then he stopped abruptly, choking back words of hurt that rose like bile in his throat. "Sorry," he mumbled as he backed off a few steps.

I wanted to shout at him for lumping me in with the bigoted white people. But when I saw the torment in his eyes, I knew it was my turn to reach out. As I placed my hand on his arm, I could feel the anger surging through his body; it was the rage felt by generations of his ancestors. It was then that I began to grasp the real chasm between Negroes and whites. A picture flashed through my mind: a deep, wide gorge that developed over time as a river of pain eroded the walls, deeper and deeper. In this quick glimpse of understanding, I sensed what a labor of words and action it would take to bridge this chasm. And I wanted to be part of that work.

I dropped my hand from his arm and said, "I'm sorry too." This was not the Luke I knew—the casual, teasing Luke, the Luke who gently explained truths about Mississippi to me. But I realized that this side of Luke was also part of who he was.

And to understand Mississippi, I needed to know this other version of Luke.

~~~

On Jane's last night in the safety of Western College for Women, we arrived early for the evening session. It was obvious that we volunteers and the SNCC trainers felt as worn-out as the auditorium looked with its overflowing wastebaskets along the walls and debris scattered about: a jacket here, a soda bottle there. It had been an intense week unlike anything I'd ever experienced in my life.

Bob Moses spoke on what was the last evening for the first group. He reminded us that we needed to write to our congressmen to ask for protection throughout the summer. As he talked in his calm, quiet way about what the Freedom Summer Project meant, and the vision of SNCC and its umbrella organization, the Council of Federated Organizations, I felt my tired spirit rising, infused with the idealistic importance of the work we were about to embark on. I again felt that sense of hope for change and a better future lifting us all up—volunteers and trainers, alike—above our weariness, our fears, our cynicism. I hoped we could carry that optimism and daring out of this worn-out auditorium and leave all its debris behind.

The singing began then, the songs that had come to mean so much and brought our arms and our spirits together each time. Around midnight, we stood as one with arms crossed and hands linked—Black and white together—and ended with the one song that united us the most: "We Shall Overcome." We stood tall as we sang strong and felt strong. These were the words that gave our summer work meaning. These were the words that told the world what we intended to accomplish. And, more importantly, these were the words we believed.

~~~

The cafeteria filled with chatter on Saturday morning, carrying a feeling of excitement and anticipation. I looked up as Luke and Silas sat down at our table. They would also be leaving that day to begin their work with voter registration.

"Are you anxious to get back to Mississippi and get to work?" asked Jane.

Both Luke and Silas nodded. "Three guys are already on their way back to Meridian...left in the middle of the night," Silas said. He told us that Congress of Racial Equality (CORE) workers Mickey Schwerner and James Chaney and a volunteer named Andy Goodman were driving down. "They want to talk to the people at Mount Zion Church out near Philadelphia, Mississippi. A while back, Mickey and James had talked to them about having a Freedom School there. But a few days ago, the Klan burned that church down."

Luke and I exchanged a glance. That was the incident he'd told me about earlier in the week, right after it happened.

Silas went on, "The night of the fire, well, earlier that evening, there'd been a committee meeting at the church. On the way home, some of 'em had been stopped by the Klan and beaten, then the Klan went back and torched the church. All that was left was the big church bell. That's why Mickey and James are going back. Want to talk to the folks, though, by God, there ain't much to say about something like that. It's nothing new."

Jane and I felt our spirits drop, our shoulders sag. This isn't what we wanted to hear this morning. Suddenly no longer hungry, I pushed away my bowl of oatmeal.

~~~

A few short hours later, we all gathered around the buses and cars bound for Mississippi. I gave Jane a last hug goodbye. "Stay safe, "I whispered in her ear. Jane climbed on the bus then leaned out the window with the others gaily shouting goodbye and waving. Luke and Silas got into one of the cars. The vehicles chugged off and the echo of shouts, laughter, and singing floated in the air for a while. I stood as the remaining Freedom School volunteers and staff drifted away and watched for a few lingering seconds.

The day after that first group left, a new group of volunteers crowded onto the campus. They were so eager and enthusiastic. They glowed with anticipation. Watching, I began to detect in them the same inexperience and naiveté the SNCC staffers had seen in my group when we'd first arrived. These kids carried with them the same careless laughter, guitars, and comfortable air of self-confidence. *Would they lose all that in the upcoming week,* I wondered, *once they heard the stories we'd heard, once they saw the wounds carried by Reverend Ed King, Jim Travis, and the others we'd learned about?* Right then I felt older and sadder, yet I marveled at how far I'd traveled in one short week.

After breakfast, my suitemates, Mary Etta and Ann, who were also staying this week for Freedom School training, squeezed into the auditorium with me for the introductory lecture. The air-conditioned room was as packed as it had been the week before, even though many of the SNCC trainers had gone ahead to Mississippi with the voter registration group. The place had been cleaned over the weekend, the debris carted away, and the stories, the words, the sharing, and the songs were all gone. I missed the familiar faces, especially Jane's.

When Bob Moses came forward, just like last week, he drew an outline of Mississippi on the blackboard and told a little about each area.

From all I'd learned in the past week, I felt a closer identification with each area: Amite County where Bob Moses had been working since 1961; McComb, a town where five Negroes were killed this year; and the Delta where I expected to be headed in a few days.

Bob Moses gave the overview as before, but this time his talk had a rather philosophical tone, referring to Albert Camus's novel *The Plague.* "This plague doesn't just affect Mississippi. It seeps its way across the nation. If we can crack Mississippi, we can crack everywhere. Having you white students involved will get the attention of the country. Your involvement is so important."

Bob's style was so low-key that it might be easy for some to dismiss him, but his words were always powerful and full of meaning, and it was impossible not to pay close attention. I for one felt he was speaking directly to me. As usual, he assured us that if we decided not to make the trip to Mississippi, he understood.

As he was speaking, two of the SNCC trainers standing near the doorway bent toward each other. Then two more. Then three. Then Marcus stepped up to the edge of the stage and motioned Bob over to him.

After a moment, Bob returned to the center of the stage, and an expectant hush filled the room. He looked out at us and drew in a deep breath. "Yesterday morning, three of our people left Meridian to check on a church that was burned in Neshoba County." Bob's firm, calm voice carried throughout the auditorium. "They haven't come back, and they haven't been heard from."

I gasped. My hands flew to my face. Around me, the murmurs grew into tense, anxious voices: "Who were they? What could've happened to them? Who was hunting for them? What happened? What happened?"

When I spotted Rita Schwerner walking onto the stage to stand beside Bob, I grabbed Mary Etta's arm. I'll never forget Rita's voice. It was strained but painfully controlled.

"My husband, Mickey Schwerner, James Chaney, and a summer volunteer named Andrew Goodman went to investigate a church burning yesterday and have not returned. All night, our people in Mississippi have been trying to locate them. We just learned this morning that they were stopped and arrested in Philadelphia, Mississippi, and they were released last evening. The FBI has been notified but wasn't sure if they had jurisdiction yet."

She swallowed hard and stood a little straighter. "Gather by your geographical area and wire your congressmen. Beg for them to get federal protection for all the workers in Mississippi. Get your families to also call those legislators." Rita then walked over to the blackboard, erased some of the map of Mississippi, and wrote: James Chaney—CORE staff; Michael Schwerner—CORE staff; Andrew Goodman—Freedom Summer Project volunteer. Then beneath the names, she wrote Neshoba County—Disappeared.

4

Don't you let nobody turn you 'round,
Turn you 'round, turn you 'round.
Don't let nobody turn you 'round.
Keep on a-walkin', keep on a-talkin',
Marchin' on to freedom land.
—"Don't Let Nobody Turn You Round", Negro Spiritual later adapted for the Movement

The silence lasted for a moment before we all jumped into action. "New Yorkers over here," someone shouted.

"Massachusetts here," called another.

Groups formed quickly, and the noise level rose higher and higher. As I made my way to the group from New York, I glanced to the stage and saw that Bob remained where he was, his head bowed, and Rita Schwerner stood by the blackboard still holding the chalk, her shoulders drooping. I wanted to put my arms around her. Maybe the message wasn't true. Maybe they'd be found safe. But there wasn't time to wish anything else. It was time to stop thinking and do something.

I was learning that it's not only words that carry power, it's what's behind them, what's attached to them. Reading about the hatred in Mississippi was disturbing. Hearing the stories this past week about the violence was even more so. But having them attached to people I had met and to a place I was going made the words come alive in an ominous way.

Those of us who had met the three missing workers shared what we knew of them, making them more real to the others. Luke had told me a lot about Mickey and Rita Schwerner. Like Luke, I also admired them simply because they were spending these years working for such an important cause instead of trying to get their careers started. Mickey's size might have made him intimidating, but his friendly nature overcame that. James Chaney seemed quieter than the others and looked younger. He had started in the Movement working for change when he was still in high school down in Meridian.

Just last week, Andrew Goodman had introduced himself to the people we were sitting with during dinner. He was a drama major at Queens College. Someone at the table had teased him about liking poetry, but he'd laughed it off. With dark eyes and dark hair that fell down his forehead, he really looked like the poet he admitted to being.

The next day, in spite of the shocking news, the workshops continued as we followed our printed schedules. I listened to the leaders, but in the back of my mind, there was always one lingering question: where were the three? It was hard to think of anything else. Ever since the announcement, the mood on campus was subdued, but we understood that classes must go on. I was trying to find strength from something Luke had said to me: that we would be in the Black community and they would be looking out for us.

But I couldn't shake the following thought: *who was going to look out for* them?

~~~

Later, before we had finished lunch, Bob Moses announced an optional meeting afterward called, "Why Do I Want to Go to Mississippi This Summer?" At this point, that was certainly a valid question.

Vincent Harding led the discussion at the meeting. He and his wife, Rosemarie, came from an interracial voluntary service center in Atlanta as representatives of the Mennonite Church. He explained that they worked with SNCC, CORE, and the SCLC to serve as counselors, reconcilers, and participants, saying, "We believe the Movement calls us to go beyond the comfortable places in our lives. We believe that many of you, if not all of you, are also called. What do you think? In other words, why did you want to go to Mississippi this summer?"

When we'd been sitting comfortably around the bonfire, Luke and I had talked about reasons why the volunteers were willing to join with SNCC for the summer. It was difficult for me to explain my motivation.

The truth was that my feelings—not my logical thoughts—had prompted me to come, feelings that things were unjust in the South and I could in some way help make things better. In the space of the past few days, however, I realized that I'd had no clue about the degree of violence I'd be facing. In my naiveté, the injustice did not extend beyond signs designating "white" and "colored." I had not seen the depth of difference in this Southern culture in my own country. And, yet, I believed in what SNCC's mission statement said. I had faith that "hope would end despair and love would transform hate."

~~~

The rest of the day's workshops gave us the materials we would be using for teaching in the Freedom Schools. The curriculum had been put together in March during a meeting that the National Council of Churches sponsored. Educators, ministers, and SNCC workers had met together and worked out what they felt needed to be taught. During dinner, those of us who would be teaching in the Freedom Schools went over what we'd learned. Several had already graduated college with teaching degrees, so I listened closely to their suggestions.

When Bob Moses entered the room and went to the microphone, my fork froze halfway to my mouth. Bob's glance swept around the room as he clicked on the microphone. "About the missing workers....The car was found by two Choctaws fishing a few miles from Philadelphia. It was badly burned, but it *is* Mickey Schwerner's blue station wagon. However, the three young men were not with the car."

Bob's voice slowed, emphasizing the importance of the words. "They have not been found. The FBI is now treating it as a kidnapping, so please keep contacting your legislators."

He started to turn away, but when he came back, my stomach clenched. *Don't say it....Please don't say it,* I thought.

But then Bob picked up the microphone and said, "I fear they are dead."

~~~

Bob Moses's words knocked the breath out of us, rendering us unable to speak for a moment after he left the cafeteria. But soon our voices rose louder and louder. "Could it be true? But there weren't any bodies found. Maybe they're still alive and are being held prisoner somewhere. Maybe they got away somehow and are hiding out. Maybe they're hurt and someone has taken them in but hasn't let anyone know. Maybe...Maybe...Or maybe they really *have* been killed. Could they truly be...dead?" The words tasted sour in my mouth.

A week earlier, we were idealistic college students looking forward to an interesting summer experience, and now someone was talking about death. The death of one of us because of the work we'd be doing.

A Columbia student sitting next to me muttered, "I just want to get drunk."

"Me too," agreed another. "There's a cool place not far away where we can have a bonfire and some beers. It's in a little clearing in those woods behind the school."

"I'm in," added another student. "Let's spread the word."

I walked slowly out of the cafeteria with my suitemates, Mary Etta and Ann, my shoulders sagging from the thoughts weighing so heavily on my mind. "What do you want to do?" I asked.

Ann shrugged. "Let's go to the bonfire. It's better than sitting in our rooms worrying."

"Do you know where it is?" asked Mary Etta.

"Uh-huh," I admitted. "Luke and I went there last week."

"Oh, really. You and Luke?" Ann raised an eyebrow.

I scowled at her. "Sure. After an evening workshop. Almost everyone went. It was no big thing. But it's a neat place. Logs to sit on around a fire pit. It's this way."

I turned down a walkway behind one of the dorms then led them down a path headed toward a mix of pine and hardwoods. We fell into a line of small groups of students all going to the same place.

As we entered the clearing in the middle of the woods, several students were already building up a bonfire. Others had brought six packs of beer that were being distributed. Ann brought back three cans. We each grabbed one and found a log to perch on.

The first sip I took added to the bitter taste in my mouth, but it was somehow satisfying, just what I needed, so I took another swallow. The pungent smell of burning wood filled my nostrils, and the swirling smoke stung my eyes.

I thought about Luke and the time we'd spent here together. We'd shared our stories that evening, and it had been a special time of getting to know each other better. I'd wondered then if our worlds could ever be equal, could ever meet in some safe place. Now, on this night, I doubted they ever could.

A large group of us gathered around the hissing, spitting flames of the burning pine wood and talked about anything but Bob Moses's announcement. As our conversations grew louder, the laughter became more frequent. The smoke seemed to carry away our fears and concerns, circling around and around, up over the tops of the trees silhouetted against the still golden skyline. For that brief time, I felt like a college student again, and I'm sure I wasn't the only one.

~~~

In the morning, the sky was gray and cloudy. It would've been a perfect day to sleep in, but I grumbled my way up and walked to breakfast with Mary Etta and Ann. The clouds were rolling in, seemingly angry and threatening to dump rain on us all. They were the perfect backdrop for the prevailing mood.

The downpour started as we finished lunch. Dark clouds roiled and boomed and clashed against each other. We rushed to our classes shielding ourselves from the rain with umbrellas, jackets, or notebooks.

Staughton Lynd, the leader of our Freedom School group, rose to speak. He was one of the few whites who had led any of our sessions. A Quaker from the North, he stood casually before us. Even with a bachelors and masters from Harvard and a doctorate from Columbia, this young man didn't look much older than some of the volunteers.

He read us a paragraph from our packet:

"The aim of the Freedom School curriculum will be to challenge the student's curiosity about the world, introduce him to his particularly 'Negro' cultural background, and teach him basic literacy skills."

All I could think was: *how in the world do I do that?* As Mr. Lynd spoke, though, I saw what my role would be. I would not be working with younger children as I'd envisioned, but high school students.

The Freedom School teachers were there to help the students learn how to question and, more importantly, to *dare* to question. The job before us was to give those young people the tools they would need to move forward, to become the Negro leaders that places like Mississippi so desperately needed. What was expected of us was more than challenging. I prayed that I could do it. It seemed so academic or philosophical rather than practical. I wished Jane was there to bolster my confidence.

The afternoon workshop continued with information about the kind of material we'd be covering. First, though, they gave us some statistics about Mississippi that shocked me: the percentage of white high school graduates was 42 percent; for Negroes, it was only 7 percent! Both numbers astonished me.

The message we took away from that session was how different the Freedom Schools must be from the regular schools for Negroes in Mississippi.

~~~

That afternoon, word went around like gossip in a small town that CBS would be airing a special report that evening called, "The Search in Mississippi." We all crammed around the TV in the lounge after dinner.

The advantage of having the media here, I could see now, was that everything had been recorded from that first week. The show began with film of James Forman, SNCC's executive secretary, speaking to the first group when we'd arrived the previous week. His large, intimidating presence was obviously holding our attention as he gave the warnings we had since heard over and over. "I'm just wondering if people in this room understand...that people should expect to get beaten. They should expect to spend [time] in jail," he said. "They should expect possibly somebody to get killed.... [We] raise these questions so if people want to turn back, they can turn back now without going through this whole week without understanding the tremendous dangers that are involved." I remember his speaking to us last week, but those particular words had not resonated with me then the way they did now.

As Forman spoke, the camera panned across the audience to show the earnest faces of last week's group of volunteers. Suddenly, I recognized Andy Goodman's face as he sat among the audience only a week ago. In the video, he was simply another volunteer watching James Forman, listening to the warning, and probably believing such a thing would never—could never—happen to him. Yet he'd been in Mississippi for only a day before he went missing. Twenty-four hours!

I wanted to weep for him, for his parents, and for us! I never imagined living in such a world where this might happen to a young man I'd met, a young man who simply wanted to be a poet.

After James Forman finished speaking, Walter Cronkite identified Andy and pointed out that he was missing with two others who were part of the Freedom Summer Project. The report went on to say that two hundred sailors from a naval base in Meridian—the first federal forces dispatched by the US government into Mississippi—had come to search the swamps near where Mickey Schwerner's car was found. The newsreel showed the sailors spreading out into the snake- and mosquito-infested bogs.

Later, some of the volunteers I recognized from last week give their reasons for going to Mississippi. We cheered when we learned that 150 lawyers had met at the Columbia School of Law and would be coming down to join the three Negro lawyers in Mississippi who worked on civil rights cases. This gave me renewed hope that if any of us volunteers or the SNCC staffers were thrown in jail, there would be a chance of being rescued.

Some of the news report was infuriating to watch. Many of us shifted in our seats, grumbling angrily while we watched Senator James Eastland say, "We have more peace and harmony in Mississippi than any other state in the union." Then he asserted that there was no problem with the "coloreds" in Mississippi. "We don't have any racial fiction...friction." Phillip and I exchanged an amused look at the slip of the tongue.

After others spoke, Fannie Lou Hamer briefly told her story. Then James Silver, a professor at the University of Mississippi who had just written *Mississippi: The Closed Society*, startled us with his opening comment. He stated, "By and large, the average Mississippi Negro today is an inferior human being. I hasten to say that he is that way because he has been trained from infancy to subservience. He has been taught by his parents, who have done this in order to protect him. He has been taught that he is inferior."

On one hand, I was discouraged by Professor Silver when he said that we wouldn't change Mississippi. But I was also encouraged when he said, "When these kids go back home and tell about their experiences...then... the Civil Rights Movement has a better chance of being more than just a fad and more than just a temporary crusade. This is something that's got to be done and done for all time."

Throughout the hour-long special report, there were several times when the crowd reacted strongly to things Governor Paul Johnson, Senator

Eastland, and some of the white businessmen in the Delta had to say. The boos were loud when Eastland denied any intimidation to keep Negroes from voting. When the reporter pushed him further about such claims, the senator said, "You see, you go by what some agitator claims who doesn't live in the state and knows nothing about it."

Later, businessmen from the Delta said they were sorry the volunteers were coming and referred to us as "invaders and potential troublemakers." They all insisted that Communists had infiltrated the group and were behind the whole thing. As angry as I felt at those comments, their words helped me see what we were up against.

Governor Johnson concluded by explaining that those COFO people are "beatnik-type people...weirdos." He assured the audience that Mississippi would not tolerate those outside agitators and would uphold the law, "Mississippi-style." We roared our disapproval, comments flying like a tornado rushing through the crowd.

One woman interviewed for the news report offered her opinion. "Those boys are probably off at a beach somewhere, or if they're really dead, well, they asked for it." (All quotes adapted from video "*Freedom Summer,* PBS American Experience, produced and directed by Stanley Nelson, 2014) I didn't know which made me angrier, the words of denial of any problems or the bold-faced anger and hatred.

As the credits scrolled, we watched on the screen as the last week's training group stood and sang "We Shall Overcome." Now, almost as one body, we also stood, crowded together with hands clasped, and joined their singing. When it was over, Fannie Lou Hamer kept us singing more verses and then more Movement songs until the bruising from the hurtful words on the video finally eased a little.

~~~

On our last day, Marcus led the morning workshop, and my mind wandered as he told some all too familiar stories of brutality. He launched into a list of rules and warnings. They were laid out in the pamphlet, but I knew they were of the utmost importance so I forced myself to pay closer attention.

The previous week when Jane and I had attended that same workshop, we had later laughed together about some of the rules, particularly the last five. Now, however, as I read all the rules, they left me dejected because they served as a reminder of the danger that might lie ahead.

8. If it can be avoided, try not to sleep near open windows. Try to sleep at the back of the house, i.e., the part farthest from a road or street.
9. Do not stand in doorways at night with the light at your back.
10. At night, people should not sit in their rooms without drawn shades.
11. Do not congregate in front of the house at night.
12. Try to avoid bizarre or provocative clothing and beards. Be neat.

That evening, James Forman, who had just returned from Mississippi, began the talk. He looked as if he'd just stepped out of the news report, except that he was a little rumpled and wearied. Still, his voice carried the same power as always. He reminded us of the sacrifices already made in Mississippi: Herbert Lee, Louis Allen, Medgar Evers, and so many others, many who were never found or identified. He assured us that SNCC knew the seriousness of the task before us and would understand if anyone chose not to go.

Bob Moses followed Forman to the microphone. In so many ways, the two men were complete opposites. While Forman's voice kept our attention with its strength, Bob Moses gathered us up gently and brought us close as he spoke to us of good and evil. It was perhaps more effective.

Bob again used a literary reference, but this time it was from *The Lord of the Rings.* He spoke of the weariness involved in the struggle of good versus evil. That weariness was a visible part of him that day; it was apparent in his stance, in his face, in his voice. Yet, I could discern a strength and purpose that rose above the fatigue and was part of his very essence. That resolve was what captured us and kept us willing to walk with him into whatever the future held.

5

All three sections of the Freedom School Curriculum—the Academic Curriculum, the Citizenship Curriculum, and a Recreational Curriculum— were intended to promote the following principles:

1. The school is an agent of social change.
2. Students must know their own history.
3. The curriculum should be linked to the student's experience.
4. Questions should be open-ended.
5. Developing academic skills is crucial.
—Freedom School Instruction Pamphlet

The previous evening, both Bob Moses and James Forman had urged any reluctant volunteers to leave, but I heard at breakfast that almost no one had left. We enthusiastically flowed out of the dorms with our luggage, packs, sleeping bags, and guitars and made our way to the cars and buses. The charter buses would take us as far as Memphis where we would switch to the Greyhound line.

This second week's send-off to the Freedom Summer Project had a different feel than the previous week. The Saturday before, there'd been singing, shouting farewells, and laughter. I missed the laughter.

The singing started hesitantly as the buses rumbled their way out of Oxford heading south. I was glad someone started singing the freedom songs. As always, the music of the Movement pulled us together as one so we no longer had the uncomfortable feeling of singularly tilting at windmills like the knight-errant Don Quixote. I was not alone. The singing made me feel part of something bigger, something vital, something urgently important.

I watched as the moon, which was just beginning to wane from being full, skimmed along above the treetops, staying with us on our journey. By this time, the volunteers were quiet, wrapped in the individual comforters of their own thoughts or, perhaps, dreams as they slept. The bus carried us on through Kentucky and into Tennessee, humming steadily down two-lane macadam roads. Finally, at dawn, the bus maneuvered into Memphis and stopped at the Greyhound station where we disembarked to find the right bus to take us to Jackson, Mississippi.

As we traveled south, the early morning sun revealed the scenery of the Deep South: the red clay soil, the occasional tall, thin, piney woods, and flat fields of cotton. If we had hoped for *Gone with the Wind* plantation homes atop lush, green knolls to break the monotony, we were sorely disappointed. Instead, we occasionally passed an unpainted, tin-roofed shack, lonely and uncared for.

Getting off the bus in Jackson, the heat blasted us from all sides. Mississippi's summer heat was definitely different than what we were used to. The volunteers were sorted into smaller groups, some going south and some staying in Jackson. Those of us getting our assignments through the Jackson headquarters were soon delivered to the COFO office on John R. Lynch Street, a sad-looking white plaster building on a block without much else.

Stepping across the cracked and broken sidewalk, I entered a beehive of activity where at least fifteen workers filled the main room, each person busy with a project. A professional-looking woman greeted us. Her crisp white blouse and denim skirt were a stark contrast to our disheveled clothing. "Welcome. I'm Ruth Schein," she said. "You'll be here until tomorrow while we decide which town you'll go to. You'll be in District Two." She pointed to a map tacked on the wall along with dozens of notices, articles, and lists of rules. "So until you get your assignment, try to find a way to be helpful here in the office. You can stash your belongings in a corner for the night. Freedom School teachers, you can select books from the donated supplies. Check with Suzy in the other room. She has mail for some of you." With that, Ms. Schein smiled her dismissal.

The room was crowded with desks and tables, two mimeograph machines, and a couple of sagging couches. I quickly staked out a faded, green tweed eyesore and placed my suitcase and pack on it then set off to explore the headquarters.

The sound of hammering drifted in from a second room, so I

peeked inside. The room was awash with an odd mix of scents: the smell of mimeograph ink, the mustiness of an old building, and the aroma of sawdust reminiscent of freshly cut lumber.

When I introduced myself to the girl I believed to be Suzy, she handed me a thick envelope. It was from Jane and just what I needed! I headed back to the ratty couch, tearing open the envelope on my way.

The letter began in Jane's familiar handwriting, inserting swirls whenever possible and always slanting uphill in her optimistically enthusiastic way.

Dear Lenore,

The Williams family I am staying with is wonderful, so warm and accepting in spite of the danger our being here puts them in. I share a room with the two daughters, so now they have to sleep together in one small bed while I get the other.

The work of getting people to sign up to register to vote is hard, and it is so hot here! We start on one street and knock on every door. There is so much poverty! People have jobs, but they can't seem to make it from payday to payday because their income is so low. Most couldn't get by without their vegetable gardens, and they almost never have meat with their meals. There's never enough money to make repairs on the houses, so they keep sinking into disrepair. The children run around barefoot. It is heartbreaking!

People say that they can't sign up to vote because they would lose their jobs, or they're too old to start with "all that mess." It's very discouraging, but we will persist.

One evening when I got back to the house, I must've looked disheartened because Mrs. Williams came up to me, put her arm around me, and said, "Don't you worry, sugar. Folks will begin to listen and not be as scared. Change will come because of your bein' here. Don't be discouraged."

Well, how could I feel down after that? She's had a lifetime—generations, really—to be discouraged and yet she's holding out hope for change. It's got to come, and I'm so proud and humbled to be part of that change.

That was so like Jane. I stopped reading and looked around. This office was obviously a hub for Black and white SNCC and COFO workers coming in and out, scurrying around, some laughing with others, some frowning or looking intensely at their assignments. Whether they were staff

51

members toiling for ten dollars a week or volunteers working for ideals, they were all doing it for the Movement, investing themselves because they had hope that things would change. I vowed to be like Jane and try to keep that sense of hope alive in myself this summer so that I could pass it on to my students.

~~~

After a brief lunch break of peanut butter and jelly sandwiches, I used the afternoon to plow through haphazard boxes of books and collect any I thought might be useful for my future classes. But it was discouraging work. Hundreds and hundreds of books had been donated as a result of an article in *Harper's Magazine*, but many were copies of *Reader's Digest* or old encyclopedias. They smelled moldy and unused. Almost none were by or about Negroes. I did gather a few authors of note, such as Langston Hughes, John Steinbeck, Robert Frost, and others. I took books of several reading levels, art books, plays, and even a few children's books. I was also pleased to find a dozen well-used copies of *To Kill a Mockingbird*.

After pulling all I could from the last box I found stuffed under a table, I sat back on my heels. *What will be useful?* I wondered to myself. When I asked a few of the workers here, they said "Whatever you think might be helpful." Truth be told, I didn't find that answer helpful at all.

All the instructions we'd received in the workshops were so vague and I wanted specifics. I packed up my selection of books in an empty box and wrote my name across the top so it would go to wherever I was headed the next morning.

My task complete, I retrieved a Coke from the refrigerator in the back room and made my way to the couch, settling in on the worn cushions. Leaning back, I closed my eyes and ran the coolness of the bottle across my face. The hum of activity continued around me—voices calling to each other, the constant clank of an old mimeograph machine, the whir of the fans set in strategic places—and all of it provided another kind of music of the Movement.

Suddenly, a discordant note interrupted my thoughts: Stokely Carmichael, SNCC's field organizer for Greenwood, was giving one of his lectures. I had seen that side of him when he was debating against the effectiveness of nonviolence with Reverend James Lawson in one of the training workshops. Stokely could be intimidating because his whole body conveyed the intensity of his convictions—including the frown lines creased on his high forehead—but when a smile burst upon his face, it was like an abundance of sunshine and love. Although I could understand and appreciate Stokely's passion, I was relieved not to be working closely with him over the summer.

~~~

That evening, the official assignments were handed out. Bob Moses stood in front of us holding a clipboard. "For Freedom Schools in Sunflower County under Mac McLaurin's direction, you'll leave in the morning in three cars that'll take you through the Delta and drop you off at your assigned locations. Be ready at 9:00 a.m. Those in Ruleville and Mystic Springs, you'll be picking up your supplies in Greenwood." Then Bob began reading off names, finally getting to my area. "Phillip Wilson and Karen Wright, you'll be in Ruleville. For Mystic Springs, we've got Lenore Rogers and Elizabeth Stanton." I looked around the group and smiled at the other girl I assumed was Elizabeth. She was about my height but a little on the plump side with thick sandy-blonde hair and a friendly face.

Bob added one important comment. "Those of you going to Sunflower County, we suggest you take advantage of our showers here tonight or early in the morning. It might be your last chance for a real shower."

After the assignments had been handed out, Elizabeth and I sat in a corner getting to know each other as we went over preparations. I liked Elizabeth right away, and it seemed like we would work well together. She had a calm about her and a ready laugh.

She had just graduated from Syracuse with a degree in education and her certification for teaching junior high school math and science. I was more than happy to turn that area of academics over to her so I could focus on history and English. Together, we'd try to tackle the other goals that COFO had put before us.

~~~

The next morning, I woke to sounds of activity already buzzing around me, then took my turn for a shower. The three station wagons parked in front of the COFO building were almost loaded with our boxes of books, so after a quick breakfast of cold cereal, Elizabeth and I folded ourselves in the second vehicle and the convoy was ready to embark on the final leg of our journey.

Bob Moses instructed the drivers to go past the Medgar Evers home before they left Jackson. He wanted us to face what had happened there.

Stopping in front of Evers's ranch-style home, we got out and self-consciously walked up the driveway. Curtains in the windows of nearby houses drew back as we passed.

One by one, we placed our hands on the blood-soaked concrete. The heat from the cement burned the image of the murder deeply into my mind. My heart ached for the young children I could picture waiting inside, hearing their dad come home. But instead of the sound of the door opening and the familiar, "I'm home," there was the sound of gunfire. The scene was beyond anything I could visualize. And yet, there was the bloodstain on the pavement, an ever-present reminder.

Back in the car, my thoughts jumped from Evers's murder site to the three missing civil rights workers, people I had come to know. Such events were the reality in Mississippi, and now, I was actually there too. I felt some of the Freedom School excitement ebb from me, leaving me not only saddened but angry. And with that moment of anger, I began to understand Stokely Carmichael a little better.

~~~

After that stop, the car ride through Jackson was quiet and subdued. Gazing out the window, I saw a different kind of poverty than I'd seen in the tenement houses of New York. In the poorest of the Negro sections of Jackson, the homes looked like little more than worn down, tar-paper shacks. Even so, there was some space around them, and I caught an occasional glimpse of a garden or a bed of petunias by a front stoop. The expressions on the faces of those we passed, however, were the same as those in the tenements—that haggard look of hopelessness, too tired to smile.

Before leaving the outskirts of the capital city, the drivers of the two cars pulled around to the back of an Esso service station. Derryle, our SNCC staff driver, announced, "If any y'all need a restroom, best go here. We won't want to stop anywhere between here and Greenwood. Won't look good to see mixed races riding together in a car. We'll just need to keep going once we leave here." I looked around the car in surprise. Besides me, Elizabeth, Phillip, Karen, and Derryle, Marcus was also with us, hitching a ride to Greenwood. Four whites with two Negroes.

I hadn't given it a thought, but now the realization struck me like a blow. I had to be aware of things like that. This was no longer a conversation at a training session in Oxford, Ohio. This was now a new reality—my reality. I climbed out of the car and headed toward the restroom.

~~~

We'd been driving about an hour when we made our way through Yazoo City. I didn't know when we would actually be in the mystical area known as the Delta, but I figured we must be there because cotton fields interrupted by occasional tiny villages surrounded us along the route. I noticed that when we went through the towns, Derryle and Marcus faced straight ahead but their eyes darted back and forth to the mirrors.

As we entered Greenwood, we drove a few blocks down a wide street lined with small wood-frame and brick houses. We finally came to a stop in front of a two-story building with the metal number 616 tacked near the front door.

"Here we are," said Derryle, shifting the vehicle into park. "The SNCC offices are on the second floor.

As we got out of the station wagon, the heat rose up from the asphalt, engulfing me after the temporary relief from the breeze as we drove. Inside, we climbed the stairs to find a scene much like the one in Jackson, with lots of busy people. Several came from the back room to greet us, including Luke.

"Luke! I thought you worked in Ruleville!" I exclaimed.

Luke chuckled. "I *am* working in Ruleville. Just had to be here today. Good to see y'all. Welcome to the Delta." He shook Marcus's hand with one hand while patting his back with the other—the male equivalent of a hug—then did the same to Derryle. Next Luke took us around the room and introduced us to the Greenwood staff. Some seemed very busy, while others stretched out on their sleeping bags.

Elizabeth and I made our way to the boxes of supplies. I was surprised and pleased with what we found: pencils, pads of paper, an atlas, two abacuses, and flash cards. One whole room was set up as a library full of more donated books. I was pleased to find ten more copies of *To Kill a Mockingbird*.

As I glanced at a wall of announcements, I noticed that someone had posted the most recent articles about the missing civil rights workers. It was the first thing people asked every morning, but after we heard the usual "no news," there was nothing left to say.

After choosing my supplies, I sought out Luke. I found him in the back room, bent over a workstation in deep concentration, his closely cropped hair outlining his face. I strolled up beside him and said, "Luke, tell me everything you've been doing since you left Ohio."

He looked up and laughed as he raised a hand to show me the flyer he'd been working on. "When I'm not out canvassing, trying to get folks registered to vote, I'm working on this kind of stuff."

"Any problems?"

"Nothing real bad," he said before reeling off some things as if he were reading a shopping list. "A volunteer's car was hit by a bullet in Canton. In Holly Springs, some tires were slashed and some beer cans were thrown at volunteers. Williams Chapel in Ruleville was firebombed last Thursday. Not much damage, but it could've been a lot worse. We found eight plastic bags of gasoline outside the building. There's been an increase in harassment, phone calls and such. And some homes, especially further south in the McComb area, have been bombed.

"But on a more positive note, I've been working with a team of two of the volunteers going door to door to get folks registered. We got three who said they'd go with us to the courthouse and try to register. We're working with them now to teach them what they need to know."

After catching up with Luke, my group had a hurried lunch at the Greenwood office. In addition to the usual peanut butter and jelly sandwiches, they offered us bologna—a rare treat.

We wasted no time after lunch getting packed up and ready to get back on the road. Phillip and Karen would get off at Ruleville, then Derryle would drive Elizabeth and me on to Mystic Springs. At the last minute, Luke decided to hitch a ride to Ruleville with us.

The news both pleased and worried me. I liked Luke, but because of our training in Ohio, I knew I had to be very careful. Fannie Lou Hamer had held a workshop for the girls and, in her very blunt way, told us that any relationship between the races could not even hint of being romantic or sexual in nature. She had been very clear that the danger for the Black person would be disastrous.

Even so, moments later as we loaded up the cars to leave, I happily moved over so Luke could climb in beside me for the trip from Greenwood to Ruleville.

Derryle drove through residential areas then cut through to a main street. "I'm going to take y'all the scenic way out of town so you'll see more of Greenwood."

It was an attractive town, complete with an imposing, gray-columned courthouse and a huge Confederate memorial. Derryle spoke with bitter sarcasm as we passed the monument, which rose tall against the blue sky. "Y'all don't want to miss this tribute to white power," he quipped. Steps led to a base with Confederate soldiers on each side and a stone pillar rising to a final figure on top. No one said a word as we drove on. We crossed the river and drove out of town along Grand Avenue, which was impressively lined with stately oaks.

Soon we were back in the countryside. Out of the blue, Phillip brought the conversation around to what was on everyone's mind. "We couldn't believe what we were hearing when Bob Moses made the announcement about Mickey, James, and Andy. How did everyone here react when you all got word about them?"

Luke's mouth formed a hard line. "It was rough. Still is. We know they're dead," he said somberly as he shook his head. "We know it, but we got to find them. So many people have disappeared. But with the FBI involved, they're bound to find them and get the ones who did it. 'Course, I don't know if the FBI would even be involved if they'd all three been Negroes. While they're looking in the swamps and rivers around these parts, they're going to find a lot of bodies. They've already found two others. One was cut in half, and the other had its head cut off."

"Oh my God!" My stomach knotted.

"Yeah, but they're Negroes so no one paid any attention," Derryle spoke up.

Luke looked at me. "And you wonder why we're angry. Maybe by the end of the summer you'll understand. But y'all will go back to your northern colleges, and we'll still be down here wondering who'll be the next one thrown in the Tallahatchie River."

The anger burned in his eyes. I could only meet his glare and not flinch. We stayed silent as field after field of cotton flashed by.

Luke shifted positions as if trying to shake off his last words. "Phillip and Karen, we've got the school in Ruleville all ready for you. The kids are real excited."

Phillip smiled at Luke. "Great! I can hardly wait to get started. Do you know how many students we'll have?"

"Won't know until we start up, but we're expecting about thirty."

"How about Mystic Springs?" asked Elizabeth.

"Dunno. It's in Sunflower County, so Mac will have everything figured out for you—where you're going to stay and everything. You'll get all the details when we get to Ruleville. Mystic Springs is only a few miles out of Ruleville."

I found some comfort knowing that both Mac McLaurin and Luke would be close by. The rest of the ride went by quickly as we chatted easily about subjects that did not include bombings or harassment—or death.

~~~

Route 8 brought us to the town of Ruleville. "This main street on the white side of town was just recently paved," Luke told us. "None of the other streets are paved, so watch out for mud when it rains." Elizabeth and I exchanged a glance, not hiding our surprise. A few turns later and Derryle pulled the car into the side yard of a white house on Lafayette Street.

"This is Fannie Lou Hamer's home," Luke said. "For now, it's serving as the headquarters here."

A number of volunteers were clustered under the shade of a large pecan tree, some sitting on crude benches, some spread out on the ground. As we joined the others, their warm greetings made us feel welcome.

I whispered to Luke, "One of the rules is not to gather in front of places. How come everyone is spread out in this yard?"

"Glad you know the rules, girl," he answered, smiling at me. "We'll have another headquarters sometime, but for now it has to be the Hamer home, and there's not enough room inside for all these people. Mac has talked to the police chief and, for a while anyway, we'll be okay like this."

Mrs. Hamer and Mac came out of the house with a handful of papers to pass out the housing assignments. Mac greeted us and said, "Elizabeth and Lenore, you'll be staying with the Johnsons in Mystic Springs. Here's their address and the keys to and the address of a house you can use for the school. Chris Hexter is our Freedom School director here in Ruleville, and

I'm sure he'll be happy to help you in any way." I was glad to learn they would be putting a phone in the building since it will also be the SNCC headquarters.

Mac went on to say they didn't expect a huge turnout in Mystic Springs, so Elizabeth and I would be the only teachers for that school. Harry and Anitra, the SNCC staff members stationed in Mystic Springs, were already over there. Mac suggested we find Brenda and Tom, the new voter registration volunteers, and have Derryle drive us over before dark. He smiled as he patted us on the back, wished us luck, and moved on to the next group. The last thing he said was a reminder to go over all the safety rules.

That warning from Mac reminded me of one of the stories that a SNCC staffer from Greenwood shared during the Ohio workshops. Three of them, Bob Moses, Randolph Blackwell and Jimmy Travis, had finished working around seven thirty or eight and had gotten in their car to drive to their host family's home in Indianola. They knew that for hours a car had been parked outside the office with some white men in it. That wasn't unusual. But, as always, they had called in that they were leaving and where they were headed, so someone would know if they didn't show up. As soon as they started driving, the car with the white men pulled out right behind them and began following them. Then, on a stretch of road where there wasn't any traffic, the car of whites pulled up alongside the SNCC car, which Jimmy Travis was driving. Jimmy tried to speed up, but the other car hit the gas too and, once again, pulled up next to the SNCC workers. All of a sudden, one of the whites stuck a gun out his window and shot right into the SNCC car, hitting Jimmy. The other two SNCC workers managed to pull the car to a stop and get Jimmy into the back seat then took him to the hospital in Greenwood.

I recalled the icy feeling that had danced through my veins hearing that story during training. I especially remembered that staffer's expression as he told the story. He'd shaken his head and said, "They shot Jimmy then drove off. They just beat it on down the road." Luke had pointed out Jimmy Travis to me during that week of training, but I never got to meet him.

If I think of all the terrible stories, I will really second-guess what I'm doing here.

Elizabeth waved me over to the group in the shade. "Come meet

59

Brenda and Tom," she called to me. I took a deep breath, let it out, and joined them.

Brenda was outgoing, a bubbly, friendly kind of person, while Tom was quiet, almost shy. I wondered how they would do with the voter registration work.

"We'd better get going," suggested Tom. We looked for Derryle, our ride to Mystic Springs.

As Elizabeth and I walked to the station wagon, she shook her head and exclaimed, "God help us!"

I grimaced and added, "Amen."

6

Start by doing what is necessary, then what is possible,
and suddenly you are doing the impossible.
　　—Saint Francis of Assisi

As Ruleville got smaller and smaller in the rearview mirror, I wished Mystic Springs was a little closer than the "few miles" Luke had said. Continuing west, Route 8 led us directly into a residential area of Mystic Springs with brick and white-painted homes, their expanses of lawn neatly trimmed with flower beds or boxwood hedges shaded by tall oak, pecan, and magnolia trees. Derryle drove us down a commercial block housing a bank, a drugstore, a café, and a J.C. Penney.

As the car clattered over some railroad tracks and onto an unpaved street, Derryle said, "I'm driving you the long way around so you can see a little of the area." When we passed a strip of painted cinder block buildings, each huddled under a faded awning, he added, "This will be your part of town this summer."

I noticed a thrift shop, a diner offering barbeque, a liquor store, and finally, on the corner, the only two-story building, which sported a sign for Wang's Grocery.

Derryle made a left turn and then another onto Lee Street. The houses here were mostly one-room wide and not much deeper. Cinder blocks held up sagging front porches crowded with rockers, or worn-out sofas, and tired Negroes whose eyes followed us as we drove down the dusty street. We waved, but only the children waved back.

Derryle pulled up in front of a slightly larger home that boasted a screened porch across the front of the house. "This is where you'll be, Lenore and Elizabeth. The Johnson family. They're real nice. You'll like

61

them. Brenda, you'll be with Anitra a few houses down, and Tom, you'll be with Harry. That's about a block away."

As we pulled our suitcases from the car, a heavyset woman wearing a bib apron over a flowered dress hurried out of the house. Her hair was held back in a tight bun, but several tendrils escaped, softening her appearance. "Welcome. Welcome," she said, wiping her hands on her apron. Her smile was warm and friendly. Two young girls followed her and hung back slightly.

She reached for our suitcases. "So you'll be my summer girls. I'm so glad to meet you. I'm Maybell Johnson, and these are my girls, Anabel and Serene. Anabel, she's fourteen. Gonna be in your Freedom School. My baby, Serene, she just ten. Come in. Come in. My husband, Horace, will be home soon. He works at the filling station."

In the flurry of collecting our things, saying goodbye to the others, and being shepherded into the house, Elizabeth and I found ourselves settling into a back bedroom with a double bed and a painted bureau. Anabel and Serene had followed us to the room and were watching from the doorway. "We emptied them top two drawers for y'all," said Anabel, pointing toward the bureau.

I looked around. "This is your room?"

They giggled and nodded.

"But where will you be sleeping?" asked Elizabeth.

They both turned slightly, and Anabel pointed to the front of the house. "We gonna sleep on the porch with Mama and Daddy."

"We're sorry to take your room," I said. "We don't want to be any trouble."

Mrs. Johnson made her way into the room. "It's no trouble. Why, we all like sleeping on the porch in the summertime anyway. Now, y'all just settle yourselves and then we'll have some supper. The outhouse is out that back door, and you can wash up at the pump at the kitchen sink. I put towels for y'all on the chair. Mrs. Willa Mae Parker down the street had some extra."

That evening seated at a table that took up most of the kitchen, we enjoyed the best meal we'd eaten in days: fried chicken, mashed potatoes, collard greens, beets, sliced tomatoes, and biscuits. Wiping drops of perspiration off her forehead with her apron, Mrs. Johnson hardly sat during the entire meal as she jumped up to refill a water glass or add to an empty plate. The kitchen was even hotter than the rest of the house in spite of a fan in the doorway, but that didn't hurt our appetites at all.

Upon arriving at home, Mr. Johnson, a wiry man of medium build, had been taciturn and somber. During the meal, he simply looked down at his food, eating slowly and steadily.

After finishing my dinner, I laid my napkin on the table and said, "What a delicious meal, Mrs. Johnson. Thank you so much, and thank you for letting us stay here. We don't want to be a burden to you."

Elizabeth nodded her agreement, her mouth full of a biscuit.

Mrs. Johnson's laugh came from a place deep inside her. "Ain't no trouble. I wanted to fix a special dinner for your first night. We're so proud to do our part for the Movement. Things got to change, and you'll be helping make that happen. I want things better for my girls. Got to start sometime, and now is the time."

~~~

After dinner, Mrs. Johnson refused to let us help with the cleanup. "Maybe another day. My girls can do it very well. Y'all have had a long day. Come sit a spell with us and watch television," she said as she ushered us into the main room, where a picture of a white Jesus hung on one wall. Pictures of President Kennedy and Martin Luther King Jr., which were clipped from magazines, were tacked to another wall and fluttered gently in the breeze from the fan. Underneath them, family photographs covered the top of a small bookshelf holding a partial set of encyclopedias.

Mr. Johnson headed toward a big, brown upholstered chair and dropped into the permanent dent in its seat. He kicked off his work boots, stretched out his legs, and leaned back, sighing into the chair's comfort. Mrs. Johnson removed her apron and eased down on the couch. Elizabeth and I settled in beside her.

Mrs. Johnson smiled at us. "When the news went from fifteen minutes to a whole half hour last fall, we wondered how they'd fill up all that time, but they do. They sure do." She turned to her husband. "Which do you want tonight, Horace? Walter Cronkite or Huntley and Brinkley?"

"I dunno. I guess Cronkite."

"Anabel, come in here a minute and get us CBS," Mrs. Johnson called.

"The young people are better at these technical things, you know. We can get all three channels here, although sometimes Anabel has to fiddle with the rabbit ears to get reception."

We sat through the thirty minutes of Walter Cronkite without hearing any more about the three civil rights workers, then Elizabeth and I excused ourselves to work on our school preparations.

Back in the small room, we dumped all the materials from our packs onto the bed in a storm of pamphlets, notes, mimeographed instructions, and notebooks. "How will we ever organize all this?" Elizabeth asked, her brow furrowed.

I picked up the first set of materials we had received: three pages of safety instructions, seven pages explaining our legal rights if arrested, one page on how to set up a Freedom School, a fourteen-page guide with curriculum outlines, and three pages on how to lead discussions integrating real-world situations into classrooms. And that was only the beginning.

Elizabeth pulled her hair up into a ponytail then held up another page. "Here are the guiding questions we're supposed to incorporate into all the discussions: Number one: What does the majority culture have that we want? Number two: What does the majority culture have that we *don't* want? Number three: What do we have that we want to keep?" She shook her head. "Doesn't this sound more like a college seminar? How do you think these kids will respond? Do you think we can have some realistic discussions?"

I shrugged. I really had no idea. I picked up the outline of the curriculum. "Do they really expect us to start off by saying: 'What is a Negro?' My God! What are the Negro high school kids going to think when two white girls ask them that?"

"Dunno. I guess we just have to go with it and see what happens. I mean, educators met to set this curriculum. They must know something we don't."

I looked at her, my eyebrows raised with skepticism. Sighing, I went back to studying the material...and praying it all worked out.

By midnight, the heat had only slightly abated. I lay wide awake in the double bed trying not to move so I wouldn't disturb Elizabeth. I wondered if she was doing the exact same thing. The last time I had shared a double bed with someone was at a slumber party when I was in junior high. But that had only been for one night and with air-conditioning.

I'm not sure what I'd expected on my first night in Mississippi. Perhaps intimidating police officers slapping nightsticks against their thighs or angry whites driving by and shouting threats and insults while waving Confederate flags. They hadn't shown up yet, but the oppressive heat had. I'd been warned to expect it, and it was living up to my expectations with no wisp of breeze coming through the open window.

What I hadn't expected was the warmth of Mrs. Johnson's welcome, the sweet shyness of Anabel and Serene, the generosity of an unknown neighbor sharing her towels, and an amazing meal. Those good things made me think of the possibilities that the days and weeks to come held.

~~~

As usual, morning came too early for me, but Elizabeth was already up and dressed in khaki Bermuda shorts and a Syracuse T-shirt. As she sat on the side of the bed and tied her sneakers, she said, "Wear something you don't mind getting dirty. I'm sure we'll need to do some cleanup in our classroom since it's not in a church."

Mrs. Johnson greeted us in the kitchen with a warm smile. "I made y'all a good breakfast today since you got a lotta work ahead. I made fried eggs, biscuits, and grits. Y'all ever had grits before?"

We both shook our heads as we sat down across from Anabel and Serene. "Has Mr. Johnson already left?" asked Elizabeth.

Mrs. Johnson chuckled. "Oh my, yes. This is the middle of the morning for him. Now, when you're through, Anabel and Serene will show you to the school."

I smiled at the two girls who were watching us intently while we ate. It was Serene who finally spoke up. "I never been near no white folk, nor talked to any, and here you are, staying in our very own house! I can't hardly believe it!" She put her hand in front of her mouth to stifle her giggles.

"Serene!" her mother admonished. "We talked about that. Now don't be calling attention to them or making them uncomfortable. Just treat 'em like regular folks, remember?" She looked at us. "Don't pay her no mind. She don't mean nothin' by it."

Elizabeth answered first as she reached for the last biscuit. "It's no problem. We're both the same way. We've never stayed with any Negroes before either."

After breakfast, Anabel proudly offered to lead us to the school. Mrs. Johnson loaded the four of us down with cleaning supplies, brooms, mops, rags, and a cleaning mixture she'd made from white vinegar. We went out the backyard and made our way past chickens scratching for food and a well-tended garden. It was already filling up with a variety of vegetables, including beans, cabbage, squash and tomatoes, with the tops of carrots, onions peeking out of the ground.

Elizabeth and I followed Anabel through a small copse of scraggly oaks then across a weed-covered lot to an unpaved street that skirted a row of tar-paper shacks. Anabel took us to the last house and climbed the two wooden steps of the drooping porch. Our shoes scratched against the rough wood as we followed her to the door.

"This is it," she announced.

I glanced at Elizabeth and dug in my purse for the key Mac McLaurin had given us earlier. "Well, here we go," I said as I pushed open the door.

We stood for a moment as our eyes adjusted to the dim light and our throats tightened from the dust and heat. The musty smell of a shuttered-up building overwhelmed us. Disturbed dust mites and cobwebs swirled across a floor littered with Coke and beer bottles, a single shoe, yellowed newspapers, cigarette butts, a ripped mattress, and, upon closer inspection, what appeared to be used condoms. An open doorway revealed a smaller room in the back.

Elizabeth and I exchanged a look of horror then burst out laughing. Suppressing a choke, I said, "Let's get some windows open."

Anabel shifted her gaze from one of us to the other. "Why are y'all laughing?"

Elizabeth patted her on the back and admitted, "This isn't exactly what we expected, but it's okay. Can you round up a few of your friends—preferably some strong boys—to help us clear this stuff out? If we stack it out front, I guess the trash collection truck will come by and pick it up."

Anabel let the momentary silence tell the story. "Could just put it in that lot across the street. People who want something will come get it."

Elizabeth nodded. "Okay." She pulled up her hair into a tight ponytail, which, by this time, I knew meant she was ready to get to work.

A little later that morning, SNCC staffers Harry and Anitra showed up with their summer voter registration volunteers, Brenda and Tom, all prepared with cleaning supplies. But by that time, we'd swept up the most unpleasant of the debris and made a path from the front and back doors.

"We'll take the back room for our office," Harry asserted, heading that way.

Having both doors and the windows open had helped with clearing the air. For the rest of the morning, we all worked hard. We sorted, tugged, and hauled, removing items, batting cobwebs, and sweeping areas clear. The conversation was minimal as if the heat had robbed us of the civility of speech. Anabel and the two friends she had found lugged the mattress to the empty lot, and then the young people went off on their own.

"Hello all," a cheerful voice called from the doorway. "Come sit a spell out here on the porch. We brought y'all sandwiches and sweet tea. Time to take a break."

We all walked to the front porch and, suddenly, I realized how dirty we were. All six of us apologized for the way we looked. The two women smiled and introduced themselves as Mrs. Logan and Mrs. Dawson from down the street. "We knew you'd have a big cleaning job today," Mrs. Dawson said as they handed us water bowls and washcloths. "We're so proud y'all have come to teach our young'uns," said Mrs. Dawson as she passed around cheese sandwiches to all of us.

We sat around the edge of the porch and got to know our two Good Samaritans. "We got a friendly neighborhood here, and we do the best we can with what we have," Mrs. Logan began. "Down that away," she gestured to our right, "straight down the street and over the railroad tracks, you'll get to the white part of town. I'd be careful going that way if I was you. Won't find them as friendly, I'm thinking. You can get everything you need 'round here. Wang's Grocery has plenty, and there's a laundry next door to it, plus we got a great barbeque place. Now, over another block behind us is all the juke joints. I'd advise you to stay away from them too," she said with a little laugh.

"And only two blocks that way," Mrs. Dawson pointed away from the white part of town, "is our church, New Hope AME Church. You're welcome to worship with us anytime."

Harry thanked her and added, "They'll be some mass meetings held over at Williams Chapel in Ruleville. Y'all might think about going over there. Got some real good preaching and singing."

"Oh, I know Reverend Joe D. Story. He's a fine man and brave to let them have those mass meetings," Mrs. Logan said as she turned to the volunteers. "Churches that allow the meetings get bombed. They do and I—"

Just then, a pickup truck screeched around the corner and barreled down the street with its radio blaring and a white boy leaning out the passenger window. Two teenagers in the back were hanging on tightly to the sides of the truck bed. When the truck slowed, the boy in the passenger seat yelled, "Go home, you nigger-loving Yankees! We don't want you here!" The rest of the insults were lost in the noise of the engine and their raucous laughter as they made their getaway, but we did not need to hear the words to get the message.

A cold knot twisted in the pit of my stomach. I felt as though I'd been slapped in a startling, primitive way. My shoulders slumped as I put down the rest of my sandwich, my appetite suddenly gone.

Mrs. Logan folded her arms across her chest. "Humph. Now don't y'all be worrying about boys like that. They just full of hot air. I used to work for that boy's mama. They got no class, that's all. We going to keep y'all safe here. Don't you worry none."

"Mm-hmm. Mm-hmm," Mrs. Dawson agreed, nodding her head.

The two SNCC staff members seemed unruffled by the drive-by incident, but the expressions on the faces of Brenda, Tom, and Elizabeth mirrored my own. For the first time since we'd arrived in Mississippi, I felt truly vulnerable and unsafe. The training had tried to prepare us for such an incident, but the reality of the hatred on the boys' faces made the words so much more powerful.

By late afternoon, the six of us had done all we could do for one day. We decided to keep scrubbing the next day and then start moving in the tables and chairs Mac was rounding up for us. The truck with the boys whipped by two more times, but we ignored them.

Going home without Anabel, Elizabeth and I weren't sure we could find the right backyard using the shortcut she'd shown us. We walked around the block with Anitra and Brenda then left them at the house where they were staying. Walking on, I said, "I'm ready to sink into a hot tub and soak for an hour. Preferably one with scented bubble bath."

"Ha! How do we even *take* a bath?" asked Elizabeth.

"During the training, I heard someone explaining that we might have one big, galvanized tub we can fill with water we've heated on the stove. Then we stand in it outside, pour water over us, and I guess scrub with soap and rinse with another pot of warm water."

"But what do we wear? Our bathing suits?"

"Oh my God! I don't know. Let's see what the girls do."

Elizabeth moaned. "I can't wait that long. I need a bath today! Let's just ask Mrs. Johnson."

As we climbed the steps to the door of the screened porch, Elizabeth whispered to me, "Do we knock or walk right in?"

I shrugged. "Both I guess." I knocked loudly, opened the door, and called hello.

Mrs. Johnson came from the kitchen. "Come on in," she said. "You don't need to knock. My goodness, you live here now. You're welcome to go in and out whenever you want."

As we followed her into the kitchen, she gestured to the chairs at the table and continued, "Tell me all about your day. I hear you had quite a mess to clean up. Sit down now and I'll pour y'all some nice, cold sweet tea. And those Findley brothers coming by and yelling like that. Shame on them! Don't give them a bit of care."

She handed us our drinks and added, "Now, I'm sure you'll want to clean up. There are washcloths and towels on the chair, and I've been warming up a pan of water. I'll bring it to you with some soap."

"Well, uh, how do we...uh...where do we wash up?"

Mrs. Johnson stopped midstride. "Why, in the bedroom. Just have a little scrub bath. You know, dip the washcloth in the water, soap it up and scrub a little, then rinse and do some more."

It wasn't the bubble bath we were longing for, but we did feel refreshed after we'd cleaned up. Afterward, we helped Mrs. Johnson prepare supper. Elizabeth set the table as I snapped green beans.

When Mr. Johnson arrived, we quickly crowded around the kitchen table. We knew by then that Mr. Johnson was a quiet man, but on this particular night, I sensed there was more to it. I wondered if Elizabeth noticed it too.

In the middle of the meal, he set down his fork, leaned back, and said, "Heard today that a man o'er in Ruleville lost his job for having some freedom folk staying at his house."

The silence that surrounded us throbbed with emotion—anger, fear, shame, and guilt all wrapped up in the fleeting moment like a gasp of pain.

My voice trembled, "Should we find another place to stay?"

Mrs. Johnson looked from us to her husband, her eyes wide, as she bit her bottom lip. She waited for his reply.

He stared at his plate as if the answer he was seeking was written there. After a moment, he looked around at each of us. "We'll never get anywhere if we don't take a stand. If y'all were brave enough to come down here, we have to be brave enough to provide you a place to stay." He picked up his fork and continued. "That's the whole of it," he said as he began eating again. The rest of us sat frozen for a minute.

Elizabeth and I both had tears burning in our eyes as we choked out, "Thank you." Two simple words that could not begin to convey the profound realization I had of what courage really looked like.

7

Let there be peace on earth,
And let it begin with me.
Let there be peace on earth,
The peace that was meant to be.
With God our creator,
We are family.
Let us walk with each other
In perfect harmony.
—"Let There Be Peace on Earth"

Mac arrived in the late morning with two tables and a good number of chairs. He promised more chairs for the next day and said he'd see us over in Ruleville that evening for a mass meeting at Williams Chapel. He laughed and joked with Harry and Tom as they unloaded the supplies. It was reassuring to see his familiar, smiling face.

When we told him what Mr. Johnson had said, Mac shook his head, his mouth a thin, tight line. "I'm proud of Horace for hanging in there. I think it'll be okay for y'all. The whites push back more with the voter registration people than the Freedom Schools group. Whites don't figure that as much power comes from education as it does from the vote. Humph. They'll learn soon enough. Anyways," he said as he herded us back to work, "I think y'all will be fine. Don't worry."

~~~

After supper, the six of us crowded into Harry's car and headed to Ruleville. Elizabeth and I were especially excited to be going to our first mass meeting. During training, we'd heard a lot about their importance to the Movement.

Harry drove carefully, not even a mile over the speed limit. As we approached the church, he muttered, "Uh-oh. I expected this." Several police and sheriff's cars were circling the area around the church. We pulled into the parking lot as if nothing was wrong and walked stiffly toward the church. But out of the corner of my eye, I watched two deputies copying down Harry's license plate number.

By the time we made our way into Williams Chapel, I was more interested in finding a certain familiar face. I finally saw him a few rows up. He turned and waved to me. "Come on," I urged Elizabeth forward and edged into the pew. "Hi, Luke," I said, giving him a warm smile. He scooted over to make room for us.

The stifling summer heat filled the room along with more people than could comfortably fit. In spite of electric fans placed in the windows and a multitude of Williams & Lord Funeral Home cardboard fans fluttering frantically, I felt perspiration forming on my upper lip. I dabbed at it with a tissue, grabbed a fan, and started waving it frantically as if I'd been a southerner all my life. When Luke looked at me and chuckled, I gave him a quick elbow jab.

Fannie Lou Hamer went to the front and began singing her favorite civil rights song, "This Little Light of Mine." Then she led us from one freedom song into another. The congregation rose, swaying, belting out the words, and clapping with the rhythm as joy spread across our faces.

When the singing stopped, Luke leaned over and whispered, "This was where Mrs. Hamer was inspired to go register to vote. This is hallowed ground, girl."

I looked around at the inside of Williams Chapel. The simple church was bruised but not broken from a bombing attempt not long ago. *Hallowed ground?* I thought. *Yes, I could see that.*

I believed it because of the spirit surging from the voices lifted together in song. I heard the pain in the words, in the tenor notes tugging at the heartstrings along with the soprano and bass voices all singing of hope. I found myself nodding. *Hope. There's hope in this place. That's what'll make a difference.*

"Brothers and sisters," Reverend Story's voice pulled me from my thoughts. "I said, brothers and sisters...are you with me tonight?" The "amens" and "yes, sirs" gave a resounding reply.

"And why are we here, gathered together in this place? This place that has been bombed. This place that has white police officers noting all who are here tonight." People shook their heads and muttered angrily. "But the scriptures say...the scriptures say, 'I will not be afraid of ten thousands of people who have set *themselves* against me all around.' So we will not be afraid because the Lord Jesus, the Lord Jesus, he is walking beside us, is he not? He is walking with us through this troubled land."

The crowd shouting "Amen" and "Preach it" distracted me at first. Back home, our sedate congregation never spoke out during the sermon. But soon I began to feel the rhythm of Reverend Story's words and the answering rhythm of the congregation.

Reverend Story continued. "We are not walking alone...no sir. I want you to look around you. We are not alone because we have these young people who have come from all corners of the country. They have come here to help us, to help us get registered to vote, to help set up Freedom Schools and community centers."

"Amen."

"Look around and you can see them. Now, they don't look exactly like us, do they?" Laughter rumbled through the congregation. Luke returned the elbow jab.

"They don't look exactly like us because something is different about their skin, isn't it?"

I smiled self-consciously. For the first time in my life, I was in a situation where I was the racial minority. I was "the other" and, although everyone was so friendly, I felt different and a little uncomfortable.

I could tell Reverend Story was enjoying this. "But they can't help that. It was the way they was born. We've been working hard down here to get every Negro registered to vote, to establish our Mississippi Freedom Democratic Party, and now these young people came down to help us. Can I get an 'amen'?"

"Amens" flooded the room.

"They're working with us, standing side by side with us. Now, I ask you, if these young people have come to walk with us, shouldn't we be out there walking too?"

By now, people were standing and clapping their hands. Tears pricked my eyes. I knew, as they surely did, that there would be consequences for what we were doing tonight: this mass meeting. There would be consequences because of actions those in the congregation might take in the future. Of course, I realized these good people wouldn't rush to the clerk's office in the morning, but the seed was there. This is how it would begin.

Between the power of the singing, Reverend Story's energetic preaching, and the heat, I was wilting by the end of the meeting. But as I joined in the singing, I felt less like an outsider. It was a good feeling.

When Mrs. Hamer walked to the front, everyone knew what was coming, and we rose, holding hands with our arms crossed. She started with a plaintive note that hovered a moment in the silent sanctuary before all the voices joined in. As we sang, I believed that we really would overcome. I still believed that kindness was stronger than cruelty, that love was more powerful than hate, that goodness would overcome evil. I was still a believer.

After the meeting, the congregation funneled outside amidst goodbyes and handshakes. Luke walked with Elizabeth and me to Harry's car. As I ducked into the back seat, he caught my arm and spoke softly. "Good seein' ya, girl. Be careful. Stay safe." He shut the car door for me and added, "I'll come visit sometime soon."

I smiled up at him and nodded.

The six of us were quiet on the ride home. I for one would've liked a full moon to light the way along Route 8. In the darkness of the countryside, I felt a little uneasy. As we traveled down the road, I watched the quarter moon and started reciting a poem my mother used to say to my sister and me when we were little:

The moon's the North Wind's cooky [*sic*],
He bites it, day by day,
Until there's but a rim of scraps
That crumble all away.
"What?" Tom asked from the front seat.
"Just a poem my mom used to say."
The South Wind is a baker.
He kneads clouds in his den,
And bakes a crisp new moon that...*greedy*
North...Wind...eats...again!
I finished the poem with a flourish like my mom always had.
"Isn't that a little depressing?" asked Anitra.

74

I shrugged. "Just something I thought of while watching the moon." I didn't say what else it made me think of: *Would much of our work simply crumble away once we left at the end of the summer?*

~~~

The next morning, Anitra and Brenda stopped by the house as Elizabeth and I were finishing breakfast. "Wear your walking shoes," Anitra told us. "We're going to take a tour around town so y'all can get to know the area. There's town maps and county maps in your packets. Study them. You need to know where you are and to have alternative safety routes home."

I found the words *alternative safety routes* a little unsettling because it was something I never had to consider where I grew up. I was glad to have this opportunity to get to know Anitra. When she was with Harry, he did all the talking. She was an attractive young woman, about my age. She had a short, compact body and, to me, it fit her personality. She dressed with a flair for colors that highlighted her caramel-colored skin. While most of us wore khaki Bermuda shorts with sleeveless tops, Anitra was wearing a sundress with deep pink and golden yellow swirls. She held herself in tightly and carried that same edgy aloofness I had encountered with most of the SNCC staffers. I knew I would have to earn her friendship, and it would not come easily.

After crossing Railroad Avenue, we kept our eyes straight ahead as we passed the police station and jail on our right. Further down the road was a large grocery store.

"You probably won't ever have to come here," said Anitra. "Wang's has everything you should need."

The coffee shop and newsstand with a beauty shop next to it looked appealing. "I pointed in that direction. What about going in there?" I asked. "Would we have a problem?"

Anitra shrugged. "Hope not, but you never know."

At the corner, we turned left and passed an impressive Baptist Church: a sturdy brick building that took up almost the whole block. Elizabeth paused as she looked up the steps at the massive wooden door. "This looks like my home church. Would I be welcome there on Sunday mornings?" she asked.

Anitra simply snorted.

After the church parking lot, we turned left again and passed a few shops, a bank, and a drugstore. The downtown looked like any small town, with people going in and out of businesses and occasionally greeting one another. At first glance, it seemed so nice and friendly. But with my newly opened eyes, I saw that, except for Anitra, there were only whites in this part of town, and some of them gave us wary—even angry—looks.

We passed an inviting-looking café with red-and-white checkered cloths on the tables. "How about eating an occasional meal at the café?" I had to ask.

"That would probably be okay as long as you're not with any Blacks. Of course, *we* can't eat there."

I stopped and looked at Anitra. "Hearing about segregated places and actually seeing them are such different things!" It really hit me what the "racial divide" really meant.

Anitra didn't say a word. I hurried to catch up.

We passed the J.C. Penney store then crossed Railroad Avenue again as we headed back to what Anitra told us was called "Niggertown." I winced every time I heard that word.

We walked down a block until we were in front of Wang's Grocery. I peeked in the window; it appeared to be a clean, well-stocked store.

"As long as they have bread, peanut butter, and jelly, we'll be okay," Brenda quipped. We all smiled, knowing the truth of that.

Elizabeth turned to Anitra. "I'm surprised to find a Chinese grocery store in the Delta."

"Many towns in Mississippi have Chinese grocery stores. The family usually lives in the back rooms, but the Wang's live upstairs. Their kids go to school with the Negro children."

In the next block, Anitra paused in front of a small brick church. "This is my church, New Hope AME Church. You'd definitely be welcome here."

I gazed at the neatness of the yard and the well-kept exterior of the church and observed that it was considerably larger than the schoolroom we'd been assigned. Anitra started to continue on, but I touched her arm. Despite thinking of the hard work we'd done to get the donated school building into shape, I had to ask: "Do you know why we couldn't use that church for our Freedom School?"

Anitra nodded. "Yeah. When the mayor heard y'all would be here, he stopped the city from paying for the church's water and canceled the church's tax exemption. Those are two benefits all churches are supposed to get in Mississippi. Then the insurance company canceled the church's coverage. You can imagine how vulnerable a Black church is here in Mississippi if it doesn't have insurance."

"Can the mayor do that?" Elizabeth gasped.

Anitra grimaced at our naiveté. "Sure can...especially when the White Citizens' Council runs the town."

Damn! There's that white thing again, I grumbled to myself. Anitra's expression made me uncomfortable yet angry, learning of another injustice. However, there was no point saying anything to Anitra, so we turned left and made our way back to the school and SNCC headquarters.

"Are you from this area?" I asked her as we walked.

"Jackson," she replied curtly.

"Oh. Have you been up here in the Delta long?"

"A while."

This conversation wasn't going anywhere, and we were almost to the school, so I gave up. Back at the SNCC office, the four of us pulled Cokes out of the refrigerator and sat at the table. Elizabeth, Brenda, and I chatted for a moment about buying groceries we'd need for our lunches, and Elizabeth started a list.

Anitra sat quietly for a few minutes then spoke up. "Y'all want to know what the power of the White Citizens' Council can do?" Her question cut into our conversation with the sharpness of a knife.

Elizabeth put down her pencil and replied, "Of course."

"Last winter," Anitra began, "a number of people in Leflore County were 'agitatin'' to register to vote. The white county supervisors tried all kinds of things to stop them, but when nothing worked, they simply cut out the federal surplus food program. Last winter was an especially hard winter, and the sharecroppers were really desperate. They needed those basics that the surplus food program supplied—things like rice, flour, and cheese. So word went out that we needed help, and Dick Gregory brought in fourteen thousand pounds of food and distributed it through the SNCC office."

The three of us sat quietly, absorbing yet another example of injustice at the hands of whites. These were bitter pills to swallow. Our emotions ran the gamut of shame, embarrassment, anger, and determination in our commitment to work with SNCC in whatever way we could. But we remained silent. What was there to say anyway?

For the first time that day, Anitra smiled at us. "But the story has a good ending. When someone came to apply for that help, a SNCC worker would suggest they first walk on down to the courthouse and register to vote since they were already in town and then come back to get their supplies. So, in the end, cutting off the surplus food supply really backfired for the white establishment because the SNCC workers were able to show people the connection between the power of the vote and actually having food. They demonstrated that if Blacks could vote, they could elect people who would look out for them. It's something we remind them of when we're trying to get them registered."

Brenda lifted her Coke bottle in admiration and we all joined in. The clinking of the glass bottles together was a joyous sound.

~~~

With the little we had available, Elizabeth and I continued trying to make the schoolroom look bright and inviting. But it was discouraging work, somewhat like making Cinderella's ball gown without the fairy godmother.

We had enough chairs, tables, and supplies to get started, and someone had improvised shelves along the wall and filled them with the books Elizabeth and I had found. We looked around our classroom. It was small and neat and as ready as we could make it. Elizabeth and I were too.

~~~

That evening after dinner, Mrs. Johnson insisted that we sit with them to watch the news. I was embarrassed that I'd forgotten an important event was happening that day, but the Johnsons were not about to let us miss it. We took our usual places in front of the television for the news broadcast and watched as President Johnson signed the Civil Rights Act of 1964. It was July 2. President Johnson sat with an arsenal of pens in front of him to enact the legislation that President Kennedy had submitted before he was assassinated. After President Johnson finished signing, he turned to Martin Luther King Jr. and handed him the first pen.

"Look at that!" exclaimed Mr. Johnson, pointing at the television. "First one to Dr. King. First one!"

With tears shining in her eyes, Mrs. Johnson watched as President

Johnson handed pen after pen to Robert Kennedy to give to other honored recipients. She said, "And all those to Robert Kennedy, naming people they should go to. Maybe Mac will get one. Or Mrs. Hamer. There's so many that deserve one."

The Johnson family had been leaning forward as if to be closer to the important event. When it was over, they settled back into their seats, smiling at each other while Walter Cronkite continued the evening news report.

"This is a big day for us," Mr. Johnson remarked as he turned toward Elizabeth and me. "A big day."

The family was still talking about it after watching *Rawhide* when Elizabeth and I headed back to our room. We'd witnessed history in a unique way, and I could hardly wait to discuss it at the school.

Later that night as I was quietly making my way back from a last trip to the outhouse, I caught a glimpse of Mr. Johnson removing a shotgun from the hall closet. He put a handful of shells in his pocket and headed to the front porch for the night. The euphoria of the sweeping legislation had been swept away by the reality of what Negro people experienced every day and every night in Mississippi. I returned to the back door and double-checked that I had locked it securely behind me.

~~~

On Saturday, the two Mystic Springs SNCC staff members, Harry and Anitra and the four of us volunteers, Elizabeth, Brenda, Tom and I, decided to celebrate the Fourth of July with a picnic lunch in the town park, a right denied to Negroes until two days prior with the signing of the Civil Rights Act. Anitra and Brenda brought items to make sandwiches along with potato salad, paper plates, and plastic forks. Their host family had also made brownies for them to share. Mrs. Johnson provided an old quilt to spread out on and sent us off with cups and a jug of her sweet tea.

It was no surprise that the park was full of families, even though Mrs. Johnson had told us that most would come in the evening for the fireworks. Nevertheless, she advised us to be back home before dark, saying we could see the fireworks from their front yard.

At the park, all the picnic tables and shady spots were taken. The sound of people relaxing floated through the air with conversations, laughter, and parents calling to their children to come eat. On the outskirts of the park, there were a few small groupings of Negroes who seemed to be testing the waters of a newly integrated public space.

When we entered the park, the jubilant sounds evaporated and conversations stopped as people stared at us. We received hostile looks as we drove a wedge between the picnickers. Despite the ensuing silence, the overwhelming sense of hate was unmistakable.

We sidestepped some teens tossing a Frisbee and spread our quilt near a giant oak whose shade a white family had claimed. I smiled at them as we arrived. The mother started to smile back until she saw Harry and Anitra with us. Setting out our picnic, we couldn't miss the glowering looks of the parents as they muttered under their breath to each other. The two blonde daughters stared open-mouthed at our mixed-race group.

The parents looked at us with such disgust as if we were some dirty animals ruining their picnic lunch. It made me feel uncomfortable and angry in some obscure way, so I shifted around to avoid facing them.

When I sensed someone approaching, I expected the worst. But, instead, I looked up to see a familiar, handsome face. "Luke! What are you doing here?" I exclaimed.

Luke chuckled and greeted everyone in the group. "Marcus went off with some friends, so I borrowed his car and came to see what y'all were up to. Mrs. Johnson told me you were here integrating the park. Whatcha got to eat?"

I laughed. "So you only came to get a free meal? I know your type." My smile quickly disappeared when I heard some commotion coming from the nearby family. The father had jumped up, thrown down his napkin, and was stuffing everything in the picnic basket while mumbling curses. The two little girls were sobbing as the mother pulled them to their feet and grabbed the blanket they'd been sitting on.

The father glared at us. "Y'all have no business here!" he snarled. "This here is our place, our park!" He snapped up the basket and turned to leave.

As the parents rushed them away, the two little girls cried, "Why do we have to leave Daddy? Why?"

I felt stunned as tears filled my eyes. My heart ached because I knew how those parents would answer their daughters' plaintive question.

"Come on," Harry said, jumping up without missing a beat. "Let's claim that spot in the shade."

We quickly moved under the tree. I joined the enthusiastic chatter hoping no one noticed my display of emotion. Luke sat down next to me and gently touched my arm. "Yeah," he said softly, "that's what happens when you're a Negro. But now with the Civil Rights Act, they can't make us leave like they used to. It's a new day, girl. Be happy."

For a brief moment, I looked into his eyes—those eyes that held generations of emotions. I nodded and smiled then asked, "How's everything going in Ruleville?"

~~~

Sunday morning presented a problem for me. *Should I try attending a white church or go to New Hope AME Church with the Johnsons? Or should I stay home and sleep in?* The Johnsons had invited Elizabeth and me to go with them, and Brenda had said she would stop by on her way to a white church in case we wanted to join her.

Elizabeth was tucking in her blouse when I got back from my morning trip to the outhouse. "What are you going to do?" I asked her.

She zipped up her skirt and said, "I thought about going with Brenda to try that Baptist church. It's the closest. But I don't know. It doesn't feel quite right from what Anitra said. Still, it would be the kind of service I've gone to practically every Sunday of my life."

I nodded. "Sure....But we're here staying in the Johnsons' home. They've welcomed us in like family. Wouldn't it be an insult to them if we went to that white church?"

Elizabeth sat down on the edge of the bed and sighed. "I've had all those same thoughts, Lenore. I know it's a white church, but the fact is, I'm white. I think I'd be more comfortable at a traditional white service." She paused then added, "I don't know what to do!"

"Well, I think I'll go with the Johnsons to show support. At training, they encouraged us to do that."

When Brenda arrived, she convinced Elizabeth to go with her to the Baptist church. But my mind was made up; I was going with the Johnsons.

I smiled at the hurry-scurry atmosphere that morning as Mrs. Johnson barked orders at each of her family members: "Anabel, don't you wear that pink dress no more. It's getting entirely too short. Serene, pull up your socks so the ruffle shows good. Now Horace, make sure you got your tie on straight. I'll come fix it for you. Oh, where did I put my gloves?"

I tried to stay out of the way and be ready to go when the family set off walking the few blocks to the church. Mrs. Johnson called out a greeting to everyone we passed along the way, and Mr. Johnson tipped his hat. He seemed to stand straighter and step more firmly dressed in his dark suit and carefully ironed white shirt. Anabel and Serene walked ahead, waving to friends.

When we arrived at the church, Mrs. Johnson guided me through the small groups chatting before the service and introduced me to everyone. "This is our Freedom School teacher, Lenore. She's my girl for the summer."

Reverend Hamilton Hendricks shook my hand. "I was so sorry we couldn't offer you space here. The finance committee simply couldn't approve it with the risk involved."

"I do understand. I was sorry too."

"I've been thinking about an alternative, though. If it works out, I'll get back to you." He excused himself to greet others, leaving me to wonder what he might have up his sleeve.

The only other Negro service I'd ever been to was the mass meeting in Ruleville. A Sunday morning service was quite different. The hymns that the choir sang were not the freedom songs but were equally as powerful in the way they stirred up the congregation.

"What a friend we have in Jesus," the choir began, the pianist striking the beat behind the voices. I didn't see any hymnals, but I knew the words by heart. The soloist belted out, "Yes, Lord! Yes, Lord!" When we got to "What a privilege to carry" and the rest of the congregation added "to carry, Lord," I knew this wasn't going to be the way we sang in my church. Several in the congregation were moving with the music, their raised arms swaying in praise and worship.

Reverend Hendricks leaped into his sermon with the energy of a sprinter, and his enthusiastic style carried the congregation along with him. "Psalm 18 verse 6, brothers and sisters, listen to what it's saying. If you have troubles, I say, if you have troubles or pain or difficulties, cry out to the Lord like David did. Listen to his Word, his Word when it says, 'In my distress I called upon the Lord, to my God I cried my distress.' And listen, brothers and sisters, listen to what God does. 'From his temple he heard my voice.' He heard my voice and he will hear your voice when you call to him in your distress. Can I get an amen?"

I left the church service feeling that I had definitely been to church and worship had happened there. While the Spirit hadn't moved me to stand up and shout out, "Yes, Lord!" at any point, I felt that I was part of the service.

After church, almost everyone stayed around outside at the picnic tables under the live oaks for a potluck meal. Dish after dish was marched out from the tiny church kitchen: macaroni and cheese, cold fried chicken, ham, cornbread, more garden vegetables than I'd ever seen, banana pudding, and a berry cobbler that Mrs. Johnson had brought.

The conversation swirled all around me—words and laughter that signified bonds, ties, and deep connections. For the first time in a long, long time, I missed that same feeling I'd experienced as a child in my church and community. With my parents divorced and living in different places, I no longer felt like I had a home to go back to.

I wandered through the cluster of people while some women set up the meal. Several people spoke to me about the Freedom School and what they hoped it would bring to the Black community. One couple stood on the edge of the group while we talked, and finally, after a while, the woman spoke up. Her Afro framed a pretty face with high cheekbones, dark brown eyes, and full lips. "This is what bothers me, young miss," she began. "We welcome you into our midst. The white man notes that you visited us or taught our children. Then you go back home, and we're left here with Mr. Charlie's wrath and brutality. Now how does that really help us? Huh?" She stood with her arms crossed over her chest.

I felt flustered for a moment as I tried to remember what I was taught about this kind of confrontation in my training. "I do understand what you're saying, ma'am, and, honestly, it's a valid question. There are two things I can say in response. First, there *are* people who are going to stay after the summer. SNCC and COFO are working on getting teachers and leaders to keep the Freedom Schools and community centers going. The second thing is more important. By all of you registering to vote and then actually voting, you will have the power to change things here. That's what needs to happen so that white people who don't care about your rights won't be in power anymore."

"Do you really think that'll ever happen here in Mystic Springs?" a man scoffed.

"If I didn't believe it, sir, I wouldn't be here. If Mac McLaurin and Mrs. Hamer can get a proper delegation seated at the Democratic National Convention in August, a lot could turn around. Getting registered and voting is the key."

"Quiet, y'all. Pastor Hendricks is going to bless the food," someone called over the noise of all the conversations, saving me from any more discussion.

When the Johnsons and I got home from church, Elizabeth and Brenda had already changed into shorts and tops and were sitting on the front porch.

"Well?" I asked. "How was it?"

They exchanged a glance, and Brenda confessed, "The service itself was okay."

Elizabeth snickered. "They definitely knew who we were and we were *not* welcome at all! We should never have gone to that church!"

8

1. Why are we (students and teachers) in Freedom Schools?
2. What is the Freedom Movement?
3. What alternatives does the Freedom Movement offer us?
—Guiding Questions, Freedom School Curriculum

I had no trouble waking on Monday morning. It was the first day of school, and the entire household was up and bustling around.

Wearing my professional-looking shirtwaist dress, I stood in front of the bureau's mirror rolling my hair into a French twist, hoping the overall effect would make me look older. I had debated bringing any jewelry but finally decided on wearing my circle pin. No self-respecting college girl was without one. I pinned it on and gave my reflection a confident smile, even though I didn't feel confident at all.

Anabel and Serene were finishing up their breakfast as Elizabeth and I sat down.

"Good mornin'! Good mornin'!" Mrs. Johnson greeted merrily. "I fixed you girls a special breakfast today," she added as she set out a platter of pancakes that could have fed twice as many people. They looked delicious, but with the knot in my stomach, I wasn't sure I could eat anything. I noticed Elizabeth take a stack of three.

Anabel insisted on carrying some of the bulging notebooks Elizabeth and I had packed for the first week's classes. We were prepared for almost anything, although we were quick to admit to each other that we hadn't a clue what to expect. As we followed Anabel's shortcut to the school, my senses heightened. I felt more aware of the sound of the birds, the branches brushing against us, and the smell of earth and grass as we crossed the vacant lot. Then finally, we reached our destination: the Freedom School!

I unlocked the door, opened the windows, and started the fans the church had loaned us—except, of course, for Sundays and Wednesday evenings. Elizabeth got out supplies for the day and looked around the room full of empty chairs. I held up crossed fingers to Elizabeth, hoping that those seats would soon be filled with eager students. With a deep breath in and out, we moved toward the door to greet any early arrivals.

Just then, Anabel, who'd been waiting outside for her friends, entered with two girls and sat at a back table.

"Anabel, bring your friends up front and introduce them," I called to her.

The girls looked at each other and shyly moved to a table in the second row.

"I'm Lenore Rogers. Elizabeth Stanton and I will be your teachers. What are your names?"

Both girls looked down and spoke softly. "I'm Autumn Stokes."

"And I'm Thelma."

"We're glad you're here." I gave them my brightest smile then Elizabeth and I moved to greet others coming into the room.

In the next half hour, many more students had arrived. Elizabeth counted eighteen, not including seven adults and younger children crowded against the back wall. I tried to memorize something about each one to help me learn their names. Sadie wore her hair in one tight braid, Naomi's was in several small pigtails, while Cora's hair was short and soft around her face. It was harder with the boys. All of them had closely cropped hair, except Josh who sported an Afro.

There was an undercurrent of conversations among the students, who occasionally cast wary glances our way.

At nine o'clock, I stood a little straighter and seriously wondered if I could do this. Elizabeth began first, and her confident manner gave me the boost I needed. We introduced ourselves, explained what the Freedom Schools were about, the importance of the students speaking up and giving their opinions, and what we would be covering. We assured the students that this was a safe place to speak the truth. We reminded them that they could call us by our first names, which we'd written on a blackboard Mac had unearthed for us. Once we started going over the familiar curriculum, I began to feel more comfortable.

Then it was time to really begin teaching. I opened with, "The first unit we're going to cover is called The Negro. We'll be looking at what it means to be a Negro. Imagine I had just landed on a spaceship from outer space and met you on the street. Suppose I didn't know anything about the earth. If I asked you, 'What is a Negro?' what would you say? How would you answer that question?"

Many of the students squirmed in their seats. Most of them looked down, avoiding eye contact. When two boys glanced at each other, I was sure they were thinking: *What is this crazy white woman asking?* Thank goodness our training had prepared us for this. Marcus had told us not to expect anyone to speak up at first—maybe not even the entire first day. Even so, the longer the silence went on, the more the butterflies flitted in my stomach.

I paced back and forth across the front of the room, looking at the students and listening to a room full of silence aside from the sound of shifting bodies. "Anyone?"

"Depend if you white," came a muffled a reply, which was met with guffaws from the back row of boys.

I took another deep breath. "Okay...forget I'm an alien. Assume that I'm from a country that has never had any Negro people, and I'm really curious when I see you. What would you say?" The only response was the sound of a creaking seat as someone shifted positions.

I looked over at Elizabeth, but she only gave me an encouraging smile. Returning my gaze to the class, I said, "I know it seems like a ridiculous question, but remember what Elizabeth and I explained earlier. During our time in the Freedom School, we want you to really look at what it means to be a Negro today. So let's think about that question. What is a Negro? You are all Negroes. What does it feel like to be you?"

An older boy in the back, who was small for his age and dressed in a clean, white shirt and jeans, stood up. "A Negro is a Black person, ma'am, and if you're a white person, that's all you'd care to know. You wouldn't want no truck with a Black person." He looked around to the nods of agreement and sat down.

I wanted to hug him for giving me a response. I could imagine what would happen if I really did that, but it made my butterflies go away. "Great observation. I think you're probably right about that. Now let's look at why that is. Remember, we told you that in this school there are no right or wrong answers in our discussions. We want to know what your opinions are and why. You are allowed to speak freely here; you can even say things that are negative about white people."

I looked at these young people, who had come to school this

morning with some kind of expectation in their hearts, and my shoulders slumped. "Look, I know it's stupid for your white teacher to be asking you what a Negro is. But the educators who wrote this material thought it was important. They want you to think about and express things that you haven't been able to do in your regular school. This is the place for you to really face what your lives are like, so you can be able to move forward. So, again, tell me in your own words, what is a Negro?"

"A Negro is a person who got no rights. He a nobody," called a boy sitting near Anabel.

"He a nobody to whitey. But a Negro's somebody in his own community," commented another.

Heads swirled around to see who had dared to use the term *whitey* in front of me and Elizabeth. She and I smiled at each other and nodded. *Now we're getting somewhere,* I thought.

"Remember, we said this is a safe place for our discussion." Elizabeth smiled at the boy who had used the term *whitey* then continued. "One of you said that a Negro has no rights. But what happened last Thursday? Did that make things different?"

Anabel spoke up. "The president signed Civil Rights Act. It's s'posed to make things different, but I dunno if it will."

"Yeah. If the whites here don't want things to change, they won't."

Again there were nods of agreement. Finally, Thelma spoke up, "My parents think that because it's a law, things *will* change."

"That's what Dr. King says," someone concurred.

"Yeah, I guess it's possible for things to get better." Anabel shrugged. "Maybe."

Again the room fell silent, but I felt a pulse of excitement boiling beneath the surface. It seemed like it wanted to burst forward like racehorses straining at the starting gate.

I continued the lesson by suggesting, "Let's look at that Civil Rights Act and see what it says." I pulled out our copies from the piles of material on the table behind us. Elizabeth and I had been studying them all weekend. I held up my copy. "This has been described as landmark legislation. Does anyone know what the phrase *landmark legislation* means?" I noticed more students were looking up, no longer averting their gaze.

The young man in the white shirt stood up again, "It means it's very important. It's a law that might change things."

"That's right. What's your name, young man?" Elizabeth asked.

"Cornelius, ma'am."

"Thank you, Cornelius. Yes, this is important legislation that might change things. Let's look at what it might change. It's divided into eleven sections called titles. Title I is about voter registration. It says that it's *illegal* to apply unequal application to voter requirements."

An older woman in the back of the room leaned forward on her cane and asked, "Do that mean we don't have to tell what the Constitution mean when we try to register to vote? I know this school ain't for the likes of me, and I was goin' to sit quiet back here and try to learn something, you know. I'm sorry. I couldn't help but ask that question. I want to vote sometime before I die."

I felt appalled to realize that this woman, who was probably three times my age, had never been allowed to vote. "That's an excellent question, ma'am. May I ask your name?" I smiled at her as I walked toward the back of the room.

As all eyes turned toward her, she gripped her cane more tightly. "I'm Willa Mae Parker."

The name sounded vaguely familiar as I struggled for an answer to her question. "Mrs. Parker, what this law says is that now the requirements to register are the same for everyone, white or Negro. So if you're asked to interpret the Constitution, then every single white person trying to register must also be required to interpret it. Everyone must be treated the same under Title I."

A hum of whispering followed my answer. Mrs. Parker sat back, her lips pulled together, and shook her head. I could see she wasn't the only one having this reaction. They clearly realized this law wasn't going to make it any easier for Negroes to register to vote.

"Title II and III are similar to each other, and they're important ones. They say that any discrimination based on race, color, religion, or national origin in hotels, motels, restaurants, theaters, and all other public spaces is against the law. Title III also prohibits state and municipal governments from denying access to public facilities on the grounds of race, color, religion, or national origin. So what does that mean for everyone?"

Hands flew up, but several people simply called out their responses.

"No more colored restrooms or drinking fountains."

"I'm going to sit down in that café and order me a big ice cream sundae, and I'm going to take all afternoon to eat it." There was a great deal of laughter in response to that one.

"We can go to the state fair!"

"When we travel now, we don't need no green book."

Elizabeth broke in. "I'm sorry, but what's a green book?"

A low rumble moved through the students and their expressions became more open. They were going to teach this white teacher something she didn't know.

Cornelius stood again. "*The Green Book* is a guide Black people use when traveling. It tells the places where we can stop to eat, to spend the night, gas stations where we can use the bathrooms, things like that. Places that are safe for Blacks."

I filed this away as yet another thing I had no idea existed. I continued, "Thanks, Cornelius. So back to our first question: what is a Negro? Class, would you say a Negro is someone who until July 2, 1964, didn't have the same rights as white citizens, and it was white citizens who held the power to determine and control the rights they *did* have?"

At first, faces flickered with looks of wary puzzlement that such a statement should come from a white person. Then gradually, confident nods, "yeahs," "yeses," and "yes, ma'ams" followed.

I stopped pacing. "It's true, right? But let's look at this further. What does it feel like to be Negro under those circumstances? Who's willing to share? What does it feel like to be a Negro, to be you?"

The students looked around at each other. After a while, a petite, dark-skinned girl sitting next to Anabel, shyly raised her hand and dared to speak up. "It don't feel good when you cross those railroad tracks."

I remembered her introducing herself when she came in with Anabel. "That's a very good answer, Thelma. That would definitely help someone understand something about being a Negro." I turned to the class. "How about someone else? Tell us what it feels like to be a Negro in Mississippi today."

As the morning and the discussion went on, the room sizzled with emotion. The freedom the students sensed vibrated around the room, bouncing from one young heart to another. I saw them becoming more confident about expressing their feelings, putting words to understandings they hadn't fully realized before. This was a beginning, an important one.

Their responses were also leading me to some new understandings. I felt a tightening in my chest, and I wanted to shout, "This isn't the way life should be. This is wrong!" I had known all this, of course, but to hear it sputtered out by young people who should be concerned with dates, clothes, movies, and music—to see their expressions full of hurt and anger—made a painful impact on me.

By the end of the session, we managed to get the class to come up with a few universal feelings of what it's like to be a Negro. We wrote them on the blackboard:

1. A Negro is taught to fear white people. Black people must always show respect toward whites because white people have all the power.
2. Within the Negro community, individuals are shown respect in their churches, businesses, and organizations, etc.
3. A Negro is a person who needs to use faith and education to move forward.
4. A Negro is a person with a history of strong people.
5. A Negro is a person who must get the vote.

When the class left for a lunch break, I let out a long sigh that felt like it had been held in all morning.

An hour later, even more students crowded into the room. As they settled around the tables, Elizabeth handed each of them a blank piece of paper and a pencil.

Right away I assured them, "This is not a test. The people who set up these Freedom Schools want you students to have some input into how they are conducted, so they're simply asking for your opinions. The first thing they want to know is, why are you here in the Freedom School? Elizabeth and I shared with you this morning why we are here and what we hope for. This is a chance for you to tell us why *you* are here.

"We're going to take fifteen minutes for you to talk to those sitting around the table with you. Ask each other: Why did you come here today? What do you hope to learn in the next few weeks? Do you want to do things that include art or music? Do you want to act out plays or role-play? Do you want us to review basic skills in math, English, or science? Do you want to spend time talking about Negro history? Basically, we want you to write out your thoughts about the Freedom School and what you want from it. Go ahead and talk to each other for a few minutes to help you get some ideas, then start writing about why you are here. We'll collect all the papers in a few minutes. Remember, you can be completely honest."

The afternoon passed quickly. We talked about starting a newspaper and, after much discussion, the students voted on a name for the paper:

The Freedom Story. I gave a brief overview of the book *To Kill a Mockingbird* and said that even though it was written a few years earlier, it was still very much like life in Mississippi today. We explained that we'd discuss it more in a later class, but they where to start reading it on their own. We handed out all the copies Elizabeth and I had collected.

Later, Elizabeth and I tried to decipher the written answers to our questionnaires and remember the comments the students made regarding what they wanted from the Freedom Schools. It became very clear that what they wanted and COFO's vision for the schools were basically the same. They wanted an education on par with the white schools and for the untold story of Black history to be told.

~~~

The week flew by for us. By Friday, there were almost thirty students coming to the school each day. Luckily, Harry, Anitra, Brenda, and Tom had begun working on door-to-door voter registration, so we were able to expand into the back room.

We took turns having students of different grade levels work in the back room on improving certain skills, but whenever it was time for a discussion on Black history, everyone wanted to be in the main room. Unlike that first morning, there was no longer any holding back on sharing opinions, asking questions, or arguing with each other. For us, the days were invigorating and exhausting, thrilling and troublesome.

Learning what it was like to live as a Negro in America stunned me. I was beginning to realize that I would never completely understand. I thought of the Luke I knew and the Luke I wanted to know and felt sad knowing that I could barely reach that generations-deep Luke.

At dinner on Friday evening—biscuits with butter beans, turnip greens, and fresh tomatoes from the garden—Elizabeth and I recounted the week's highlights to the Johnsons. "Our biggest problem is that we're so overcrowded," I said.

"And that makes it even hotter," Elizabeth added as she buttered a biscuit.

"Don't see why y'all don't use that empty school," said Serene.

"What empty school?" Elizabeth and I asked in unison.

"The old Lee Junior High over on Oak Street. Been empty since they merged it into the high school."

"Oh my gosh! That would be perfect. How can we find out about using it?" Elizabeth exclaimed. "I wonder why Mac didn't get it for us?"

"You'd have to talk to the school board president. I reckon that's probably why Mac couldn't get it," Mr. Johnson replied.

"But that's ridiculous," I sputtered.

No one spoke for a moment. "Well, the school board is white, of course," said Mrs. Johnson.

I shifted uncomfortably. My whiteness kept slapping me in the face.

"I suspect Mac talked to them," Mr. Johnson continued. "He's good about trying to touch base with the town leaders when he goes into a place in Sunflower County. I know he always makes hisself known to the police chief, lets them know what he's about, you know. Sometimes that helps, sometimes not."

I set down my fork. "Well, we'll give it a try anyway. What's the board president's name? We'll get in touch with him tomorrow. It's Saturday, so we can both go see him."

Mr. Johnson chuckled softly and shook his head. "You can try, young lady, but don't expect him to let y'all use it. His name is Stanley Williamson. He owns the insurance company in town, the Land Title Company, and some more. He's also the police chief's brother-in-law. And on Saturday, he'll be out on the country club's golf course, so I don't think you'll catch up with him."

~~~

On Saturday morning, Elizabeth and I figured we had plenty of time to accomplish our mission. We got Mr. Williamson's number from the phone book and called him from SNCC headquarters. No one answered at his home, so we couldn't even leave a message. We hoped to catch up with Harry and Anitra to get their advice, but they were out working on voter registration with Brenda and Tom. We also called the insurance company to ask for a meeting with Mr. Williamson, but our calls went unanswered there too.

We stayed at the school doing a little clean up. But even with the fan blowing directly on me, I was too hot. "How do people function in this heat?"

"Some people actually have air-conditioning," answered Elizabeth.

"Do we know any of these people?"

Elizabeth put down the papers she had been studying. "No, but maybe we could borrow Harry's car and go to the movies or at least to Ruleville to sit under the pecan tree at Mrs. Hamer house. I suspect there's always some members of our group there."

"Great idea! Now all we have to do is find Harry and get the car keys."

That chore took longer than we thought it would, and the morning was almost gone by the time we managed to convince Harry to lend us the car. Before we left, we told Harry of our attempts to reach Mr. Williamson.

"I'd suggest you forget about it," he said. "There is no way he'd ever let us use that building for a Freedom School."

I frowned. "But that doesn't make any sense."

"Makes white people's sense," Harry muttered.

"We'll see about that," I replied.

After a quick lunch of peanut butter and jelly sandwiches, Elizabeth said, "Let's swing by Oak Street and look at the school on our way out of town."

Moments later, we parked in front of Lee Junior High, a sad-looking, one-story, dilapidated building. We got out and walked across the weed-infested lawn. Most of the windows were broken, and racist graffiti bruised the walls. Peering inside, we could see that any room with anything left in it had been completely trashed.

I shook my head. "This is unbelievable. How would you feel if you were Negro and you came by this place every day. I don't think there's any way we can make this usable. I mean, what would it cost to replace all these windows, get the walls painted, and clean up the rooms?"

"I can't imagine," said Elizabeth. "Let's get to Ruleville and talk to Mac."

I felt disheartened as we drove down the street of run-down, shotgun houses anchored by the defeated building that was denigrated by vicious graffiti—a disgrace that had once been a school.

~~~

We were only a few miles down the road when I gasped. "Oh my God! We forgot to call Gail in Greenwood and report that we were leaving Mystic Springs!"

Elizabeth groaned. "Well, can't do anything about it now. Drive carefully. Don't speed or anything."

The stretch of two-lane road in front of us that was dotted with cotton fields on each side loomed longer and longer. Ruleville had never seemed so far away. I tensed up with every car that passed us until, finally, we pulled into Mrs. Hamer's yard. As we hoped, several SNCC staff members and volunteers were there under the pecan tree.

We were especially glad to see Karen and Phillip, the teachers in Ruleville, to compare notes on the first week of classes. "How was it?" I asked.

Phillip smiled. "At first we couldn't get them to say a word. Now we wish we could get them to quiet down."

Karen laughed in her gentle way. "Not really. We love to hear how eagerly they're questioning. Next week we're going to have them pick a person from Black history and portray them to the class. I got a bunch of clothes from some thrift shops that they can use as costumes."

"What a great idea!" I said. "Mind if we copy it? You can borrow our idea. We've had them start a weekly newspaper."

"Every idea helps," said Karen.

Just then, Mrs. Hamer came out, looking tired as she limped toward us in a pair of scruffy slippers. She set a pitcher of ice water and some glasses on a table, greeted us, then sat down on one of the benches. Her skin shone with perspiration as she wiped her face with a tissue.

I poured a glass of water and went and sat beside her. I held out the glass to her, but she shook her head.

"Mrs. Hamer, can I ask you something? A personal question?" I'd learned that Fannie Lou Hamer was someone who would be absolutely honest with a person, and I wanted such an opinion now.

"Of course, baby. Anything."

"After all you've been through, what your family has been through, how can you not hate us white people?"

She was quiet for only a heartbeat. "I can't carry that much hate around, child. It would burden me down too much. And we've got too much work to do."

95

I sipped the water as we sat in silence.

Turning toward her again, I said, "I've learned so much since I first set foot on the campus in Oxford, Ohio, and I know I still have a lot to learn. I'm grateful for this opportunity. But I wonder, can we really make a difference in the few weeks of summer that we'll be here? It seems like such an uphill battle, and I don't think attitudes will change. Can we really do anything to make life better here? Will what we do matter at all?"

She chortled as if there was an easy, obvious answer. "Oh, yes, it will matter! If you get one person signed up to vote, if you get one child to learn that their voice can be heard, then yes, it will matter. If we can get our Mississippi Freedom Democratic Party delegation seated at the Democratic National Convention in Atlantic City in August, we will have finally made a real change. And look at what your being down here means. Almost every Negro adult you meet and shake hands with has never had a white person address them as mister or missus and put out their hand to shake. Don't you never think that you being here don't matter."

She patted me on the knee as she slowly rose. "It do matter, baby. Surely it do." She picked up some empty glasses and the empty pitcher and headed back inside, leaving me comforted and affirmed.

Wiping the perspiration from my face, I joined the others. The group was sharing stories and laughing as the afternoon flowed slowly around us. Carol set up a knitting class. Someone brought out a guitar and was softly strumming popular tunes. I tried not to look for the one face I hoped to see. Actually, it was Elizabeth who saw him first. She nudged me. "There's Luke," she whispered.

I waved him over, and he sat down beside me. "What's up, girl? Whatcha doing over in my town?"

"*Your* town? I thought this was Mac's town."

Luke's smile broadened. "Well, you're speaking the truth there. At least this part of town. How'd your week go?"

As I told him about the students' reactions to the information and questions, I found myself getting more and more enthusiastic. In the retelling of events, I saw that each day had gotten better and better. Finally running out of steam, I sat back and said, "It was a great week. How was yours?"

Luke eased into a more comfortable position. "An interesting thing happened Thursday. I wasn't there, but Mac told me about it. A known segregationist came to the COFO office just asking questions—like he wanted to understand what we were about, you know? They had a friendly discussion. Well, some white person must've seen his car parked there or seen him walking in the office and didn't like it, so they went to the police to complain about it. The police came and told the guy to leave. When he didn't, they charged him with disorderly conduct, and they actually fined him—one of their own! They couldn't stand the idea of a white person being friendly with us," Luke said as he shook his head in dismay.

I scrunched my face into a puzzled expression. "That *is* strange. And hard to understand." I thought about it for a moment then asked, "How is the voter registration going?"

"Slow going, Lenore, that's for sure. And I get it. I understand about being scared to simply try to register. Look at what happened to Herbert Lee and Mrs. Hamer, even to..." He stopped himself before saying the names Mickey Schwerner, James Chaney, and Andy Goodman, whose bodies still hadn't been found.

There was still no word about what had happened to the three missing civil rights workers even with the FBI assigned to the case. The SNCC staffers and volunteers had all gotten sick of hearing whites say on the news that it was a hoax, that the three were off partying somewhere, and so on. But where were they?

"Elizabeth and I will also be helping with the voter registration on free evenings. What's the best way to approach people, to reassure them?"

Luke shrugged. "Hard to say. For y'all white people, you need to develop some level of trust before you go trying to get them to sign up. Get to know them as individuals in your neighborhood, y'know what I mean? That you're teaching in the Freedom School is important. They'll know you care by you doing that."

"Okay. Thanks. There's something else I wanted to ask Mac about, but I don't want it to sound like I'm complaining about the building he found for us. There's an old school on Oak Street, but it's in terrible shape. It was abandoned, and every window has been broken, doors are bashed in, there's graffiti on the walls. There's no way we can get it ready now, but I wondered if it would've been possible to get it ahead of time—"

"Whoa, Lenore. Hang on right there," Luke interrupted. He was leaning toward me with his chin jutting out and his eyes narrowing. "Don't you think Mac already tried to get the best places for schools and community centers in Sunflower County? He knows the system, and he worked it the best he could to get things ready for the Freedom Summer Project." Luke wagged his finger in my face. "Don't you dare go whining to him about that. You're looking at that from a white point of view, and that don't work down here." His eyes flared with anger.

"I...I'm sorry, Luke," I stammered, but then I felt a burst of anger myself. "But for God's sake, I didn't mean it as a complaint against Mac! I'm only trying to find the best possible place for the students. We get more every day, and soon we won't be able to fit them all in at one time."

Luke spat out his words. "Then think of other ways to handle it. Have split sections or something. Meet outside. Be creative. Every Freedom School is crammed full of people, which shows how badly they're needed. Find out from teachers in other schools what they're doing instead of coming here criticizing Mac."

Luke turned away slightly, and I wanted to do the same. We sat there for a while with a silent wall between us.

Soon, Elizabeth headed over. "Anytime you're ready to head back, I'm ready. There's a Dairy Queen on the edge of Ruleville, so we can get some burgers and fries...and milkshakes," she added with a smile.

I hopped up and said, "I'm ready. Let's go." I started after Elizabeth, stopped, and then turned back toward Luke and barked, "I *wasn't* criticizing Mac! Don't be so damn sensitive about everything I say!"

I left quickly before he could respond. Sometimes it's important to have the last word.

9

Adversity is like a strong wind....It also tears away from us all but the
things that cannot be torn, so that afterward we see ourselves as we really are...
—Arthur Golden, *Memoires of a Geisha*

As we opened the door of the Dairy Queen, the aroma of french-fries called out to me. Suddenly, a cheeseburger, fries, and a milkshake became my idea of a perfect meal, and they instantly put me in a better mood.

We had called in our plans before leaving Ruleville so we felt more comfortable on the drive back. I shared with Elizabeth the conversation I'd had with Luke. By then, some of the sting had left and what remained was some practical advice. I mentioned all the suggestions Luke had given.

Elizabeth kept her eyes on the road ahead as she drove. "Well, Karen and Phillip are as crowded as we are. They're having some classes outside."

"But it's so hot!"

"True," Elizabeth agreed, "but they get under shade trees. Any big enough trees near the school? I don't...oh, Lord, no!" she exclaimed as she looked in the rearview mirror at the flashing lights of a police car. "I didn't see them coming up, but I know I wasn't speeding!" She pulled the car slowly to the side and stopped as blue and red flashes washed over us. We looked at each other, eyes wide, my fear reflected in hers.

I never thought this would really happen to me. *Oh my God, how were we taught to handle situations like this?* I thought as I tried to push down the rising sense of terror.

The uniformed cop who approached the driver's side window didn't look much older than either of us. The sinking sun glinted off his aviator sunglasses as he put both hands on the rolled-down window and leaned close.

"Was I doing something wrong, officer?" asked Elizabeth, gripping the steering wheel more tightly.

"I'll ask the questions here. License and registration. You too," he gestured toward me.

I wanted to protest, but I remembered the words of attorney Jess Brown: *Don't be thinking you can give some sheriff or deputy a lecture on your constitutional rights.*

I fished my driver's license out of my purse without a word. Elizabeth handed him the documents and tried to look innocent.

While the deputy sauntered back to his car, I wiped my sweaty palms and said, "What's he doing? Can you tell?"

Elizabeth glanced in the rearview mirror. "Copying all the information from our IDs. Damn!"

He returned and handed back our credentials. "Get out of the car," he snarled.

"What!" Elizabeth and I exchanged a frantic glance.

"I said, 'Get out!'" He slapped his palm against the roof of the car. "Both of y'all. You tryin' to resist an officer of the law?"

We jerked the car doors open, and the contents of my purse spilled onto the floor as I swung my legs out. I started to reach down to pick up my things but thought better of it. I was so frightened that I wasn't sure my shaking legs would hold me up.

"Stand in front of the car, hands on the hood," he barked.

The heat from the car's hood seared my hands. My throat was dry, and my heart raced. *Breathe in. Breathe out.* I thought as I forced myself to regain control.

The police officer paced behind us, leaning nearer each time. "The registration says this car belongs to a Harry Cooper. Did y'all steal this car for a joyride?"

His face was so close I saw the pimples on his cheeks and smelled the tobacco on his breath. "No," I answered, "Harry lent us his car so we could run an errand."

"And where does this Harry live?"

The SNCC safety rules were imbedded in my memory. *Do not travel with the names and addresses of local contacts. Never give anyone any information about your local family* "I don't know where he lives. We just see him occasionally at the Freedom School."

The young officer reached for his handcuffs but paused as the police chief's car pulled up.

The police chief took his time getting out of his car. When he did, he hitched up his pants and looked over at us. "Whatcha got here, Donny?"

"Could be a pair of car thieves," the officer answered. "Car don't belong to them. The license plate is one we got from that mass meeting last week."

"Well, well," murmured the chief as he made his way toward us. "While we're tracking that down, I wonder how these little ladies'll do in jail with all the weekend drunks. Might give them second thoughts about coming down here and telling us how to live our lives. Thinking they're better'n us."

When the police chief beckoned the officer a little distance away, Elizabeth and I glanced at each other, trying to convey a strength we didn't feel—or at least I didn't.

After a few moments, the officers returned, and the sheriff slowly looked us over. I flushed, feeling violated and powerless. I wanted to cry. I wanted to be furious. But I continued easing my breaths, calming myself by remembering our training. I could tell Elizabeth was doing the same, biting her lip, eyes closed.

The chief chuckled. "Well, you college girls are in luck today. Seems like we don't have room in the jail so we're not taking you in. I saw some of y'all at church Sunday so I know you're good Christian girls, aren't you?" He paced a moment behind us. "Yup. Good little Christians come down here to teach us to be good to the Negras. Well, our Negras are just fine without y'all. We don't have no trouble with 'em. The sooner you realize that and go home, the better it'll be for all of us.

"Now we're going to let y'all go," the police chief continued as he yanked us by the arms, shoved us in the car, and leaned in Elizabeth's open window. "But we got your names now. Next time y'all won't get off so easy." He spat out the side of his mouth, went back to his car, and drove away.

Elizabeth and I sat there trembling for minutes after the two cars left.

"My God! I've never been so scared in all my life!" Elizabeth remarked.

"Me neither." I still hadn't stopped shaking. "But that feeling! Oh my God! The feeling that even though we hadn't done anything wrong, we were powerless. That was the worst! It was...it was horrible!"

While we sat there for another few minutes, I reached down and collected my purse and its contents. I grabbed a tissue and wiped the perspiration from my face and hands. "The training didn't quite prepare me for the reality, though."

Elizabeth sighed. "We'd better get back. When we do, I'll call Greenwood and report what happened."

We reported in, returned Harry's car, and walked the two blocks back to the Johnsons' house. Harry had been sympathetic about the traffic stop, but he didn't seem disturbed by it. Of course, he'd been stopped countless times and arrested several others, as had pretty much everybody in SNCC. Elizabeth seemed to be putting it behind her, so I didn't want to keep rehashing it. I wanted to call my mom, but I knew she'd tell me to come home, and I wasn't ready to do that. What I really wanted was to talk to Jane...or Luke. But couldn't do that either.

Elizabeth went inside to give herself a sponge bath while I sat on the front steps. The sun was beginning to set, so I watched it slowly sink behind the tree line. It first appeared as a golden circle then only flames. Over time, the sky became a muted mauve and lavender before it turned to dark purple then black. And still, I sat there.

When I saw the first star, I began quietly reciting, "Star light, star bright, first star I see tonight, I wish I may, I wish I might, have this wish I wish tonight."

The sound of the screen door thumping shut startled me. Serene plopped down next to me on the steps. "You wishing on a star?" she asked.

I smiled at her. "Yeah. My mother taught me that."

"My mama taught it to me too."

"What would you wish for?"

"Oh, different things, like a bike, or when I was little, I'd wish for a baby doll that looked like me, things like that." Serene shifted on the step and wrapped her arms around her knees. "But you're not s'posed to tell wishes or they won't come true."

"That's what they say," I agreed. I pulled Serene close in a hug and said, "I hope you get every single thing you ever wish for."

But now that I'd learned more about Black life in Mississippi, the futility of that desire made me want to weep.

~~~

Sunday morning there was no discussion about which church to attend. Brenda and Elizabeth were joining me and the Johnsons. I still felt shaky from the incident the day before, so simply staying in bed had some appeal, but I opted to go back to New Hope Church and was glad I did.

That afternoon, Elizabeth remarked that she had to do some laundry. We'd been rinsing out our under things and T-shirts after our scrub baths, but the time had come for a larger washing. "Do we ask Mrs. Johnson for some bigger tubs and heat the water?" I wondered out loud.

Elizabeth went to ask. When she returned, she said, "Mrs. Johnson said that Mrs. Parker has a wringer washer that we can use. She's the one who let us use her towels. Just lives two doors down. Let's go."

I was looking forward to seeing Mrs. Parker again so we could talk more about registering to vote. Mrs. Parker was a short, wiry woman with immense energy even though she used a cane. She reminded me of a bird as she flitted in and out of the back hall where the washing machine filled the area. Her hair was just starting to go gray and her eyes had the filmy covering of cataracts. She told us her husband had died six years earlier from the "sugar sickness."

She explained to us exactly how to use the ancient machine, patting it with pride and saying that her four children had purchased it for her. As we waited for the clothes to swish through the wash and rinse cycles, Mrs. Parker kept up a running commentary on the Mystic Springs community. She told us about each and every neighbor and people at church, those whom we could count on and, more importantly, those whom we needed to watch out for. As she nattered on, there was no need for us to make a comment. We only needed to listen.

Mrs. Parker had grown up in a sharecropping family, had worked in the cotton fields since she was six, and had finished only the third grade. She had birthed seven children, but only four had lived to adulthood. The two sons had moved to Chicago and had families there; her two daughters and their families lived nearby.

Elizabeth and I listened with interest. Mrs. Parker's story could have been the universal story of that generation of Negroes in the Mississippi Delta. Her grandmother had been born in slavery. Mrs. Parker lowered her head and shook it as if in homage to her ancestors who had endured that terrible time. She held up a hand for us to wait as she shuffled out of the room. She returned a few minutes later with a frayed cigar box that she proudly opened, and gingerly lifted out a worn, graying doll made from a corn husk.

She gently touched the stiff, tattered remnant from so long ago and said, "It don't look like much, I know, but until my granmama were free, it were the onliest thing she owned." Mrs. Parker laid the doll carefully back in the cotton-lined cigar box. "When my granmama showed it to me, she cried so I knowed it were important to her. Said her brother made it for her. So I kep' it all these years. Silly, I guess, but it's all I got of her."

I covered her hand with mine. "Oh, no, it's not silly at all. It's a priceless thing. Thank you for sharing that with us."

"My granmama, she told me lots of stories. Told me 'bout when her brother ran off from the plantation one time. They caught him, and when they brung him back, they made all the slaves watch him get his beating. Said it was lucky they didn't cut his heel and cripple him like some slave owners did." Mrs. Parker rocked back and forth as she held the box closer.

Later that day, as Elizabeth and I walked home with our laundry to hang on the Johnsons' clothesline, I said, "What a great way to hear history. Imagine the stories that little doll could tell. Maybe we can get Mrs. Parker to bring it to school sometime."

~~~

Arriving at the school early on Monday morning, Elizabeth and I found Harry and Tom already there, coordinating their plan for the day. I could tell something was off though because Harry didn't have his usual smile and enthusiastic greeting.

I set down my bag and asked, "Everything okay?"

"Oh, sure. It's just that I got the weekly report of incidents, and it's so damn discouraging, week after week."

"What happened?" asked Elizabeth.

"The usual. The SNCC Freedom House in McComb got bombed. Another church was burned. There were a lot of arrests on trumped-up charges, and now there's a paddy wagon in Greenwood that the townspeople call the 'Nigger bus'. Plus there's the usual bottle throwing and threats and spitting on us. The same as always. Oh, and Luke got physically thrown out of the clerk's office for accompanying a woman to register."

"Luke?" I felt a rush of concern. "Was he hurt?"

"Nah. It's the usual stuff. It gets discouraging, that's all."

104

I patted Harry's arm and went to work. Harry hadn't even mentioned me and Elizabeth being stopped. Perhaps it wasn't as bad compared to all the other events.

Elizabeth covered the morning lesson of making math less of a mystery for the students. There was no doubt that teaching was her gift. Seeing the faces of Earl, Roy, Thelma, and others light up with understanding was a joy. When I weighed the list of incidents that Harry had mentioned against the positive results of a Freedom School, I agreed with the message of our training. The cost was worth it. Progress was happening.

After our thirty-plus students left for lunch, Elizabeth and I turned the fans directly on us, and I began to feel a little cooler. Even so, I took a wet cloth and wiped the perspiration from my face every five minutes as I cleaned up the room.

As Elizabeth erased the blackboard, she said, "My grandmother once told me 'horses sweat, men perspire, and women come aglow.' I believe I've really come aglow a lot lately."

I laughed heartily and had to agree.

~~~

My turn to teach came after lunch. "Time to work on our weekly newspaper," I announced as I wrote *The Freedom Story* at the top of the blackboard. "What kinds of stories or news do we want this week?" Before I could make suggestions, ideas were soaring around the room.

"We could interview one of you teachers."

"Let Anabel write another poem."

"We could tell all the things we can do now that the Civil Rights Act's been signed."

"Yeah. Yeah, let's do that," several responded.

I smiled. "I think we have a consensus. Who knows what the word *consensus* means?"

Hands flew up while voices called out the answer. "Whoa! Hold on," I interrupted. "One at a time. Thelma, what does *consensus* mean?"

"It means all of us agreed to something."

"Not all of us," Josh called out. "It don't have to be all of us, just most of us, right?"

"Right, Josh. It means a general agreement. So let's talk about the article. How should it start?"

The class worked with that for a while, canceling out each other's suggestions until they finally reached an agreement on the best opening and beginning content.

Anabel suggested listing all the things they could do with the signing of the act.

"No more 'colored' and 'white' signs," began Earl.

"But that ain't happened yet," grumbled Autumn.

I stopped writing on the board and turned to face the students. "Some of these things will take time to implement. Will they be done, though?"

The yeses were so loud and emphatic they could've been heard all the way to Ruleville.

I had to smile. "And why is that?" I asked. "Why are you so sure those things will happen?"

The class quieted down and looked to each other for a response. I heard Mamie's soft answer. "Because now it's the law."

I caught my breath. It was the first time Mamie had opened her mouth in class. It was my triumph for the day. "That's right, Mamie! Thank you. Because it's the law now. And how can we get more laws like it made?"

"By voting," answered Mamie again, this time a little louder, "and getting people in office who will change things."

I beamed at her and turned to the class. "Exactly. Now can you see how important it is to vote? You get the power you need by having laws that support your rights. That's why we need to get everyone registered to vote. Talk to your parents about it. Talk to your neighbors."

"Miss Lenore," came a voice from the back row. "What's *implement* mean?"

"Glad you asked, Roy." I swung the blackboard to the other side and wrote the word *implement*.

"This is one of those words in the English language that can mean two things." I loved that the students were asking questions, wanting answers and information. I seized the opportunity to give a quick reminder lesson about verbs and nouns, then we continued working on the newspaper.

My favorite weekly column included one of their student essays about what it meant to be a Negro. They had each written one during our first week's study on that subject. The one selected for this week was a powerful poem.

What Is It Like to Be a Negro in 1964
by Harter Pearl Shaw

It is 1964 and I can enter the door and not ride in the back of the bus.
    I can drink from the water fountain and how disappointed to know
It doesn't taste any different from the colored and so,
It's 1964 and what do I see ?
The visible signs removed the invisible scars within me.
I know things are better, I can enter the store,
Yet you are still watching me as before.
Fair housing, you elevated the cost.
The location you're the agent, you're the boss.
You hire me, I am out in the cold. I never complain, I have a goal.
I hide my invisible scars, they are hard to see.
I keep striving because others are depending on me.
I am thankful for the year 1964 for the accomplishments and failures,
And for those who fought and opened the door.
The scars are invisible, they helped me to succeed.
Never give up and always believe.

The day sped by in a blur of voices and teaching moments, both for the students and for me and Elizabeth. The students' eagerness and enthusiasm lifted our spirits with the power of a strong wind. That strong wind, however, also left us exhausted.

~~~

Dinnertime at the Johnson house had become a time of lively conversation. Anabel always began with a report of what had happened at the Freedom School, and I enjoyed hearing her accounting. I used it as a barometer of what I had hoped to achieve. Often, there were some interesting insights.

"Naomi shouldn't sit in the back with them boys no more," Anabel told us. "She keeps them from listening good."

Elizabeth raised her eyebrows. "Thanks for mentioning that, Anabel. How did you like the class today?"

"It was good. I 'specially like when you tell us about important Negroes like that Ida B. Wells and Frances Watkins Hooper."

"Frances Watkins Harper," I corrected her gently. "Yes, she was an amazing, strong woman at a time when that was not easy. Her poetry shows what life for Negroes was like then."

Anabel nodded, her mouth full of cornbread.

Mr. Johnson spoke up. "I heard that the FBI opened a big office in Jackson last week. Brought in lots more agents. I sure hope they find those boys' bodies soon."

I stopped eating and looked at him. "More agents is a good thing, right?"

Mr. Johnson shrugged. "It might be a good thing for finding the boys, but it don't make no difference for us Black folk, 'cept maybe in the searching they'll find more of us. They've already identified two bodies they found earlier. They was boys from Alcorn University who'd been working for voter registration. They'll find a lot more bodies of Negroes before it's over."

The Johnson family continued eating as if that were every day conversation.

Serene broke the quiet. "I wish I could go to the Freedom School. It's not fair."

Elizabeth answered. "I wish you could too. I wish we could make it open for students of all ages, but we don't have the room or the teachers right now. We'll keep working on that, though. Maybe after the summer, there can be something in addition to your regular school."

Mr. Johnson leaned back as his wife spooned more black-eyed peas onto his plate. "Heard the SNCC and COFO people are getting ready for a Freedom Day in Greenwood. What's that all about?"

"Harry or Anitra could tell you more about that," I answered. "SNCC has declared July 16 as Freedom Day when, hopefully, a large number of Negroes will go to the courthouse to register and the SNCC staffers and volunteers will be there to support them. There will be Freedom Days all over the state to let the public know about the Mississippi Freedom Democratic Party and to encourage them to get involved."

Mr. Johnson leaned back and wiped his mouth with his napkin. "Sounds like a place where there might be trouble."

"Sadly, that's true," agreed Elizabeth. "But things need to change here in Mississippi, don't they?"

All four Johnsons were silent. Mr. Johnson finished his black-eyed peas then continued. "Jobs is what needs to change. We're lucky because I got a good job at the filling station and Mrs. Johnson's got cleaning jobs, but for those that farm, it's a rough life. Out on the plantations, a body is always in debt to the owner. That there is where things need to change. We need more jobs for Negroes. Ain't no way to get ahead unless there's more jobs for us."

Mrs. Johnson sat back down after refilling her husband's water glass. "That's true. Both Horace and I grew up working in those cotton fields. Pay wasn't much then, but now you got to pick a hundred pounds to get paid. Pay is three dollars."

"I don't see how a sharecropper can ever make a living!" exclaimed Elizabeth.

"It's rough. That's for sure. He usually end up in debt to the owner every year."

"Well then what can he do? What *does* he do?" Elizabeth asked what I was also thinking.

Mr. Johnson scoffed. "He takes the midnight bus to the North. Nothing else he can do."

~~~

After dinner, Elizabeth and I walked down the block to meet up with Brenda and Anitra. It was our turn to work on voter registration. Our instructions were to meet Harry and Tom in front of their house then divide into teams and start in the nearby blocks.

Harry took Brenda and me with him. Brenda reminded me of Jane—a real people-person, outgoing, and enthusiastic. I always enjoyed her company. I hoped this would give me a chance to get to know Harry even better. He impressed me as a hard worker and a take-charge kind of guy.

As we walked, Harry did share more of himself. "Grew up in Dallas. My dad's a cook, and my mom's a maid. They always preached education to me. I graduated from Fisk in Nashville last year. That's where I met the crowd that got me into SNCC: Diane Nash, James Bevel, John Lewis, all those guys."

I asked, "Had you planned to do something else before you started working in the Movement?"

"Oh, sure. Accounting. I'm a numbers guy. Lots of Black businesses need someone to keep the books. I'll get to that someday, but this work has got to be done first."

I admired his willingness to work for SNCC at ten dollars a week when he could be making a lot more.

We followed Harry to the first house. He climbed on a porch of a wooden home that sagged with a sense of despair. The door hung crookedly, and the screen was torn out at the bottom. An old man, his face lined and weather-beaten, sat back in his rusty chair and eyed our mixed-race group.

"Good evening," Harry began in his friendliest tone. "I'm Harry Cooper with the Student Nonviolent Coordinating Committee." He held out his hand. Slowly the older man reached out and shook it. Harry introduced us, and we all shook hands and made small talk for a while before Harry said, "We'd like to talk to you about voting. Are you registered to vote?"

The old man scoffed. "No, never seen no need for that."

Harry smiled and continued. "I understand. But it's a different time, and now your vote can matter; it can make a difference. We're establishing the Mississippi Freedom Democratic Party so we can have a say in what happens in our state in this next election. We're talking to everyone in the Negro community because if we all come forward and register and then vote, we *can* change things."

The old man put up his hands as if to stop an onslaught. "No. No, nothin's ever going to change in this state. Now, you need to leave before the police come through. They see me talkin' to you, they'll come back and hassle me and who knows what all. So go on, now."

Harry tried to explain more about the Mississippi Freedom Democratic Party and to encourage the man to change his mind. But the old man placed his arms across his chest and sat back farther in his chair, getting quieter and shaking his head.

As we walked to the next house, Harry whispered, "Well, maybe a seed was planted, and he'll be more receptive when we come back."

But the next three houses were much of the same. Leaving the last one, I couldn't resist saying, "Lots of seeds, Harry, but when do you get the harvest?"

10

In the matter of classroom procedure, questioning is the vital tool... The value of the Freedom Schools will derive mainly from what the teachers are able to elicit from the students in terms of comprehension and expression of their experiences.

—COFO Freedom School data memo

Tuesday morning's class was one I was especially looking forward to. It was time to look at the history, *their* history. I was interested to hear what the students had learned about how life for Negroes had developed in our country.

I smiled at the students, sitting squeezed around the few tables, their eyes looking to me. I imagined that it was not always like that in a regular school setting. One of the best parts of a Freedom School was the eagerness of the students.

"Today we're going to talk about your history. By that, I mean the story of Negroes in America. So where does that start?"

"Slavery?" suggested Autumn.

I nodded. "That's right, Autumn. Good answer. The accepted date for the first slaves in this country is 1619 when they arrived in Jamestown. Now, I'm sure you have learned about slavery in your history classes, but I'm curious. What did your textbooks say about it?"

There was a ripple of amusement running through the room. Roy put it into words. "They said that the slaves were treated well, had all their needs met by the plantation owner, and were so happy they would sing in the fields as they worked."

Open laughter followed, but it wasn't the laughter of joy. It carried pain, hurt, and anger.

111

Cornelius raised his hand and added, "And those textbooks, Miss Lenore, they were the secondhand books from the white schools, and those kids had written all kinds of nasty stuff about Negroes in them."

"Yeah, I've heard about that. I hope that when schools are actually integrated, you won't have to be working with secondhand books anymore." I was glad Cornelius no longer felt he had to stand up to speak in class. I was also proud that he felt comfortable acknowledging such abuse to a white teacher.

I walked to the blackboard where I had written a column of names. "Let's look at some Negroes who did important things during the time of slavery." I pointed to the first name. "Harriet Tubman. Does anyone know what she did?"

We worked down the list of names. Even though during our training we had been told these young people had not been taught their history, I was still surprised at how little they knew about it. We spent the morning with stories of people like Sojourner Truth, John Brown, and Robert Smalls, who in 1862, with his crew and their families, sailed a Confederate ship out of Charleston Harbor—a Confederate-controlled port—and to Union waters and freedom. Smalls eventually became a US congressman from South Carolina. We also talked about people in the arts like the poet Phillis Wheatley and astronomer Benjamin Banneker. I remembered our trainer saying, "Make these people real to them. Make the kids see that Negroes— *their people*—were making important contributions in this country even back during times of slavery." I hoped I was doing that.

We talked about the Emancipation Proclamation and what it meant for the slaves and told some stories about the Reconstruction period. The students were amazed when I informed them that 1,500 to 2,000 Black people held office during the Reconstruction, many of them from Mississippi.

I asked them, "So how many Negroes hold elected state or federal offices in Mississippi today, in 1964?"

There were no guesses.

"Absolutely none," I answered for them. "Even though Negroes make up 42 percent of the state's population, not a single Negro has held an elected office in Mississippi since Reconstruction. What happened?"

"The Jim Crow laws," suggested Thelma.

I nodded. "That's right. Good job, Thelma. The Jim Crow laws set up the situation we have today of Negroes being held down as second-class citizens with no voting power." We talked about the landmark case of *Plessy v. Ferguson* in 1896 when the Supreme Court declared "separate but equal" was acceptable, therefore, making segregation legal.

I glanced at my watch. "We have covered a lot of your history this morning. I know it's about lunchtime, so we'll stop for now. Keep reading *To Kill a Mockingbird*. We'll be discussing that book next week."

~~~

After the morning class finished, Elizabeth and I made our usual peanut butter and jelly sandwiches. She ate quickly and began setting up the science experiment she had planned for the afternoon session. I wasn't needed, so I wrapped up my sandwich, grabbed my bag and a Coke, and headed out the door.

Looking up and down the street, I thought about where to go. I needed time to myself, so I figured the town park would be a good destination.

Once I got there, I noticed an empty picnic table under a large, sheltering oak. I settled in with my lunch and my book. I had brought three books with me for the summer, mistakenly thinking there would be time to read: Sylvia Plath's *The Bell Jar*, David Wilkerson's *The Cross and the Switchblade*, and today's choice, Mary McCarthy's *The Group*, a novel following a group of Vassar girls throughout their lives.

I was engrossed in the first chapter and had finished my lunch when someone's shadow fell across my book. I looked up.

"Hey there." A tall, blonde girl about my age smiled at me. "My name's Jenny. Jenny Williamson. I don't want to disturb you, but I was sitting at that other table and I noticed we're both reading *The Group*. Don't you just love it?"

"Hi, Jenny. I'm Lenore Rogers. Nice to meet you. I'm only on chapter one, but I think I'm going to like it."

"You will." Jenny settled herself on the opposite bench. "So are you new here or just visiting?"

"I'm here with the Freedom Summer Project, teaching in the school."

Jenny nodded, her smile a little less bright. "I thought so. We don't get many new faces in Mystic Springs." She straightened the gold bracelet on her wrist. "I don't mean to be too personal, but I can't help but wonder: why did you decide to come here?"

I studied this stranger's face, trying to see the hostility I expected. Instead, I sensed that Jenny was actually curious. I tried to frame an answer to avoid making her defensive. The trainers had touched on how to do this at one of the workshops, but, at this moment, I couldn't remember their suggestions.

"Well, I'm going into my senior year of college," I began, "and my major is child welfare work. So when SNCC came around looking for summer volunteers for the Freedom Schools, community centers, and voter registration work, it seemed like a good way for me to spend my summer because it ties into what I want to do after graduation."

"Hmm. Interesting." Jenny looked around a moment then continued. "You know," her finger traced an imaginary design on the table, "a lot of people don't appreciate your being here. Some actually resent it."

"A lot of white people, you mean. Yes, I know that." I decided the less I said, the better.

Jenny changed the subject. "I just finished my senior year at Ole Miss. I'm an Alpha Chi."

"A what?"

"Alpha Chi Omega. You know, the sorority."

"Oh, of course. So what will you do now?"

"I'm working in my father's office until my fiancé finishes his master's degree." She stretched out her left hand, wiggling her ring finger bearing a glittering diamond ring.

I acknowledged it with a quick nod. "So this is your hometown? You grew up here?"

Jenny smiled. "Born and raised. It's a wonderful place to live. I love it."

"I really haven't had a chance to explore Mystic Springs," I admitted as I glanced around the park and the town beyond. "Tell me about it."

"Well, it's a small town, of course, yet it has everything we need. But we can easily get to Jackson or Memphis for shopping or the fine arts and such, and it's easy to get to Ruleville or Greenwood for the movies, bowling, or roller-skating. Everyone knows each other and looks out for each other, you know, like in all small towns. We have wonderful community events, plays, concerts, and things. We grew up with good schools and a library, a wonderful church, and the country club has golf, a pool, and tennis courts. It's a great place to live."

I nodded, but I couldn't hold my tongue any longer. "Mm-hmm... but the things you mentioned are only available to white folks."

I waited for her to get mad at me, but instead, she leaned forward and earnestly tried to explain why I wasn't looking at things correctly.

"Yes, but the coloreds have their own part of town and their own activities. They don't want to mix with us either. I know they're protesting to end segregation and all, but it's not good to mix the races. Who knows what that might lead to."

Before I began to say what I was thinking, I suddenly remembered Jenny's last name. "You said your last name is Williamson? Are you related to the Williamson who has the insurance company?"

Jenny's expression brightened. "Yes. My daddy owns that."

"And he's the president of the school board?"

"Right. So...," she said, her voice becoming wary, "how do you know all that?"

"We'd been wondering about using that old school building on Oak Street, and someone suggested we call him about it."

She shrugged. "I don't know anything about those old colored schools."

There were so many sarcastic, nasty responses swirling through my mind, but I took a deep breath. "Well, we have another site anyway," I said politely. Jane would've approved.

Jenny looked at the slim gold watch on her wrist. "My lunch break is over. I'd better get back to the office. Look, there's hardly any young people our age in town. A few of us meet at the Methodist church on Sunday evenings for ice cream just to be social; there's no real program. You're welcome to come, if you want...although I wouldn't talk too much about why you're here if I were you."

After Jenny left, the smell of her Joy perfume lingered in the air along with the echo of her words. I was caught in a fog of anger and frustration. Would it mean anything to try and change Jenny's mind and reveal the racism? Mac or a SNCC staffer might need that connection to Mr. Williamson in the future, and I didn't want to ruin any potential opportunity.

Actually, we girls might enjoy visiting with others our age on a Sunday evening, but how could we bring Anitra? Impossible! Or how could we go and leave Anitra out? No way! *All I wanted to do was sit quietly, sip a Coke, read a good book, and not have to face the challenges of racial problems, and look what happened.* Scowling, I slammed my book shut, gathered my things, and headed back to the Freedom School.

~~~

At dinner I mentioned meeting Jenny Williamson. Mrs. Johnson, who knew about everyone in Mystic Springs, gave a rundown of the family. "Mr. Williamson grew up in Mystic Springs, but his missus is a city gal from Jackson. They both grew up with money. They live in the biggest house in town. Have you seen it? It's a big white house with columns in front and a long paved driveway on the edge of Main Street. Jenny is their only child. Lands sakes, that girl don't lack for nothing. Whatever she wants, her daddy gets it for her. Soon as she turned sixteen, she got a brand-new sporty convertible. The sweet sixteen party they threw for her at the country club was the talk of the town."

"Maybell, hush up," Mr. Johnson interrupted. "Nobody care about all that."

"I'm just giving our summer girls a little background. That's all."

I smiled at Mrs. Johnson and confessed, "Jenny was friendly to me, but...," I tried to think of the right words to say, "I mean, she seemed interested in us being here, but she was...well...the things she said weren't hostile or angry, but they were really racist. She was obviously brought up to think that way, to think that the way things are between the races here is perfectly normal."

There was silence around the table until Mr. Johnson pointed his fork at me and said, "But it *is* normal for Mystic Springs. The way life is here is the way it's always been. The whites don't want it to change, and the Blacks are afraid to try to make it change. That's the whole of it, right there."

Elizabeth and I exchanged a quick glance. "Yeah, I know that's true," said Elizabeth, "but the reason we came down this summer is because we believe by us being here to work with you, by showing the nation that things need to change, laws will be made to help you not be afraid to try. We believe things can be different."

I nodded. "You must've believed a little bit that change could happen. Otherwise, why would you be brave enough to open your home to us and let Anabel come to the Freedom School?"

Mr. Johnson let out one of his rare chuckles. "Lenore, what I believed is that Mrs. Johnson said we had to do this, and I knowed for a fact that she weren't going to back down. And believe you me, when that woman has her mind made up, there's no changing it."

Mrs. Johnson smirked at her husband and swatted him with her napkin as we all laughed. I drank in the comfortable casualness of family around the dinner table. It was something that had been missing in my own family. The Johnsons including Elizabeth and me in that circle made it even more special. These were moments to be cherished.

A gift is not always wrapped up in a box, I thought, *but the ribbon around it, holding it together, is often something very simple that connects people and ties them together for a unique and precious moment.*

~ ~ ~

It rained all night, sending the streets and yards into a slippery, muddy mess. The next day, the dark clouds overhead seeped into everyone's moods. The students seemed to lose a little of their motivation, and I'm sure I wasn't the only one who felt more tired than ever. It was not shaping up to be a good day.

I was especially frustrated because Harry relayed a conversation he'd had with Mac. Mac thought we should be doing even more with the Freedom Schools, like adding adult education classes in the evenings to teach people about nutrition, literacy, and voting issues. *Really?* I grumbled to myself. *Between the school and voter registration, I'm stretched as thin as I can possibly be.*

This summer wasn't rolling out as I had envisioned it back at Barnard. For one thing, there was the heat—the constant, energy-sucking blast furnace that never let up. There were also mosquitoes and flies and other little insects I wasn't used to. I hadn't had a real shower in weeks. And there were the tensions that flared up between us, even as we were trying to work together. What bothered me most, though, was that I was almost never alone. As an introvert—a person who gets her restorative energy from moments by herself—that was the hardest.

I sighed, hoping the day would get better. Elizabeth had taught her math session while I wrote reports in the back room, squeezing in around Harry's voter registration workers. When it was time, I gathered my teaching materials and joined the class.

Thelma, Autumn, and Cornelius crowded around. "It's newspaper day, Miss Lenore. What essay are you going to pick?" asked Cornelius.

"They're all good. Do you want me to select yours for today?"

Cornelius nodded enthusiastically.

I sorted through the pile until I found Cornelius's neat handwriting. I took the sheet of notebook paper and read to myself:

My life as Negro teenager can be described as living in a cloudy bubble. I was comfortable inky bubble because I never had a clear view of what was outside. Although I was aware of another world outside, I thought that I would be invisible in this "other world." I sensed that my desire to burst my bubble was hopeless, for I knew that it was reinforced with hate and inequality because of my skin color. If I stepped out of my bubble, I was always conscious of my behavior and surroundings, always careful to stay in my place and follow the teachings of my parents.

I knew that there was more to life, but I felt trapped and dared not dream of experiencing more because I was stuck in my bubble. As a high school student in an all-Black school, I recognized that I was limited in what I could do. The only role models I knew were my teachers, my parents, and the Black nurses in the community. I never had new textbooks and the school system did not provide any, so my parents went to the secondhand bookstore to purchase outdated books for me. But then in 1964, there appeared to be hope because of the decisions that the federal courts gave. Knowing that the courts can make laws but not change hearts. I'm grateful for my Negro teachers and my parents because they encouraged me to be the best I could be in spite of the fact that I was still living in my cloudy bubble.

There was a beat of silence. "Wow, Cornelius! This is great!" I left Cornelius beaming as I took the essay into the back room to be added to the newspaper and mimeographed for later distribution around the community. In spite of all the negative thoughts I'd been having, these kids were so ready to learn, so thirsty for knowledge. They made it all worthwhile. Compared to their lives, how could I dare complain about mine?

Setting Cornelius's essay down, I noticed the latest list of incidents lying on Harry's desk and scanned it.

Clarksdale: Negro volunteer chased out of white Laundromat, picked up by police for failure to signal turn, taken to jail and beaten. Charged with resisting arrest. Out on $64 bond.

Clarksdale: Chief voter registrar closes office for next few days.

Reason: court is in session; no time for voter registration.

Canton: Man threatened with job loss if youngster continues in Freedom School. Youngster stays.

Laurel: Gas bomb thrown at local Negro's home.

Natchez: Jerusalem Baptist and Bethel Methodist Churches burned to the ground. Home of Negro contractor in Natchez firebombed.

There were more, but I didn't want to read them. Looking again at Cornelius's essay, I saw the word *hope* and clung to that.

~ ~ ~

On July 16—Freedom Day across the Mississippi Delta—all the SNCC staffers and volunteers from Sunflower County (except us teachers) were to go to Greenwood, the county seat of LeFlore County, to support those brave souls who were going to try to register to vote. Elizabeth offered to cover the school so I could join the others, and I took her up on it.

The morning had been cloudy, but no rain was expected—just the usual oppressive heat. On the drive over, Harry gave us the anticipated warnings. "We're expecting violence, y'all, so be vigilant. Remember the training we gave you. Don't do anything that might escalate the situation. Above all, remember to remain nonviolent, no matter what happens to you."

A tight knot was developing in my stomach. Looking at the other volunteers, I sensed they felt the same way. We arrived by nine o'clock and reported in. There were protest signs ready for those marching, but my group was told to join the people from Ruleville and support those in line to register to vote. Our job was to hand out cups of water as they stood waiting to get inside, serve them sandwiches at lunchtime, and offer aid to anyone hurt or ill. We greeted our Ruleville friends warmly, and I was especially glad to see Luke this morning.

Of course, a hostile crowd was already forming on the opposite side of the street. The Confederate flags they held fluttered with the slight breeze or were waved with vigor by young men my age. When the shouts and taunts began, I tried not to look their way. There's just something ugly about people's faces when they spew hatred, and I'd rather not see it.

A long line of police surrounded the courthouse and kept an eye on our marchers as they got into formation. The police chief, Curtis Lary, used a big bullhorn to announce several times that those who wanted to register could do so, but he would not tolerate any protesters. It was odd to me that those of us marching *for* the vote were labeled the protesters, although I guess it was because we were protesting *against* the status quo.

The chief waited until it became obvious that there would be a large number of marchers. Carrying the prepared signs, they began walking along the opposite sidewalk from those in line to register to vote.

I was standing alongside our group from Mystic Springs and Ruleville as we put out cups of water on a folding table. We were separated from the protesters by the line of those waiting to register, but my heart was racing and my palms were sweaty. I was so shaky with nerves that water sloshed out of a cup as I tried to pour. Luke eased up next to me as the tensions mounted.

Somehow, those waiting to register remained calm as they stood in line, dressed in their Sunday best. They were ready for this day. I, on the other hand, was quaking in my boots, but I didn't want Luke to know that.

Chief Lary held the bullhorn to his mouth as he threatened, "You protesters have two minutes to disperse or you will be arrested." The bus waiting to take them to jail sat a short distance away. "Now you have a minute and a half."

The protesters continued their walk. Our side became more and more quiet, while the whites yelling seemed to grow louder, urging on the police.

"One minute...thirty seconds...ten seconds...five...four...three... two...one."

As soon as Chief Lary finished his countdown, the police tore into the marchers. They poked and struck them with their nightsticks and cattle prods. We heard the yelps of pain and saw people—including some elderly folks—stumble and fall, only to be hit again. Cheers of encouragement erupted from the whites on the sidelines. Those waiting to register stood tall and silent, their eyes staring straight ahead.

Tears were falling down my cheeks as I whispered, "No! No! No!" over and over. Luke and I held on to each other's arms. I don't know if he was holding me up or I was holding him back, but we needed each other at that moment. To watch the brutality was too much. And for what? For supporting people who simply wanted to vote—a right they'd been entitled to for nearly a century? I couldn't believe what I was witnessing on a summer day that should've been about picnics and baseball games. I knew I would never be the same after that day. Never.

The police rounded up all those who had been in the protest march, loaded them onto the bus, and hauled them off to jail. As Luke and I stared at each other, I felt a bond between us that wouldn't be erased. Then we went back to filling and distributing cups of water.

Harry and Anitra gathered up the protest signs that lay scattered on the sidewalk. Those waiting to enter the courthouse remained quietly in line—they were a dignified force to be reckoned with. I was so proud of them, each and every single one of them. I thought of Mrs. Parker, who was working every day studying to prepare for the voter registration test. I thought of my students who were eager to become old enough so they could register to vote and of Mrs. Hamer who was bravely going around the state educating Negroes on the importance of the vote. I couldn't help but wonder what our country could be like if everyone eligible was equally able to vote. Wasn't that what we were intended to be as a country?

The crowd of whites diminished quite a bit after the marchers were arrested, but a few remained throughout the day to try to intimidate the hopeful registrants.

At the end of the day, we piled wearily into Harry's car and headed home. Harry suggested we meet after dinner. By then, he should've received a report from Greenwood headquarters about the results of this historic Freedom Day.

Even though all I wanted to do after we ate that evening was crawl into bed and pull the covers over my head, I was anxious to learn the results and how those arrested had fared. Elizabeth walked back with me. I was grateful that she didn't question me. I had given a bare-bones report at dinner to her and the Johnsons. It was all I could muster.

Soon after we all arrived at the SNCC office, Harry was ready with some information. He began with those arrested. "They're still in jail, although several lawyers are on their way to try to get them out. In Greenwood alone, there were 111 arrested."

"What about the other locations?" I asked.

"Cleveland did the best because a state representative named Charlie Capps kept everything under control with both whites and Blacks. About twenty-four of the forty in line to register actually got to fill out the forms. The others were turned away for the usual reasons: not enough or proper ID, not filling things out correctly, you know the drill.

"In Canton, two Negro men were arrested, and we heard they were pistol-whipped before the lawyers could get them out of jail. But overall, I would say it was a great day because so many turned out, including those who tried to register and those who came to support them."

~~~

By Friday, things were looking up. The Mississippi heat had dried the mud, so we were back to simply dealing with dust, mosquitoes, and no-see-ums. For our history lesson, we were using Ruleville's idea of dressing up to role-play important people in Black history. With the help of homemade costumes and outfits from the thrift shop, each student depicted the life of a historic Negro.

We had expected a lot of Rosa Parks and Martin Luther King but were delighted with the dramatic renditions of Harriet Tubman, Sojourner Truth, and Frederick Douglass. Sadie came dressed elegantly in a colorful robe with lots of Mardi Gras beads draped around her neck as Madam C.J. Walker, the first Negro female millionaire of hair care and makeup fame. Four of the boys came as the Greensboro Four who had started the sit-in movement in 1960. They had wrapped red bandages around their heads and arms as brutal reminders of the violence against Negroes.

The mood lightened up when Anitra belted out some operatic-sounding notes as she presented Marian Anderson, the famous singer that Eleanor Roosevelt championed. Bearing a bag of peanuts that he shared with the class, Earl came as George Washington Carver. Cornelius wore a sailor's cap and told the amazing story of Robert Smalls. What impressed me the most was the way the students had done their research and had found courageous, strong, successful people that they identified with.

~~~

After supper at the Johnsons' house, Elizabeth and I went to join Anitra for voter registration work. Despite my efforts, I had failed to make any progress in developing a friendship with her. I'd asked Brenda what it was like living with Anitra.

Brenda tilted her head and thought for a moment. "She was a little standoffish at first, but we're fine now. We have great discussions at night in our shared room. She graduated from Tougaloo with an education degree, and someday she'll probably get some higher ones. She's very bright. She's certified to teach after she moves on from SNCC."

That surprised me. "*Teach!* Then why isn't she teaching in one of the Freedom Schools?"

"SNCC needed her to work with voter registration, I guess."

It dawned on me that Anitra had two reasons for not liking me: One, she probably didn't approve of me hanging out with Luke; and two, I was doing the job *she* was formally trained to do.

The deeper we went into the Negro neighborhoods, the more the level of poverty and the obvious lack of services shocked me. The worst was seeing children with bloated stomachs, indicating extreme hunger. I visited with one woman who made $2.50 a day working from seven a.m. until10 p.m. as a maid for a white family.

Everywhere I looked, I saw beaten-down people living in ramshackle houses along shabby streets. Their only hope was the vote, but that came at such a cost. *How could they find the courage they needed—courage that might cost them their meager wages or even their lives?* I wondered. After what I'd seen the day before, I would always admire the courage it took them to register to vote.

11

The burdens will always be heavy,
The sunshine fade into night,
Till mercy and justice shall cement
The black, the brown, and the white.
—Frances Watkins Harper, "The Burdens of All"

When I woke up on Saturday, my first thought was to turn over and go back to sleep. I could feel the heat splashing in languid waves through the window. I knew Harry would be anxious to get us started finding the remaining people we hadn't yet visited to get more names for the all-important Mississippi Freedom Democratic Party, but I wondered where they might be. We had covered every street in Mystic Springs and found every possible country road. At least, I always thought that until Harry took us to yet another dusty side road.

Elizabeth was already up and out, but I knew where to find her. I dressed hurriedly and made my way to the kitchen for Saturday pancakes.

Elizabeth looked up from dousing her pancakes with syrup. "Harry sent word that he'd pick us up at nine thirty, and we'll go to Ruleville." Hearing that we were going to Ruleville, the day immediately brightened.

Later, driving down the narrow road to Ruleville, Harry got us singing the freedom songs that I'd been missing: "Woke Up This Morning (with My Mind Stayed on Freedom)," and "Ain't Gonna Let Nobody Turn Me Round." Singing lifted me out of frustration and weariness.

Sitting next to Anitra in the back seat, I saw an opportunity. "Brenda mentioned that you graduated from Tougaloo with a teaching degree. I'd appreciate any ideas you have for the Freedom School."

Anitra shrugged it off, but I persisted. "Maybe if you could find the time, you could sit down with Elizabeth and me and help us come up with some plans?"

Anitra turned and looked me in the eyes. "Maybe," she said and nodded.

Harry turned onto the dusty drive that led to the Hamer home. The branches of the Cyprus trees along the narrow, rutted entry brushed against the car. Harry parked under the shade of one of the few oaks. As I got out of the car, I scanned the crowd for that one special face. Luke extricated himself from a group sitting around a boy with a guitar and made his way over to us. There was an awkward moment, a remnant from the last time we'd met, but it quickly evaporated.

"Hey girl," he said with that endearing, lopsided grin of his. We made our way to the shade of the pecan tree. After greeting the few volunteers I knew, Luke and I meandered toward the far side of the tree. There was only one lone bench on that side, which was away from where everyone was settled, so we quietly claimed it. "How's it been going?" he asked.

"Classes are great! The kids are so involved. But voter registration is so hard." Our day in Greenwood seemed like the elephant in the room, so I dared to mention it. "It sounds like Freedom Day in Greenwood was a success. But it was so hard watching those supporters get arrested!"

Luke only nodded, his lips drawn into a tight line.

"Are they still in jail?" I asked.

"Yeah. I've heard rumors that they're on a hunger strike, but I don't know for sure."

We sat silently for a moment listening to the sounds of other conversations and laughter nearby. Luke nodded toward a checkerboard and checkers on the end of the bench. "Wanna play?"

I accepted and the hour passed quickly as we used the game as an excuse for being off by ourselves. As usual, we talked about everything: what it felt like to be jailed and scary things that had happened this summer. Luke told me about one experience Mac had just before our training session in Ohio.

"Mac told me he used to think he was lucky. He'd been working with SNCC quite a while and had never been beaten. But finally, his luck ran out. Five of 'em were driving to Atlanta and the Mississippi Highway Patrol pulled 'em over. They took 'em to jail for 'investigation.' No charges, but held for 'investigation.'

"They took 'em one at a time out of the cell and Mac was last. He heard all of 'em gettin' beat before him. When his turn came, two policemen pushed him out behind the jail. One stuck his face close and said, 'Are you a Negro or a nigger?'

"'I'm a Negro,' Mac said. And the punches started. They asked another time, 'Negro or nigger?'

"Mac said again, 'I'm...a...Negro.'"

Luke exhaled deeply and lowered his head as he continued, his eyes cast downward. "The next punch decked him. He knew they'd keep beating him until he said the word they wanted to hear. They'd beat him 'til he died and not give it a second thought. So when he got back on his feet and the police officer thumped him in the chest and asked again, that time he said, 'I'm a nigger.'

"'Right, nigger,' that white bastard sneered, and then they let him leave, alive."

I grabbed Luke's hand. "Oh my God, Luke! How humiliating for him! That's terrible!" A sick feeling gripped my stomach. I couldn't begin to imagine what it took for Mac to have said that.

Luke put his hand over mine and turned his face toward me. The pain in his eyes took my breath away and tore at my heart.

The moment came swiftly to an end with the arrival of Fannie Lou Hamer. She shook a finger at me and growled, "Didn't I talk to you girls in Ohio? Didn't I warn you not to pair off and start this nonsense? Look over there. See how the windows of the hospital look over this yard. All the white folks over there can see y'all getting' mooney-eyed over each other. Don't you know that's goin' to cause trouble?"

I held up my hands, embarrassed. "But I...we...we were only playing checkers, that's all."

"Honest, Mrs. Hamer," Luke put on an innocent expression, "we weren't doing anything."

"Oh, hush up." She stood with her hands on her hips, shaking her head. "I don't wanna hear your trash. Just go around with the rest of the group. No more of this." She gave Luke a push in the opposite direction but took my arm and pulled me down on the bench again.

She stood right in front of me and looked me straight in the eye. "You listen to me now, missy. Emmett Till," she said. "Ever hear of him?"

I nodded.

"I'm goin' to remind you of Emmett Till. Emmett was a fourteen-

126

year-old boy come down from Chicago to spend time with his great-uncle here like he did ever' summer. This was back in fifty-five.

"One day, young Emmett and his cousins went by Bryant's store, maybe to buy a Coca-Cola or something. Emmett was a little bit cocky, they say. I dunno, maybe because he was from the North." Mrs. Hamer squinted her eyes at me, but I could barely meet her gaze.

"So Emmett goes inside the store. He's in there a few short minutes by hisself with that Carolyn Bryant. She an attractive white woman who own that store, her and her husband. Then Emmett's cousin comes in and pulls him outta the store. In a minute or so, Mrs. Bryant, she come out and goes to her car."

I knew the story, but I sat perfectly still, looking straight at Mrs. Hamer.

Mrs. Hamer swatted away a fly. "Now, somethin' happened. They say he whistled at her. I dunno. But later, Mrs. Bryant said he'd put his hands on her when the both of them were inside the store. I don't believe it.

"'Course, there gonna be consequences. A few nights later, Mr. Bryant and his half-brother charged into Emmett's great-uncle's house and grabbed that boy. Mose Wright, Emmett's great-uncle, he try to explain that the boy was from Chicago, that he didn't know the ways of the South, that he didn't mean nothin' by what he did, and that he stuttered so he whistled before formin' his words, that's all. Mrs. Wright offered them men money if they would leave without Emmett, but they wave a pistol 'round and say no. They took Emmett to a barn, pistol-whipped and beat him, shot him, then took him to a bridge over the Tallahatchie River and threw him in. Weighed him down with a gin mill fan fastened around his neck with barbed wire."

My hand involuntarily clutched my throat.

Shaking her head, Mrs. Hamer went on. "A few days later, some boys fishin' found his body. He don't even look human 'cause of the beatings. 'Course the sheriff wanted to get the body buried quick as possible. Didn't want nobody to see what Emmett look like. But Emmett's mom, Mamie Till Bradley, she say no. She want him taken to Chicago for burial and insisted on an open coffin, even though the sight of his body was so gruesome. She wanted the world to see what had been done to her fourteen-year-old son.

"Think of the strength it took for her to look into that coffin over and over again. Mm-hmm." Mrs. Hamer swiped a tear off her cheek. "Ever'body in America had to look too. There's many who think the Movement began with that. People finally said, 'This has to stop.'

"Now, here in the South, the white people think Black men are like sex-crazed animals. They think Black men are after white women. And those white men think they can do anythin' to protect their women." She leaned so close to me I could feel the emotion pulsing through her. "The slightest look or action on a Black man's part, honey, there's goin' to be consequences."

She drew in a long breath to calm herself. "So, baby, what you think they gonna do to Luke if they think he's after you, huh?"

I shook my head. "I...I'm sorry. I didn't think—"

"That's right, girl. You didn't think." She stood back from me. "You'd better start thinkin' from now on. Ya hear me?"

I nodded vigorously. "Yes, ma'am. I understand."

"Nothin' may happen to you, but there *will* be consequences."

~~~

The ride back to Mystic Springs always seemed longer than coming over. I couldn't get Emmett Till off my mind. "Harry," I asked, "I remember what happened to Emmett Till, but I can't remember hearing if that Bryant guy was ever accused of the murder. Was there a trial?"

Harry snorted. "A *trial*? Sure, there was a trial, if you can call it that. The jury was made up of all white men. There were supposedly two witnesses, but they couldn't be found. Turns out, they had been locked up in jail. Not surprisingly, Bryant and Milam were found not guilty.

"Emmett's Uncle Mose and his family fled to Chicago, left his field full of cotton, simply left it all. Mose Wright came back later to testify before the grand jury about the kidnapping charge, which didn't amount to anything. He and another witness left right afterward to get back to Chicago. Neither ever set foot back in Mississippi and probably never will."

Harry glanced at me from the rearview mirror. "A year later in an article in *Look* magazine, those guys admitted to the murder, knowing they couldn't be tried again."

The shock of that injustice hit me, and my anger felt like a physical burn inside my gut. "How could they not be found guilty? How is that even possible?"

Harry grunted. "The defense said that the body couldn't even be identified as Emmett. The two guys said they let him go that night, only wanted to give him a little discipline, that was all." He paused. "That's white justice in the South."

I tried to relax my shoulders, lean back, and attempt to doze, but my mind went to thoughts of Luke. What was it between us? There hadn't been anything really romantic, but from the start back at the training in Ohio, there had been a static in the air when we were together. I liked being with him. Other than Jane, there wasn't anyone else I could share my thoughts and feelings with in such an open and honest way. I felt safe with Luke. But that thought led to another very disturbing one:

Luke was not safe with me.

~~~

Saturday afternoon back in Mystic Springs, the heat seemed especially brutal as we traipsed through neighborhoods hoping to find people who might be willing to go to the clerk's office to register. It was slow work, but I did appreciate the opportunity to visit with the Negro citizens of Mystic Springs.

The typical start to a visit—after we got through a group of curious children—was, "Afternoon, ma'am. I'm Anitra Phillips with the Student Nonviolent Coordinating Committee, and this is Lenore Rogers and Elizabeth Stanton, teachers at the Freedom School. How y'all doing today? Hot, isn't it?"

We'd chat for a while, discussing the weather, learning about the person's children and grandchildren. Sometimes we'd accept a glass of water, sometimes not. Finally, one of us would bring up the newly formed political party. "We'd like to talk to you about the Mississippi Freedom Democratic Party." And then we would rush on quickly to head off any negative reaction.

"We hope to send delegates to the Democratic National Convention in August. This political party is different. When you sign up for it, your name won't be in the paper or anything 'cause signing up is not the same as registering to vote. This is simply saying you'll be part of the Mississippi Freedom Democratic Party. We hope to get at least one hundred thousand people to sign up. That'll show the state and the country that you have a voice in elections."

Whether or not the people signed, we would urge them to think about registering to vote. We'd offer to drive them to the clerk's office and mention if a neighbor would be going. We'd talk about the necessity of having a vote, give all the practical reasons, and emphasize how important it was to vote people into office who would look out for them. Some would say they weren't interested. Some would say they were behind us 100 percent but then wouldn't sign. At some point, Elizabeth or I would hand them the brochure about the Mississippi Freedom Democratic Party. "This will help explain it more. We'll leave this with you."

There was usually someone who would find a place deep inside, which gave them the strength to put their names down, and that made it possible for us to keep going.

I felt as though I had my shoulder pushing against a huge boulder. Even so, I was aware of what it took for the person to make that commitment. I honestly wasn't sure what I'd do if I were in their shoes.

Late in the afternoon, we stopped at a home where an older man sat in a rocker on the porch. Gray hair framed his wrinkled face and his gnarled hands rested on the arms of the chair, speaking volumes about a lifetime of hard work. He smiled and gestured for us to join him as we introduced ourselves.

"Glad to meet you young ladies. I'm Willard Thomas. My granddaughter Sadie is in your school. Come up on the porch and sit a spell."

"Sadie is such a bright girl. We love having her in the school!" exclaimed Elizabeth.

Mr. Thomas's eyes sparkled as he shared with us Sadie's reports about the school. It was good to hear an affirmation of what we were doing. The best part was that he signed up to be part of the Mississippi Freedom Democratic Party and planned to get registered to vote.

~~~

On Sunday morning, Elizabeth and I dressed appropriately, which meant wearing a hat and white gloves and carrying a purse. Then we walked with the Johnsons to New Hope AME Church. Anitra and Brenda joined us along the way. Anitra, with her stylish flair, made me feel almost matronly in my navy shirtwaist dress.

The members of the congregation greeted us in their usual friendly manner, except for the one couple who had expressed their displeasure earlier. When they saw us walk in, they simply turned to talk to other people. I'm not sure if I felt hurt or anger or both. Then the thought cut through my mind like a knife: that was exactly the scenario I'd witnessed many times in the North when a Negro entered a roomful of whites.

The service was as upbeat and enthusiastic as every Sunday had been. We swayed to the rhythm of the songs, even though it was a different way of worshipping than I'd grown up with. After singing "'Tis So Sweet to Trust in Jesus," Pastor Hendricks asked for and got a "hallelujah." Then he launched into his sermon, which I knew would be considerably longer than the sermons at my home church.

"Our Scripture today begins with Mark14:32," Pastor Hendricks announced. He delivered the words from the Bible with a power and authority that drew in the members of the congregation, and they responded.

Pastor Hendricks read, "They went to a place called Gethsemane, and Jesus said to his disciples, 'Sit here, while I pray.'"

"Uh-huh. Yes, Lord," called out the parishioners.

When Pastor Hendricks talked about times when God had to say no, his words became more and more impassioned. He emphasized the message, sweeping his arms to envelop the congregation. Then he dabbed at his mouth with his handkerchief.

"God knows what's best!" he exclaimed, almost bouncing on his toes. "But...but...but we got to always remember that. God knows what's best.

"Were there times when God said 'no' in your lives? What was your reaction? Did you go in your room and slam your door? Go on strike against God? Quit tithing? So therefore...mm-hmm...therefore, the challenge comes when we don't get what we want."

The message might've hit a little too close to home for me. There had been frustrations that summer, things I'd hoped would go better. *What was my response?* I wondered. *What should it be?* The sermon had planted seeds for me to think about when I had some time alone—if I ever found time to be alone.

A prayer was said for the three missing civil rights workers—Mickey, James, and Andy—and for their families. A picture of Rita Schwerner standing by the blackboard in Ohio skittered through my mind. Those sad words she had written now seemed like an epitaph. The prayer continued for the boys from Alcorn, Charlie Eddie Moore and Henry Hezekiah Dee, but now they became more real to me. I was realizing how important it was to say the names, to speak of the violence.

The prayer did not end there, however, but spun around to thankfulness for blessings and for the future. Hope...that was the key. The Johnsons, Mac, Mrs. Parker, Mrs. Logan, and Mrs. Dawson, who occasionally brought us lunch and visited a while, all of them, their lives spoke of hope. That was what I saw undergirding the Black community. If I looked back to the training, I could see it was hope in the work of the Movement that propelled Bob Moses, James Lawson, and every SNCC staff member.

As we left the church, Pastor Hendricks warmly greeted us. "Now don't forget. I'm trying to come up with a better place for y'all to have a school."

"That would be wonderful!" Elizabeth gushed. "We're up to thirty-seven students now."

He nodded. "I know. I understand your problem, and I've been praying on it. Keep your faith, girls."

Walking away, I whispered, "If anyone finds us a decent school, I believe Pastor Hendricks will have a hand in it."

～～～

The four of us girls decided to go to the barbeque place for our noon meal. It was packed, so we took our plates to one of the empty tables in the backyard. Brenda was keeping us entertained with stories of interesting encounters she'd recently had.

I wiped some sauce from my mouth and responded, "I've had some funny things happen too, but what I see is the terrible poverty and discouragement here. I—"

Anitra whipped around until she was facing right at me. "That's what really gets me about you white girls," she interrupted.

I sat back sharply. "What?" I stammered.

"You only see everything negative about Negroes. Don't you even see the wonderful sense of community we have? How our teachers are so strong and give us what we need to learn to deal with Mr. Charlie? How our churches are powerful and worshipful? How neighbors really look out for each other? No," she wagged her finger in my face. "You just see us as poor, sad, ignorant Negroes."

132

"But I...I," I held up both my hands, wanting her to stop, wanting to defend myself. Brenda and Elizabeth sat silently as I absorbed the indictment and began to face that there was some truth in what she was saying.

When I put down my hands, I held Anitra's gaze and nodded. "I do see those strengths that you mentioned. I'm sorry that you think I don't see them. I guess because I've never seen such poverty close up before I'm more aware of it. It's more in my thoughts and comments."

Anitra dropped her gaze, but her tone didn't change. "I've heard you teaching in the school. You have a lot of discussions about how bad things are, about how subservient Negro people are to white power. Why don't you talk more about the good things Negroes are doing in the world, the successes?"

"But we *do* talk about those things," Elizabeth chimed in. "We're following a prescribed curriculum so students will see how their culture has developed, so they'll think in more positive ways. If you have time this afternoon, let's sit down together. We'll show you how the material is laid out, and you can give us your ideas on how to make it better."

Anitra paused. She looked from me to Elizabeth. "Okay. I'd like that."

After that, the tension slowly tapered away leaving only a few threads like an unraveled hem.

~~~

When I thought about my high school days, the week always seemed to start so slowly. It was as though there was a rhythm inside the brick and mortar of the school, and it took a while for the students to ease back into it after a weekend away.

That was not the case at the Freedom School. Each day, the students arrived early and brought with them an electricity, a rushing forward to get as much crammed in as possible. Elizabeth and I struggled to keep up. Anitra had come up with some helpful ideas and said she would start tutoring some students in the SNCC back office. She had bubbled with enthusiasm when we went over teaching plans with her. I couldn't help but think to myself: *She's the one who should be teaching, not me.*

Does that mean I should be doing the voter registration? That work was so hard and disturbing, but there was an excitement in it too. Jane's letters

133

reflected that, and Luke's eyes shone with passion whenever he shared his convictions about it.

~~~

In that morning's literature class, I discussed the poetry of Langston Hughes. "Today we're going to look at several different ways of writing poetry as we go through *The Collected Works of Langston Hughes*. I want you to read a section of a poem and share with us what you think the poet is trying to say." I ignored the groans from the boys in the back row and deliberately called on one of them to come forward.

"Oh no! Not me, Miss Lenore," Josh objected. "Get one of the girls. I don't like that poetry stuff."

As the class giggled, I instructed, "Come up here, Josh. Read what's on this sheet of paper, please."

Josh dragged himself to the front. He looked at the paper for a moment, studying the words. He gave me a puzzled look, shook his head, then smiled, and started to read:

Good morning, daddy!
Ain't you heard
The boogie-woogie rumble
Of a dream deferred?
Listen closely:
You'll hear their feet
Beating out and beating out a—
You think it's a happy beat?
Listen to it closely:
Ain't you heard
Something underneath like a—
What did I say?
Sure, I'm happy!
Take it away!
Hey, pop!
Re-bop!
Mop!
Yeah!
—"Dream Boogie" *The Collected Poems of Langston Hughes*, Arnold Rampersad, Editor, Vintage Classics, 1994)

Josh opened his eyes wide, "Did some Black guy write this?"

"Why do you think it was written by a Negro?" I asked.

Before Josh could answer, the class was calling out responses.

"Because it's so sad!" shouted one.

"'Cause it's got a jive beat to it!" shouted another.

"The words in it are words we hear," Thelma said quietly.

The students connected with the poignant words of Hughes's "Dream Boogie." It was as relevant to their lives as it was to Negroes in post-World War II Harlem. They worked through the poem with a street-smart perceptiveness.

By the end of the morning, not only had the class learned a lot, Elizabeth and I had too. As they read through "Motto," I came to understand the poem from the point of view of a Black Mississippian. But it was while reading "Theme for English B" that I really felt touched.

As I learn from you,
I guess you learn from me—
Although you're older—and white—
And somewhat more free.
This is my page for English B.

Another swift morning and it was time for our lunch break. After the last student left, Elizabeth and I collapsed into our chairs, but we perked right up when we saw Mrs. Logan and Mrs. Dawson coming up the walk. They occasionally stopped by with sandwiches for us—mayonnaise with tomatoes fresh from their gardens—a rare treat. This was one of those lucky days.

The conversations were always interesting with those two. Mrs. Dawson's husband worked as a janitor at the police station and jail, so she often had insider information about actions against SNCC and COFO workers.

"I worry about that boy Silas McGhee over to Greenwood. He's determined to desegregate the picture show over there, and he keeps getting beat up and all. I'm afraid they're going to do something really bad to him," she said.

"Oh, I hope not!" I set down my sandwich. "I remember him from Ohio. I was in a couple of his workshops."

Mrs. Logan refilled our glasses with tea. "Well, did you hear they pulled three more bodies from the swamps looking for those three missing civil rights workers? It weren't those boys. They don't know who it is yet, but it's not those three."

I sat back stunned, realizing that it had been days since I'd even thought about Andy, James, and Mickey...or even Rita. Last time Luke and I had been together, we hadn't discussed them. I sighed as an uneasy feeling washed over me. There was the constant sense of exhaustion, the dearth of materials to meet the challenges of teaching, the frustration of the voter registration work. Another negative emotion of remembering how such violence could happen to people I knew was almost too much to bear.

Mrs. Logan patted my knee. "I'm sorry, sugar. I shouldn't have mentioned it. I didn't mean to make you sad."

"No. No, that's okay. But it's terrible that there are three more bodies. That makes five boys they've found. How can there be so many dead boys that the authorities weren't even searching for?" I looked up, questioning the two older women. Then I saw in their eyes the differences between their world and mine and the reality dawned on me. And the Langston Hughes poem "Expendable" became even more relevant.

> We will take you and kill you,
> Expendable.
> We will fill you full of lead,
> Expendable.
> And when you are dead
> In the nice cold ground,
> We'll put your name
> Above your head—
> If your head
> Can be found.

12

"Poorly educated people translate into poor people. Education is the one thing that will break the cycle of poverty. It is the only thing that will unlock the door of economic opportunity."
—Speech by Mississippi Governor William Winter to the Southern Growth Policies Board, Atlanta, Georgia, December 10, 1992

While Elizabeth and I began the afternoon session feeling wilted, the students came back to the classroom jazzed up from the morning's session. We started the first block of time looking at the geography of the United States and examining different regions and states.

The students were especially eager to hear about the North. They'd been fed the narrative that things were really good up north, that there was little prejudice, that jobs were plentiful. Elizabeth and I were burdened with the task of showing what life in the North, Midwest, and beyond might be like for them because of issues like low-paying jobs and the discriminatory practice of redlining to keep poorer people from obtaining loans.

Using the grit they'd grown up with to dig and dig to find the truth, the students' questions and discussion tore at the heart of social norms and attitudes. Their continuing to inquire was like striking a piñata with strength and hope. Our encouraging them to dare to dispute the status quo was like our removing their blindfolds.

Classes had been over for an hour and we were almost ready to leave the school when we heard a car pull up outside. Since that was an unusual occurrence, we both went to the door and peered out. Mac McLaurin and Pastor Hendricks got out of the car and joined us in the schoolroom.

"I told you I was praying on it," Pastor Hendricks began as we sat at one of the tables. "I've talked to Mac about my plan, and we think we can pull it off."

"What is it?"

Mac explained. "We want the Freedom Schools to continue after the summer and include community centers as well. So we've decided to build one here in Mystic Springs."

"Build one! Where? How?" I asked.

"There are two empty lots we're considering," Mac explained. "One's just over the tracks by the jail on Lee Street and the other is just across the street from here. We'll get as much donated help as we can get and use our organizational connections to try and raise the money. We have a community full of talented builders and such."

"And we're hoping you volunteers will reach out to your communities to get some support. So what do you think?" asked the pastor.

"Good idea!" I said as Elizabeth nodded excitedly. I immediately thought of my mother. "My mom is great at raising money for worthy projects! I'll call her."

Elizabeth gestured around her. "But how long will this take? We need the room now!"

Mac and Pastor Hendricks exchanged a quick glance. "Well, we know it's not an immediate solution," said Mac. "The hard part will be getting the lot, the permits, and all that. It'll have to go through the bank, the title company, and the clerk's office—in other words, past the white folks, and they're not going to like the idea."

My heart fell, but Pastor Hendricks smiled as the two men rose to leave. "We just wanted to let you know our plan. Got to start with a plan."

How I wished that plan would become a reality!

~~~

Elizabeth used the next morning's session to work with the students on practical math skills, including setting up a budget, writing a check, establishing a savings account, and requesting a loan.

I had been asked to accompany a group going to the county seat of Indianola to register to vote. When I arrived at New Hope AME Church, the pickup point, six people from Mystic Springs were already there. I was pleased to see Mr. and Mrs. Logan and Mrs. Dawson in the first car with Harry and Anitra. Mr. Willard Thomas, Sadie's grandfather, and a young woman named Rose Anderson would be riding in the second car with Derryle and me. But I was elated when I saw a familiar face in the back seat.

"Mrs. Parker! I'm so glad to see you today! I didn't know you'd be joining us. Mr. Thomas, it's good to see you again."

Mr. Thomas's hand trembled as he tipped his hat toward me.

I turned toward the young woman. "We haven't met yet. I'm Lenore Rogers. I teach at the Freedom School."

"Rose Anderson," she replied then ducked her head shyly.

"Well, I'm glad to see all of you and excited for you on this special day. And it's good to see you again, Derryle. How have you been?"

"Doing well. Can't complain." He put the car in gear and headed out behind Harry.

I turned in my seat toward the back. Mrs. Parker was sitting tall and her smile lit up her face, but the other two looked very nervous. "Have you lived in Mystic Springs long, Miss Anderson?"

"All my life. My daddy works for the city on the garbage truck. Mama works for the Williamson family. She's worked there for about twenty years or so now. They been real good to her."

"Oh, I met their daughter. Jenny, isn't it?"

"Right. Miss Jenny. She real nice too. Mrs. Williamson, she been giving my mama Miss Jenny's old clothes most all my life. That's where I got this dress I'm wearing today. She has some real pretty things."

"That's a very nice dress, and it looks good on you. Do you work too?"

"Oh, yes, ma'am. I work with Mrs. Freida Lawson and a couple of other ladies in a cleaning business. We take care of some of the offices in town and clean them after everyone goes home at night."

"Good for you. Tell me, how did you decide to come and get registered."

"It was at a mass meeting, ma'am. I was so moved by what the minister was saying, then hearing Stokely Carmichael and others speak, I felt I had to vote. I believe that things can get better if we have the vote, and maybe, well, maybe I could work up to a better job, like actually work in one of those offices." She shrugged and added quietly, "I dunno, maybe that's a foolish idea."

"It's not a foolish idea at all, and you're exactly right! And please don't call me ma'am. We're about the same age. Can I call you Rose and you call me Lenore?"

Rose's smile became more relaxed, and we eased into general small talk for the rest of the ride. I tried to engage Mr. Thomas in conversation, but his apprehension kept him tensely silent as we drew closer and closer to Indianola. But not Mrs. Parker. She eagerly watched out the window as if trying to take in all the views she didn't often get to see.

"How's your family, Mrs. Parker?" I asked, hoping she would start talking and lead into some of her fascinating stories. Mr. Thomas probably had some too.

"Oh, they all fine. Thank you for askin'," she replied then turned back to the window.

I sensed our passengers were wanting time for quiet contemplation as we approached Indianola. As we got closer, I could see why the courthouse could seem intimidating with its yellow bricks and columns and sturdy cupola at the top towering over us. I looked up at the building then glanced quickly at the others in the car. Rose was biting her lip, Mr. Thomas was slumped in his seat, and Mrs. Parker had a tight grip on her cane. As we got out of the car, I put my hand reassuringly on each one of them. With my firmest, most encouraging smile, I said, "You'll be fine. You practiced how to do this, and we'll be right here with you."

Harry and his group joined us as we waited, staring at a group of whites standing between us and the steps. I felt a pang of misgiving until Harry greeted some of them by name. With relief, I realized they were from the press. I figured having the press there might be helpful in reducing the threat of violence.

We marched onward up the steps but hesitated for a split second when we saw armed deputies standing in a formidable line at the top. Then Sheriff Hollowell came forward and faced Harry eye to eye in front of the group.

Harry didn't flinch as he spoke calmly. "These people are here to register to vote. We are not looking for any trouble."

There was silence for a moment as the sheriff shifted his gaze to the registrants and sneered. "They can go in two at a time. The others got to stay out here."

"You two first," he said, pointing at Mr. and Mrs. Logan. The rest of us settled ourselves along the edge of the portico. Mrs. Dawson had brought some cardboard fans, which we put to use. From his pack, Harry occasionally pulled out a thermos of water for us and later passed around crackers that we ate while the deputies took turns parading in front of us with expressions of disdain.

I was proud of those waiting to register for the calm way they sat as minutes then an hour ticked by. I supposed they were used to being forced to wait. But I wanted to jump up every ten minutes to ask what was going on, to somehow take hold of the situation and wring some order out of it.

The Logans, Mrs. Dawson, and Mr. Thomas were all turned down, even though they felt they'd answered everything correctly just as they'd been taught in the classes. The biggest stumbling block was to interpret the section of the Constitution that the clerk selected, and the clerk had the final say as to whether or not the interpretation was correct. As each one of them came out rejected, Mrs. Parker's jaw tightened and her expression grew more determined.

She and Rose were the last to go in. Almost an hour later, Rose strode out with a big smile on her face. "I did it!" she exclaimed. "Like we practiced, and I got it all done. That clerk looked like she had to swallow nails, but she couldn't find nothing wrong."

"Terrific! We're so proud of you!" The others crowded around her, beaming. Mrs. Logan hugged her, and Mrs. Dawson squeezed both of her hands, kissed her cheek, and said, "I'm so proud of you, Rose."

I glanced at the empty doorway and asked, "Uh...is Mrs. Parker still working on her application?"

"Yeah, she's 'bout done, I think," Rose answered.

For the next half hour, we had small conversations, stretched, dabbed perspiration from our faces, and paced back and forth on the portico. I heard the tap of the cane before I saw Mrs. Parker. She was moving quickly. *Is that a good sign or a bad one?* I wondered.

Mrs. Parker stopped in front of us, her eyes sparking with anger. "That white registrar, she never were goin' to let me get registered!" Mrs. Parker tapped her cane for emphasis as she spoke. "I knowed I answered good, just like we learned when we practiced. But...her...she only saw me as a dumb ol' Black lady who shouldn't be votin'. She don't know nothin'!"

I put my arm around her shoulder. "Oh, I'm sorry. That's very disappointing!"

"I'm so angry!" she growled.

"We're all angry about today, Willa Mae," said Mrs. Logan, patting her friend's arm. "But we'll keep trying. One day, we *will* get to register and we *will* vote. Someday, Willa Mae, someday."

Mrs. Parker nodded. "I tell you true, Joann, I ain't goin' to die 'til I vote. That's a promise."

I wanted to kiss this granddaughter of a slave who was teaching me the power of hope and determination.

We all bundled into the two cars. I knew that the other five had all been as well prepared as Rose. It had to be completely deflating to come through all this and still not be accepted. I felt anger and disgust at the system.

I had talked to my mother on the phone the night before. During the conversation, my mom had asked which I liked best, the teaching or the voter registration work. Without hesitation, I had answered, "The teaching. It's so rewarding and fun." Yet now, my anger could have pushed me to say that I leaned toward thinking the voter registration drive was the more important job.

I had asked my mother to organize financial help for the construction of a school and community center in Mystic Springs. She had become a real advocate of the Freedom Schools, and she was an amazing fundraiser back home. She not only enjoyed fundraising, she thrived on it. I had no doubt she would do an outstanding job for our Freedom School.

~~~

When I returned to the Freedom School in the afternoon, I immediately became immersed in the flurry of excitement that the students carried around them like a dust cloud swirling in the desert. To them, it didn't matter that there were too many bodies crammed into too small of a space. It didn't matter that materials to work with were scarce at best. It didn't matter that their teachers were young and inexperienced. What mattered was that they were being fed ideas about a world outside Mystic Springs, outside Mississippi, and beyond what they thought was their only reality. They were starting to challenge these ideas, searching them to learn truths for their lives, expressing opinions that would be affirmed. It was heady stuff that could change their futures, and it carried the power of a whirlwind along with it.

This afternoon's class was for the students to role-play events that made progress toward getting the Civil Rights Act signed on July 2. While each group performed, the rest of the class guessed the event. Then the performing group was asked to give a report on the details of the event.

Some acted out the Supreme Court decision in 1954 of Brown v. the

Board of Education. Others portrayed the Montgomery bus boycott and others the Children's March in Birmingham with Bull Connor and the fire hoses. There was a great deal of loud drama involved in the acting, and if the school actually had a principal, he would've been there in a hurry to quiet the commotion. As one of their teachers, I reveled in the sharing of knowledge and the acknowledgment of important history. Even knowing of their lack of education, I was surprised when one of the students asked me later what the Supreme Court was.

After class was over for the day, Mac and Chris Hexter, the head of the Freedom School in Ruleville, stopped by while Elizabeth and I were cleaning up.

"Y'all could still be teaching," Mac griped after greeting us. "No one is using this space."

I wanted to shake him, but I contained myself. "Mac, we don't have the time or energy to do any more. By the time we've cleaned up from one day and set up for the next, it's time for dinner. Then we have to go back out for voter registration, and that doesn't even count reading student work, planning lessons, or writing reports."

Mac looked at me with a twinkle in his eye and gave his raspy chuckle. "I know that. What I meant was we have two new girls coming in. They'll be staying just down the street with Mrs. Akers. Their job is to set up a kind of kindergarten in the afternoon after your classes, and they'll be using this schoolroom. It'll work out just fine."

"A kindergarten would be great! Are the volunteers anyone we know?" asked Elizabeth.

"One is Desiree Stone from over in Ruleville. She set up a kindergarten there. The other is Lynn Grissom. She started working on voter registration, but that wasn't goin' well. Been moved around a couple of times. She wasn't relating well to the older folks she was talking to. Before we send her home, we're giving her one last chance. Maybe you can guide her."

I couldn't help myself as groaned out loud, "Please don't let it be the Lynn I met on the first day of training!"

Mac shrugged. "She's a nice, good-hearted girl. Just hasn't found the right place yet. I'm sure you'll help her settle in. Derryle will pick them up and move them in on Saturday."

"I'll be sending over the supplies needed for a kindergarten," added Chris.

"Where are we going to put the kindergarten supplies?" moaned Elizabeth. "We don't have room for anything else."

I looked around, knowing we had no choice. "Harry and Anitra may not like it, but I'll rearrange some things in the back office. I'll work on that later. Any news about getting a lot for the new school?"

"The bank owns that lot across the street and the city owns the one past the tracks. It's land they have in case they want to expand the jail and police station. We're working on both lots, but it's not going well. In the meantime, the church has started a collection toward the cost of building and is circulating a list of people who can help, you know, construction workers, plumbers, people like that."

"Well, my mom is very enthusiastic about it. She's having a coffee Saturday morning to get donations started. I'll keep you and Pastor Hendricks posted."

Mac nodded. "We drove past that old school on the way in. It's been condemned...deteriorated too much. They're starting to tear it down. Y'all might go there with Harry's car in the evenings and see if you can salvage any materials for a school or community center. Reverend Hendricks has a group from church to do that too. Might be some good stuff. The Wilkins family from his church offered to store stuff in their empty shed."

I shook my head as the two men left. "Honestly, every time I meet with Mac I feel like he's written a new addendum to our job description," I said, exasperated.

~~~

Wednesday had become one of my favorite days of the week because it was the day the class wrote the newspaper. I worked with the students showing them how the *Clarion-Ledger* and *The New York Times* were constructed, which also gave me an opportunity to teach a class on current events. What they chose for their articles fascinated me, and I was always touched reading the weekly essay about what it meant to be a Negro. Amos, a student who'd only recently started attending class, wrote this week's essay:

What It Is to Be a Negro in 1964

A life based on the white's definition of upward mobility for Blacks. Crumbs to suppress the Black people's hunger and right to equal education, health care, housing, jobs, and justice.

Happy, disciplined children taught to respect everyone, get an education, obey the law, work hard, and trust God for all things.

Poor, having just enough, but proud to scratch and scrape for more. The meal bag was empty every Friday until Mom got paid and bought groceries.

Wearing the same pair of shoes until one or both opened their mouths, then you wired them shut and walked on.

No annual dental checkups, no fillings, teeth with cavities were extracted.

A voice crying in the wilderness of America for justice and equality.

My mom and dad saying "yes ma'am" and "no sir" to whites much younger than themselves.

Segregation, white and Black designated facilities and areas.

Black, hated by whites but blessed with the love of God and family.

Victimized, having to push through the muck and mire of discrimination and racism.

An illegitimate child from America's whoredom with slavery, without clear title to an inheritance of its promises of justice and freedom.

Fear of cops, the KKK, or other whites who thought they were privileged to kill a Black person at will.

~~~

After reading his essay, I sat for a few moments thinking about Amos. He was a lot like Cornelius—both had so much potential. How far could that ability take them? They'd never get to Harvard, but could they get to Mississippi Valley State or Tougaloo? And even if they did, what kind of future awaited them after that? I had been raised knowing I would go to college. Now I saw what a struggle it was for Blacks to get even a decent high school education. *How had Luke done it?* I wondered.

The essays helped me understand more fully what life was like for Negroes in Mississippi and what life was like for Luke. He invaded my thoughts so often, and the more I tried to fight against it, the harder it became. I'd start with the logical thought that there could never be anything between us. That thought swirled on to the truth that there *was* something going on between us. Then it flared into a cyclone of what that might mean and what disastrous consequences there would be. But every time I thought about it, I came back to where I'd started. There could never be a romantic relationship between Luke and me.

After class, the decibels rose as the students chatted and laughed their way out the door. As I looked up from my notes, I noticed Amos still lingering by the back table.

"Amos," I said, "Everything okay?"

He made his way slowly to the front of the room and stood before me. He cleared his throat. "I have to tell you, Miss Lenore. I didn't write that essay. My daddy did. When I told him about my assignment to write what it means to be a Negro," Amos lowered his gaze, "he grabbed my pen and said he'd tell that white teacher what being a Negro is like. He told me if I didn't give you that essay, he'd find out and whip me good."

"Oh, Amos!"

Amos raised his head and looked at me. "I didn't mean to cheat or nothing, honest. I would've written the same kinda thing. My daddy, though, he's lived through a lot. He don't trust no white people. He don't get what it's like here in this school, you know?"

I took Amos's hands in mine. "I understand. That essay speaks the truth, and that's what's important. That's what we want here in the Freedom School. Thank you for telling me. And really," I grinned at him, "I didn't think that essay sounded like something a student would write, but what it said was important. We'll use it in the newspaper anyway. Ask your dad if that's okay."

~~~

I had been looking forward to the time when, as a class, we would be discussing *To Kill a Mockingbird*. The students had been reading it on their own for a few weeks, and several had been sharing their opinions along the way. By putting out a plea the first day, we had managed to scrape together enough copies for most of the students. Fortunately, they were already used to having to share materials at school.

After a lively discussion about a writer's point of view, I asked, "What did you learn about the town of Maycomb?"

"They is so racist in that town," declared Sadie.

Earl laughed. "That Harper Lee lady must've lived in Mystic Springs. Sounds just like here."

Cornelius raised his hand. "I think Maycomb, and here too, has like in India, a caste system, you know. Like here there's the plantation owner on the top, then the white businessmen, and then maybe the white teachers and such, and way down near the bottom is the white trash and the Black folks."

"Yeah, that's the way it's always been, and Mr. Charlie's going to be sure to keep the Negro down at the bottom." Josh's remark brought a barrage of comments erupting throughout the room.

I rapped hard on a table. "By raising your hand, how many agree with what Josh said?"

All the hands went up, some more forcefully than others.

"Let's talk about why this has happened. What made it possible?" We couldn't have had this conversation the first day or even the first week, but now they were ready. Their eagerness was contagious. This was what made teaching them exciting.

Little by little, the discussion carried the students back in history, through the White Citizens' Council and the Klan, through the Black codes and Jim Crow laws, through Reconstruction and finally, to the beginning: slavery. There was an enthusiasm in peeling back the layers of history—*their* history. We all were coming to some new truths and awakening some previously unknown understandings.

~~~

I really missed sharing successes like this with Jane and hearing about hers, so when I got to the Johnsons and saw her letter, I tore into it. It was long, obviously hastily written on several sheets of notebook paper, but rather than including funny observations and incidents as her letters usually did, it was all about the urgency of getting Negroes registered to vote and about developing the Mississippi Freedom Democratic Party. Jane was planning to go with the group to the Democratic National Convention in Atlantic City in August, and she wanted me to join her.

The idea was appealing. Our voter registration results had me feeling disheartened. I hated that only one of the six we took to Indianola was able to pass the test, especially when I remembered Mrs. Parker's expression, how she'd defiantly held her head high as she marched back to the car, but once she got in the back seat, her lip trembled and she tightly gripped her cane. Even though Negroes were finding the courage to try to register, they were still being denied the right. Jane had experienced the same kind of thing. She wrote, "In Hattiesburg, of the seventy applying, only three were able to register. In Canton, out of the twenty-two who took the test, none passed."

The numbers across the state were demoralizing. Yet seeing the resolve and courage of the six participants on the drive to Indianola that day and seeing the proud glow on Rose's face after she was registered gave me the hope to keep trying.

I paused in reading Jane's letter when I heard voices in the living room. Someone was crying. Anabel stuck her head around the doorway. "You need to come, Lenore," she said and disappeared.

I dropped Jane's letter and hurried into the living room to see Rose Anderson in tears. Mrs. Johnson sat beside her, gently rubbing her back.

"What's happened? What's wrong?" I sat next to Rose and took her hand in mine.

"It's my mama." Rose lifted her tearful face. "Mrs. Williamson knows I got registered, so she told my mama if I don't..." The tears came in a rush. "She say if I don't take my name off the rolls, she gonna fire my mama!"

I sank back dismayed. "You don't really think she'd do that, do you?"

Rose nodded emphatically. "Oh, yes she would! She'll definitely do it! What am I gonna do? I want to vote. You know I do. But I can't be the cause of my mama losing her job. Mrs. Williamson also say if I don't get my name off, she make sure Mrs. Lawson get fired from cleaning Mr. Williamson's offices, so we'll all be out of work."

"Oh my God!" I couldn't believe what I was hearing. "Didn't you tell me your mother has worked for Mrs. Williamson for over twenty years?"

Rose bobbed her head up and down. She clasped and unclasped her hands and dabbed her eyes with a wadded-up tissue. "I'm sorry to let you down, Lenore, but I got to withdraw my name. I got no choice."

I shook my head in disbelief. "Oh, Rose, I am so sorry." I hugged her tightly and said, "That is so wrong!"

Both Rose and Mrs. Johnson lowered their heads with a sense of defeat that made me want to weep too. But instead, my anger intensified— an anger that made me want to fight against something or someone. Again, I had that brief glimpse that helped me understand Stokely. And Luke.

13

Sometimes you have to be willing to turn things upside down to make them right side up.
—John Lewis, *Across That Bridge*

I sat on the edge of the bed for a few minutes rubbing my face and trying to wake up. I had been restless all night. Elizabeth came over and sat by me. "Didn't get much sleep, did you?"

"No," I grumbled. "Sorry if I disturbed you."

"That's okay. I know you're disappointed about Rose."

"I'm more than disappointed. I'm furious! How can this be happening in our country? Those in power here are determined to keep Negroes from voting, and they can do it! They hold all the control! It has to stop, but how? How? What can we do?"

Elizabeth shrugged. "Keep trying to get them registered, I guess. In the meantime, we've got to get ready for Parents' Night."

I shook myself awake, knowing I had a long day ahead of me. We had arranged for a special event, the first Parents' Night to show the community what we had been doing. But first, there was the morning to get through.

The unit that we taught that day was called "Power Structure." Elizabeth and I led the students through a discussion of how things happened in Mystic Springs, Sunflower County, and throughout the United States and the federal government.

Earl raised his hand. "It's that White Citizens' Council that controls everything. That's what my Uncle Jake told me. He's smart. Went up North and got educated. He's got a good job up there. He told me to get out of this town. That a Black man can't get anywhere here because that White Citizens' Council will hold 'em down."

149

"And who makes up that group, that council?" I asked.

"The richest white men in town. That's Mr. Stokes and Mr. Worthington with their plantations. And Mr. Wilcox down at the bank," answered Thelma.

"And the sheriff and police chief. They not so rich, but they do what the others say."

"And don't forget Mr. Williamson who owns half the town and whoever the manager of the mill is."

Little by little, the students dissected the levels of control to see how the system operated and who had the real power. By the end of the morning, discovering what little control they had over their own lives had left them disheartened.

More than anything, I wanted these young people not to feel powerless, to feel that they had options. I saw that hopelessness in some of the older people. But without hope, what could you do? Dr. King, the leader of the Movement, was preaching hope. I wanted to preach it too.

Because it was a Thursday, we'd been able to get the New Hope AME Church board to allow us to have Parents' Night at the church. There simply wasn't room in the school for the students plus their parents.

After the lunch break, the students helped Elizabeth and me haul all the props to the church and set up for Parents' Night. The students had thrown themselves into rehearsing as Black historical figures. Some planned to reenact important events, like the bus boycott and the sit-ins. Josh was going to read some of his favorite Langston Hughes poems, and others were going to talk about how they put the newspaper together.

During the program, I noticed that Mac, who'd come from Ruleville for the event, was having quite an intense conversation with Pastor Hendricks. I hoped it was about a development for the new building. After the last applause had died down and the students and parents milled together for juice and cookies, compliments of the church's women's group, I sought out Mac.

"Do you have any news about a lot for a school?"

Mac's eyes looked merrier than usual. "We do, and you won't believe this! I wish I'd realized it myself, but I didn't. One of Brother Hendricks's members thought of it." Mac paused and gave me a big smile.

I wanted to shake him to hurry up.

"When Mississippi towns are first plotted, they're set up by sections.

There's always one section, the sixteenth section, that's held in trust for a school. As it turns out, that's where the old school was on Oak Street—on that sixteenth section. So it's already designated for a school! Here, look at this," he said, handing me a sheet of paper, "just read that first part."

I took the paper and quickly scanned the legal language about the sixteenth section of land. "So this says that the old school lot *has* to be used for a school...that the land is held in trust for a school, right?" I asked. What that meant was beginning to hit me.

"So when they finish tearing down the old school, you can have the land to build a school and community center? That's fantastic! And you don't even have to buy the lot?"

Mac's smile drooped a little. "Well, it may not be that easy. See the next part?" He pointed to the paper I still held.

I skimmed down the page.

"Although title to Sixteenth Section Public School Trust Lands is vested in the State of Mississippi in trust, laws enacted by the state legislature place jurisdiction and control over leasing and day-to-day management of the lands in the hands of the local school board where the land is located."

"Oh no. That's Mr. Williamson, isn't it?"

Mac nodded. I continued reading as he added, "And the secretary of state oversees the whole thing...but strictly in a supervisory way."

"Who is he? Can you go to him?"

"His name is Heber Austin Ladner. He's been in Mississippi politics forever. Been secretary of state since 1948. So, no, I don't think we'll get any help from him."

"I don't quite understand this. It says the land is in trust for schools, but it can be reclassified. So they can decide it should be zoned for something else?"

"I don't get it all myself. That's why I'm going to take it to our lawyers up in Greenwood tomorrow."

I continued skimming the document. "Look at this!" I read aloud the section that said if they sell it for an industrial development, then they have to give a replacement for the school.

Mac shrugged. "Those are all the details I have to find out. Best not to say anything to anyone just yet."

"I won't. Can I tell Elizabeth, though?"

"Sure, but no one else. We don't want anyone to know until we have all our plans in order." Mac paused and looked into my face kindly. "I know that trip to the registrar's office was a big disappointment to you. How're you doing?"

I fought to keep my tears in check. "I'm so angry! It's not fair! Not fair at all."

"You're right about that, Lenore. And most Negroes in Mississippi would shrug and say, 'Well, that's just the way things are.' That's why we have to show them it doesn't need to be that way. We have to keep talking to them, encouraging them. It'll be slow, slow work, but we *can* move forward. Mrs. Parker, Mrs. Dawson, and the Logans are all willing to try again."

"But not Mr. Thomas?"

"No, not yet."

I had to ask. "Mac, would Mrs. Williamson really have fired Rose's mother? After twenty years?"

"Yes, she would have, and she would've felt perfectly justified in doing so."

~~~

After school on Friday, I stayed to clear out some space in the SNCC office for the expected kindergarten things. As I worked in silence, I thought more and more about Rose's situation. I'd reread Jane's letter and saw the frustration she was feeling too, but her hope for the Mississippi Freedom Democratic Party still shone through.

I'd considered myself a knowledgeable person, but the more I learned, the more I realized how ignorant I'd been. As my sadness gave way to anger, I thought about the danger we were all in. I'd seen the latest report about incidents against COFO and SNCC workers, including the burning of Mount Vernon Missionary Baptist Church down near McComb. These injustices happened to people I knew, people I cared about. They were so much more personal now that I could no longer ignore them. These were truths I had to face.

I heard footsteps on the steps of the school and a familiar voice called out hello. *Luke!*

"Back here!" I called out then quickly set down some boxes of school supplies so I could smooth my hair as Luke entered the room.

"I brought over the supplies for the kindergartners."

As I turned toward Luke, I found myself unable to hold back the emotions of the past few days. I was so tired, so frustrated, so angry. And so very sad. Tears slipped from my eyes and down my cheeks as I tried to wipe them. I turned away, trying to regain control.

Luke took the few steps between us quickly. "Whoa, girl. What's wrong? What happened?" He gripped my shoulders firmly and turned me toward him.

I looked into his face, his strong, handsome face that I was beginning to care about too much. I wanted to tell him how heartbreaking it was to learn about his world, how I wished it were different for him, for the Johnsons, for Rose, for the students, how I wished I could always work with them to change things, but I couldn't.

"Rose was *so* happy and excited when she got registered, but all that came crashing down when some white woman threatened her mother's job." My tears came stronger now as I put words to my pain. "How can that happen, Luke? It's so wrong. There's so much here that is wrong!"

Luke pulled me close and wrapped his arms around me "There, now. I know. Lord, I know," he murmured into my hair. "But we got to believe, Lenore, that the day is coming. It's coming."

I felt the strength of his arms around me. I felt warm and safe and wished we could stay like that forever. He kissed me gently on my forehead then moved his hand and tilted my chin up and kissed me softly on the lips. I melted into the kiss with every part of me. The sound of a car passing by cut into our comfort. We pulled slowly, reluctantly apart.

"We can't do this. It's not safe." I grabbed a tissue and blotted my tears.

"I know," replied Luke, his arms dropping to his sides.

We looked at each other for a moment, then Luke reached out and pulled me close again. We kissed and kissed once more. "So how can we *not* do this?" he asked with a mischievous smile on his face.

"Luke! Think of Emmett Till. If some people saw us, who knows what they might do."

"I see only one hope for us, girl-of-mine. We'll be very, very careful, and we will work and pray for the day when it'll be perfectly okay."

I wanted to believe that. Once, I would've even thought it was possible. But now, for the first time, I doubted that day would ever come in the world I was learning about.

For the first time, I was no longer sure that good would always overcome evil.

~~~

On Saturday morning, Elizabeth and I met with the rest of the SNCC staff and volunteers to continue with voter registration. I was determined to pour myself into the work for two reasons: to do what I was beginning to consider the most important work of the summer and to keep my mind off Luke.

As we left headquarters, Harry said, "I've been talking to Mac on the phone. Derryle will be here at two o'clock with those two kindergarten teachers. He'll leave them at Mrs. Akers's place. It's only four doors down from the school, so he wants you and Elizabeth to meet them and take them to the school, you know, show them around."

I grimaced and muttered, "Oh, Lord. I don't know if I can stand this."

Elizabeth laughed. "She can't be that bad. Do you even know her?"

I rolled my eyes. "As well as I need to. She talks too much and she's just so ...so perky."

"Yeah, perky is pretty annoying."

Anitra moved forward to join us. "I've been thinking," she began. "The material y'all showed me suggested teaching a language class. I could start doing that as an extra, maybe in the back room when I'm not doing registration work."

I looked at her, surprised. "You can teach a foreign language? Which one?"

"*Français, mon amie,*" she said striking a pose. "I took it in college. It would be very beginner level, but it would be fun for some of them. And that's not all."

As we walked to our first assigned house, Anitra suggested several more ideas that would engage the students. The more she spoke, the more excited she became. *Anitra is definitely the one who should be teaching.* I'd already thought we should switch jobs, but didn't know if she'd she be willing. And, honestly, I wasn't sure I even wanted to.

By midafternoon, I'd swatted at more mosquitoes than I could count and we'd made little progress convincing people to register for the Mississippi Freedom Democratic Party. The languid heat simmered around us as we moved from house to house. Perspiration moistened our faces and discouragement dampened our spirits. Elizabeth checked her watch and patted my back. "It's after three o'clock, Lenore. We have to go welcome Desiree and Miss Perky to Mystic Springs."

"Maybe it's not the same Lynn," I groaned. "Cross your fingers."

When we arrived at Mrs. Akers's house, Elizabeth knocked on the door. Even through the rusty, old screen, I could see that familiar blonde ponytail bobbing excitedly up and down as Lynn talked to Mrs. Akers.

Lynn jumped at the sound of the knock. When Elizabeth and I went inside, Lynn smiled broadly and opened her arms wide to hug me. "I'm so excited to be here!" she exclaimed. "I knew you'd be here to greet me, so I felt welcomed already. I've lived in a couple of places before moving here, but I think this will be the best!"

She turned to Mrs. Akers, a tiny woman who was stooped over and graying. "Lenore was one of the very first people I met when we got to the training in Ohio. That's where we went for our training, you know. Up at the Western College for Women. Lenore and I met before we were even on the campus. I take that as a very good omen for my working here, don't you? It's like catching up with an old friend, isn't it?"

Mrs. Akers looked baffled by the onslaught of Lynn's words but nodded companionably anyway.

I could hardly wait to tell Jane. My worst nightmare had come true.

As we walked the few doors down to the school, Elizabeth and I explained our setup. When we arrived, Elizabeth gestured to our arrangement of the tables and chairs. "We can push some back when we get through with classes at four o'clock if that helps."

Desiree nodded. "I don't think we'll have many children, and we'll be mostly sitting on the floor, so if we could have this front half of the room, I think that would work."

I pulled out the things Luke had brought over. My body tingled as I remembered the feel of his arms holding me tightly. But along with the joy came the knot in the pit of my stomach. Even so, it made me even more anxious about Monday evening when we'd all be going to Ruleville for a mass meeting.

Desiree and Lynn were busy looking over their supplies, so Elizabeth and I headed back to the Johnsons' house. I learned that Desiree was there only to set things up, then it would all be Lynn's project. I couldn't imagine how that would work out.

"Well?" I said, "What did you think?"

Elizabeth smiled. "She is definitely perky. Poor Desiree. But at least Lynn seems nice. Anyway, we probably won't see much of them since I assume she's excused from registration work."

~~~

After dinner, Elizabeth and I were sitting on the Johnsons' front steps playing a fierce game of gin rummy when Brenda ambled up and joined us.

"Anitra went home to Jackson until tomorrow night," she said. "Now that there are eight of us, we won't all fit in Harry's car, so Anitra will bring back hers." She watched us play for a moment then added, "Aren't you bored?"

I laughed. "Us? No way. Another exciting Saturday night here in magical Mystic Springs."

"Grab your pocketbooks and come for a walk with me," she suggested.

She didn't need to ask us twice. We tucked away the cards and took a few minutes to rush in and put on some lipstick before the three of us headed out.

"Where to?" asked Elizabeth.

Brenda had a playful glint in her eye. "Let's go to the juke joints."

"The juke joints? Is that safe?" I asked. They were both over twenty-one, but I had a few months to go.

"Safe?" scoffed Brenda. "You're a Freedom Summer volunteer in Mississippi and you're wondering about being safe? Honey, there is no safe here, so let's have some fun for a change."

We strode along, but then our pace slowed. I was beginning to feel like a younger sister tagging along. "Do you think we'll have to show our IDs?" I asked, hugging my purse a little closer to my shoulder.

Brenda laughed. "Not in these places."

We had barely rounded the corner when the sound of a bluesy electric guitar and a harmonica filled the air. Brenda grabbed our arms and propelled us through the doorway under the sign for Johnny's Joint. Through the thick, smoky interior, we felt the eyes of those around the jumble of tables and even from the dance floor. Some seemed mildly curious, but a few seemed hostile. We were the only whites there. We took a deep breath and worked our way through clusters of people to an empty table in a back corner.

A slim young server sauntered up. "Whatcha all want?"

"Uh...three Buds," Brenda ordered.

While we waited for our drinks, we made idle conversation and watched the dance floor. I thought about how great it would be to dance with Luke there, but I knew that could never happen.

Again, sounding like the little sister, I said, "We shouldn't stay long. The Johnsons will be locking their doors, and I'm afraid they'll know where we've been from the cigarette smell on us."

Brenda and Elizabeth exchanged a glance and laughed. "And they might even smell the beer on our breath, "Brenda added.

I felt foolish. Maybe it was because of Mrs. Logan's warning on her first visit, but it was also partly because I felt that schoolteachers had an image to uphold. *What would Mac say...or Mrs. Hamer? But on the other hand, we are young adults on a summer Saturday night. Damn! Life is never just black or white.* Then I had to laugh because that's *exactly* what life was like in Mississippi.

~~~

Sunday morning, we all went to church together as usual. After the service, I couldn't wait to ask Reverend Hendricks about the progress on the lot for the new school.

He shook his head and said, "Nothing new. Mac met with the attorneys and they seem to feel we have a good chance. We also talked to Mr. Williamson. He's starting off with a flat 'no,' but we expected that. We'll keep trying, and we'll keep you posted."

I thanked him and moved on with Brenda and Elizabeth. We went to the café for lunch. It was interesting that all three of us ordered the pot roast dinner. Says something about our northern eating habits, I guessed.

Halfway through our meal, Desiree and Lynn walked in adjoined us. After answering questions about Mystic Springs, we sounded like any five college girls getting together. It was refreshing to talk about courses we've had, books, movies, and where we'd grown up.

When the talk turned to sororities, Brenda asked Lynn. "Are you in a sorority?"

Lynn sat up straighter, tapping her blouse where she would've been wearing her sorority pin. "Oh, yes! I'm an Alpha Chi. I just love it! All my sisters are wonderful! I can't wait to get back on campus and see them. We had great parties and did so many good things. We're all very close, like real sisters, you know?"

Alpha Chi? Alpha Chi! A plan began fermenting. I needed a way to get to Mr. Williamson and here it was: my new "best friend" Lynn and her sorority sister Jenny Williamson.

On the way back, I walked beside Lynn. "I actually met another girl who lives here and is an Alpha Chi. I'll have to introduce you sometime."

Lynn's eyes opened wide with joy. "Oh my God! That's amazing! I'd love to meet her. When do you think we can do that? I can't believe it! A sorority sister right here in Mystic Springs. This is so fantastic!"

"I'll see what I can work out. I'll let you know." I was beginning to feel like an undercover agent.

～～～

When laundry day rolled around, we were looking forward to hearing more stories from Mrs. Parker. But we were disappointed when, after greeting us, she went back to her rocker and sat with her Bible in her lap.

"Are you okay?" I asked Mrs. Parker after we'd started our washing.

"Only feeling a mite peckish, child. That's all."

"Have you eaten today?" Elizabeth asked.

"Jus' not up to cooking anything." She gave us a tired smile.

I squatted down in front of her. "What can we fix for you? Some toast? A cup of soup?"

"Don't y'all be fussing with an old lady like me. I'm fine. My daughter's coming by in a bit and she'll fix me something."

I patted her hand and stood. "I'll fix you some toast and warm milk. My grandmother always likes that."

Mrs. Parker seemed better after she'd eaten something, but she still sat with the closed Bible on her lap. I pulled a chair closer and sat down. "I know you were discouraged about not getting to register. But you'll get another chance. I'm sure that someday you'll get to vote."

She chuckled softly. "I know, darlin'. I'm goin' to keep tryin'. Folks like me, we jus' keep on keepin' on. I get my strength from the Word." She patted the Bible in her lap. When she closed her eyes and resumed rocking, I went back to doing laundry.

While I started the rinse cycle on the old washer, Elizabeth went to Mrs. Parker and asked, "Shall I read to you from the Bible while we're waiting for our clothes?"

Mrs. Parker looked up, a glimmer of tears seeping from her rheumy eyes, and held out the worn Bible. "Bless you, child," she said. "Will you please start with Proverbs Three, verses five and six? Those words, they comfort me."

Elizabeth and I took turns reading some of her favorite passages. Mrs. Parker rocked back and forth, smiling as she listened to the Scriptures. That dear woman had shared with us from the little she had: her towels, her washer, her stories, and it felt good that we could give something back. At that moment, I had the most profound understanding of the word *community*: the sense of coming together, of interconnectedness. That feeling brought a new dimension, a deeper layer to why we were there.

14

ARE YOU A REGISTERED VOTER?

If we were all voting, then things would be better in Mississippi. We would have enough food, better jobs ,better schools, better houses, paved sidewalks. People coming here this summer can work with you on VOTER REGISTRATION.

—COFO/SNCC Freedom Summer flyer

My first thought on Monday morning was that we'd be going to another mass meeting in Ruleville. Of course, the day dragged on more slowly than usual. I knew Luke and I wouldn't have a chance to be alone, but at least we'd sit together at the mass meeting. Elizabeth and I rode with Anitra in her car with the others in Harry's. She drove with one hand lightly on the wheel, the other arm resting on the open window. Her driving matched her personality: confident, completely in charge, unafraid.

Anitra kept the conversation going, brainstorming ideas for the Freedom School. Even so, the ride down that road was always long and tense for me. A knot rose in my stomach every time another car came up fast behind us. Elizabeth and I exchanged a looks we passed the spot where the police had stopped us. I wondered if I'd ever be able to travel that road without a chilling reminder washing over me.

When we entered the church, I scanned the crowd for Luke. Surely he was there, but I didn't see him. Anitra and Elizabeth found seats while I lagged behind. With a rising sense of disappointment, my eyes searched the crowd more slowly. Finally, I saw the back of his head with Silas next to him at the end of an aisle on the far side of the church. He had saved me a seat.

I wedged myself in next to Luke and turned to greet him. But when I saw him, I gasped. His face was covered with cuts and large, purple bruises. One eye was completely swollen shut.

"Oh my God, Luke! What happened?"

Luke shook his head and looked away, so Silas answered for him. "Somebody saw you two at Mrs. Hamer's. They caught up with him when we were out in the country getting voter registrations yesterday."

I couldn't take my eyes off Luke. I forced back tears. I wanted to reach out and hold him close, the very last thing I should ever do. I couldn't get any words out past the lump in my throat.

Luke simply shrugged. "Don't worry about it. It looks worse than it is."

"Oh, Luke!" There wasn't anything else to say, so I sat back in my seat, my hands gripped together, a knot settled in my stomach.

Luke gently nudged me. "How's everything going, girl?" he said softly.

How can he be so calm about it? I wondered. A warm flush rose inside me as I answered. The pews were so crowded that Luke and I were close. *How could he still want me to sit by him?* I looked around to see if anyone noticed. I was especially glad that Mrs. Hamer was way on the other side of the sanctuary. *I guess if he wants to act like it's nothing, I have to also. This is not a lesson I ever expected to learn!*

Soon the enthusiasm of the freedom songs and the preaching suffused all of us. The freedom songs always carried me to a place that felt like coming home. Standing and swaying to the music, it almost felt like Luke and I were dancing together, and sitting close during the preaching, our hands found a way to brush together. We reconnected to the Movement and connected to each other. Now I knew what the consequences of that could be.

It wasn't until Stokely Carmichael's talk that my mind went to other things. "You know we got two kindergarten teachers, don't you?" I whispered.

Luke nodded.

"With the new kindergarten, there's no chance of being alone at the school any—"

"Shh!" someone behind me hissed.

Luke squeezed my hand, but it only made me feel worse. *If we can't find time to be alone together and can't even whisper at the mass meetings, what hope is there for us? And if anyone should ever see us together...My God!*

I went back to Mystic Springs that night without even a memory of a stolen kiss because there'd been so many people around. Even when Luke leaned in the car to say goodnight, we didn't dare chance it. With the rhythm of the cracks in the concrete road, the phrase from training repeated in my thoughts, *There will be consequences. There will be consequences.* No matter what my heart said, my head said we shouldn't take that gamble. My only option was to throw myself into the work of the Freedom Summer Project.

~~~

I needed to stay extra busy, so it was fortunate that in addition to the Freedom School, registration work, and adjusting to the kindergarten program, the Free Southern Theater was coming this week. The theater group was based at Tougaloo College in Jackson, Anitra's alma mater; she'd gotten them to come and perform at New Hope AME Church. Gilbert Moses and John O' Neill had developed the play *In White America*, which offered a creative way of telling Black history in the United States from slavery to the present. I was really looking forward to it.

For the performance, we packed our students into the front pews. The troupe was going to perform in Ruleville later, so no SNCC members from there came to Mystic Springs for it, as much as I'd hoped one would.

During the play, the police chief leaned against the back wall. My stomach knotted at the sight of him. Several white citizens came in and stood alongside him. *Was one of them Mr. Williamson?* I wondered.

The performance immediately drew us in as the narrator started, "The story of the Negro in the United States begins with the slave trade. A ship's doctor aboard a slave ship in the mid-eighteenth century described his impressions."

A white actor portraying the ship's doctor told in horrific, graphic detail the conditions of the slave ship. He ended by describing how one slave had jumped off the ship to be devoured by sharks rather than live a life of bondage. In the shocked silence that followed, a Negro actress sang the hauntingly compelling lyric, "And before I'd be a slave, I'll be buried in my grave, and go home to my Lord and be free."

I rubbed the Goosebumps on my arms.

We also heard an actor playing Thomas Jefferson say, "The Blacks, whether originally a distinct race, or made distinct by time and circumstance, are inferior to whites in the endowments both of body and mind."

We listened as actors portraying freed slaves shared remembrances of slavery days. "They was heaps of niggers tried to find their folkses what was gone. But the moistest of 'em never git together again even after they got free 'cause they don't know where one or the other is."

Actors depicting Sojourner Truth, Frederick Douglass, sharecroppers, storekeepers, soldiers, and others brought their stories, their pain, and their victories and laid them bare before us.

Perhaps the audience was used to the church setting, or maybe it was because they were so involved, but loud comments of "Amen!" and "Tell it!" peppered the performance.

After a powerful portrayal of a fifteen-year-old girl trying to integrate school in Little Rock, the narrator explained, "After 1957, the Negro protest exploded with bus boycotts, sit-ins, Freedom Rides, drives for voter registration, and job protests."

One by one, the Black actors stepped forward and said, "We have implored. We have supplicated. We have entreated." And then, finally, "We can't wait any longer. NOW is the time."

A white actor stepped forward and read, "We the people of the United States, in Order to form a more perfect Union..."His firm voice continued reciting the preamble to the Constitution.

At the same time, a Black actress sang: "Oh, freedom. Oh, freedom! Oh, freedom over me!" She sang louder and louder as the words of the Constitution hung in the background. Eventually, all of us were on our feet singing with more intensity and fervor to the end, "And before I'd be a slave, I'll be buried in my grave, and go home to my Lord and be free!"(Quotes from *In White America* by Martin B. Duberman)

I wasn't the only one with tears in my eyes as we stood and applauded and applauded.

I couldn't wait to write Jane about the marvelous performance. The small cast had given these Negroes a new narrative, *their* narrative, which ended with hope. As I looked around at the students, I could see they believed in that hope. For that night, anyway.

~~~

As the days went on, I became more and more caught up in the work of the Mississippi Freedom Democratic Party. I got Harry to come to our class one rainy morning to talk about it. He went to the front of the room and began speaking without even waiting for them to be quiet.

"Y'all know we've been goin' 'round the community trying to get folks signed up to vote. What you may not know is there's even more goin' on. There's something big happening in the country, and it's starting right here in Mississippi." He pounded the desk for emphasis.

That got the students' attention. They were ready to listen.

"COFO established the Mississippi Freedom Democratic Party in April because the regular all-white Mississippi Democratic Party hasn't let Blacks participate. When the whites have their precinct meetings to elect delegates, they don't let the date or time be known, or they lock the doors so no Blacks can enter. Sometimes, if Blacks do get in, they immediately adjourn the meeting."

Earl's voice broke in. "Man, that's not right!"

"But we can do something about it. See, this is an election year. The Democratic National Convention will be in Atlantic City next month to pick who we want to run for president. We've studied the laws about it, and technically, the regular Mississippi delegation is illegal because it excludes all Black people, who represent 42 percent of the state."

Josh called out, "That's almost half the state! That ain't fair!"

Harry nodded. "Exactly. So we're going to send a delegation that will appear before the credentials committee and show that the Mississippi Freedom Democratic Party should be seated instead of the all-white one. It won't be all Blacks. There'll be a couple of whites as delegates in our group. We want to get a hundred thousand people signed up. That'll be enough to show the officials that Negroes in Mississippi want to vote."

Thelma raised her hand. "So that's another part of why y'all been going around the neighborhoods trying to get people to register?"

"That's correct. There's two important things we're doing," Harry answered. "One is to get enough people signed up to make the Mississippi Freedom Democratic Party a real thing. The other is that we need to get all the eligible voters registered at the county seats so they can vote in the election in November. But that's hard to do because a lot of them are afraid."

"Yeah. My dad said he'd lose his job if he registered," said Earl. Many in the class nodded in agreement.

Harry spread his hands out in a gesture of understanding. "Sure. We get that. If they register, they get their names in the paper for two weeks and can suffer all kinds of costs. That's why we're offering this other, safer way to be involved. They can sign up to be in the Mississippi Freedom Democratic Party and that's not made public. The next step is we'll hold precinct meetings in each district, and then those will elect delegates from the counties to go to the state convention in Jackson." He slapped his hand on the desk again. "That's when we'll elect the delegates to go to Atlantic City."

I listened carefully to Harry's explanations because I knew they'd be useful as I tried to get people to sign up. Because Negroes had been excluded since the end of Reconstruction, those in Mississippi had little or no understanding of the electoral process. I had to admit, I hadn't paid a lot of attention to it myself.

While Harry continued, I saw that Anitra was in the back office alone. The time had come for me to talk to her. I decided to head back there and jump right in.

"Anitra, we both know the truth is that you should be the one teaching, not me. Let's talk with Mac about changing places. What do you think?"

She put down the papers she was studying and looked at me, her eyes opened wide with surprise. "Honest? You would be willing to do that?" she asked.

"I...I think so," I stammered. "Yes. Yes, I would be willing, but I'd like it if I could still help with something, the newspaper, maybe."

"Sure. That's great! I've really been wanting to work with the kids. Let's talk with Mac." Anitra gestured toward the phone, her eyes sparkling with enthusiasm. "Shall I call him?"

"Uh...no. It just occurred to me. Maybe we should talk to him in person. Could we drive over to Ruleville sometime?" I tried not to grin. After all, being face-to-face was a more practical approach when trying to convince someone of something. And I really had no idea how Mac would react.

Anitra gave me a look. "Ruleville? Uh-huh." She knew exactly why I wanted to go to Ruleville, but she shrugged. "How about right after school? I'll call and let Mac know we're coming, okay?"

I nodded and went back to the classroom. I had mixed feelings about giving up teaching, but there was only a month left in the summer. If Anitra and I switched jobs, I could plan to go to Atlantic City with Jane to support the Mississippi Freedom Democratic Party. But it all hinged on Mac's reaction.

When Harry finished up his talk with the students, there was a little time left before the lunch break. "Let's plan what we'll write about in this week's newspaper," I suggested.

Cornelius raised his hand. "I think we should write about the Mississippi Freedom Democratic Party. People around town read our newspaper, and if we explain what it's all about, it would help them understand."

"Yeah," agreed Autumn. "Then when y'all come around, they'd be ready to sign up."

Anabel spoke up, "We could also include the places where they can go to sign up."

We started writing the article. As usual, suggestions flew around the room like a tornado gaining momentum. They corrected each other, changed wording, then corrected each other again.

By lunchtime, they had written an excellent article explaining what the Mississippi Freedom Democratic Party was, which showed how well they had listened to Harry and understood the importance of the initiative. I was proud of them. It was going to be hard for me to give up moments like those.

After the last student left, I stood at the doorway. The rain had stopped earlier and the air held a steamy heat, but it carried the sweet floral scent I now associated with Mississippi. Sunlight sparkled on the still wet leaves through the sycamores across the way. With puddles in the road and yard and no sidewalks to walk on, I knew there'd soon be lots of muddy footprints when the students returned for the afternoon session. I figured I'd better get the mop ready to clean the floor for the kindergarten class. I sighed and turned to join Elizabeth for our sandwich lunch.

~~~

While Elizabeth and I put everything in order after class that afternoon, I was eagerly anticipating my visit to Ruleville with Anitra. Luke might be out working on voter registration, but there was a good chance he'd be back at the headquarters when we went to see Mac. I looked up to see Anitra enter the schoolroom.

"Be right with you," I said. "Almost done here."

Anitra shook her head. "No, Mac said he had to come to Mystic Springs anyway to see Pastor Hendricks, so we're supposed to wait for him here. He should be along any minute."

My shoulders sagged as my hope of seeing Luke flew out the open doorway. Elizabeth gave me an understanding smile as she got ready to leave. Lynn and Desiree came in to set up for the kindergartners, so Anitra and I went into the back room to wait for Mac and cleared space from the table and chairs in preparation. It was a reminder of how much we needed a new building.

Maybe Mac and Reverend Hendricks had good news to share about the lot.

~~~

When Mac arrived, my first question was about the lot, but he had nothing new to report. That added to my discouragement, so it was with little confidence that Anitra and I presented our plan for switching jobs to Mac. I did most of the persuading.

Mac was hesitant at first, but he was the one involved with keeping Freedom Schools open after the summer. There was no need to remind him that schools for Negro children didn't start until November in the Delta since they were needed on the plantations for the cotton harvest. As a SNCC staffer, Anitra would still be in town and could continue teaching after I'd left in early September. I could tell he didn't like the idea, but we had a winning argument. Finally, after much discussion, he reluctantly agreed.

I was glad it wouldn't be a complete break, though. I'd still be involved with the students working on the newspaper and taking over the tutoring that Anitra had been doing. Plus, we'd get to keep our same living arrangements, which was a relief. It would be hard enough to say goodbye to the Johnsons in September.

~~~

It was my last day of teaching. Each of my students had become so special to me. I loved the way they opened up their minds and hearts and weren't afraid to share an opinion, the way they'd correct each other, the

167

way they'd work to find the truth of things. They had changed and so had I.

"It's not like I'm leaving completely," I told them. "And I want you to know how much I've learned from you. You've helped me understand a little better what it's like to be a Negro in Mississippi. Thank you for that."

Cornelius raised his hand. "You've helped us understand a lot of things too. I used to think there was never a way we could change things, but now I believe there is."

"Yeah," Josh added. "I was just biding my time 'til I could head North. Now I see that the North ain't...*isn't* necessarily the escape I thought it was."

Most of the boys nodded in agreement.

Thelma spoke up. "I used to see us stuck here and nothing would ever change. But now I've learned about people like Ida B. Wells and others. They had the strength and courage to do amazing things. We can have courage to do things too." She looked around at her classmates. "We can make a difference."

Elizabeth and I exchanged a glance. I couldn't speak with the lump in my throat. There could not have been a better affirmation of our teaching.

I went to sleep that night feeling complete in some obscure way and encouraged about the future of Mississippi because of what my students had shared today. Hope hung before the students like the gold ring on a carousel ride, and I wanted them to reach out and grab it.

≈≈≈

I jumped into Saturday's canvassing with renewed energy. Finding people willing to go to the courthouse to register to vote met with the usual resistance. However, our efforts in signing up people for the Mississippi Freedom Democratic Party were much more successful. Word was getting around that this was a completely new party to represent Blacks, and people were more willing to join the effort. I liked to think the students' article in *The Freedom Story* had something to do with that.

I also detected a subtle difference in myself. Since this was now my major thrust, I was doing it with a little more heart. I tried to get to know each homeowner a little better and to put myself in their shoes. If a meeting started off with wariness on their part but ended with friendly banter, I counted that as a success, whether or not they had signed. As Harry would say, a seed was planted. The harvest would come later—or not.

On Sunday, Desiree left to start a kindergarten somewhere else, leaving Lynn on her own. Elizabeth gently suggested to me that we needed to include her more. I grimaced but knew it was true. I probably would never admit this out loud to Elizabeth, but there was an embarrassing reason why I kept finding fault with Lynn. My last boyfriend had dumped me for a perky, talkative blonde. I had to confess to myself that I was being prejudicial. I knew that actually had nothing to do with Lynn, so I had to stop being so juvenile about it.

Since Anitra had her car now, she went home every weekend, so Sunday afternoon Brenda and Lynn came over and the four of us played bridge on a quilt spread under the Johnsons' pecan tree. I was surprised to find out that Lynn was a good bridge player. I don't know how she did it, though, because she didn't stop talking the entire time.

Lynn studied her cards. "My older brother taught me to play bridge when I was in junior high," she began. "I don't know how he learned to be such a good player. Maybe from my parents. I'll bid two clubs. My parents play bridge all the time. I guess that's why I like it so much. They've played in the same bridge club for twenty years, I think. Hmm...three hearts. My younger sister doesn't like to play as much as I do, though. She's into music. Plays the guitar. Okay. We're at four hearts. Your lead."

At the end of the afternoon, I had to admit that it had been an enjoyable way to spend the day, and I needed to stop looking for negative things about Lynn. Besides, I needed her for my plan to get the school lot, especially because Mac and Pastor Hendricks weren't making any headway toward achieving that goal.

I gathered up the cards at the end of the game. "Lynn," I began, "why don't we have lunch in the park tomorrow? Maybe that other Alpha Chi will be there and you can meet her." Elizabeth raised an eyebrow, but Lynn was thrilled.

"That's a wonderful idea, Lenore!" Lynn gushed. "I'd love that! It would be so great to have a sorority sister right here in Mystic Springs. I can't wait to meet her. I'll meet you at the school at noon, okay?

~~~

169

What I learned canvassing a neighborhood on Monday morning was that no one was home during the week except the older citizens. I especially enjoyed visiting with them, maybe because my grandparents were so special to me. Those visits made the morning pass quickly. The conversations always started slowly, though, hesitantly, their eyes never quite meeting mine. I longed to say, "You're safe with me. Don't worry." But I knew I'd have to earn that trust. Sometimes as we sat together, they'd share a story and reach over and pat my hand. It made me feel as if I'd been given a gift. I'd come to realize the fragility of the thread that connects us to each other.

Our team made it back to the school in time for me to meet Lynn for lunch. As she and I walked to the park, she didn't stop talking the whole time. I sank into a fog of her words, praying that Jenny would be at the park.

She wasn't.

After lunch, Harry picked up Brenda, Tom, and me in his car. By this time, we were reaching out into the countryside. "We need to be careful about setting foot on the plantations," Harry said. "Lenore, Brenda, and Tom, you guys will stand out because you're white. Usually, only Anitra and I would cover them. But now that she's teaching, I'll have to ask Mac how to do this, since I'm not supposed to go by myself."

We found enough small, hardscrabble farms to keep us busy throughout the afternoon. Our approach there was very different. In town, we mostly sat on porches and visited because it was the end of the workday. But in the country, we'd walk alongside a farmer and his wife, trying to keep up while they continued checking cotton bolls or performed some other chore. If Harry hadn't brought extra water, I might not have made it. I liked canvassing in town in the evenings and on Saturdays better.

It was almost dinnertime when Harry returned us to headquarters. We could hear laughter as we approached the school, so I peeked in to watch Lynn and a dozen kindergartners sitting in a circle on the floor. They each had a hand covered with a white sock, and each sock had a face drawn on it. Lynn, with her expressive face, held their complete attention. She asked questions and the students used their sock puppets to answer. Gone were the shy, quiet children! And yet, Lynn had them all under control. I was amazed. Obviously, perky worked with kindergartners. I was chagrined by my previous attitude toward her.

When I arrived back at the Johnsons' house, Serene greeted me at the door by announcing, "Lenore, you got a big, fat letter from your mama."

I sat on the bed and opened it, removing a handful of checks and a long letter.

Dear Lenore,

You will be so pleased with the response from my coffee social to raise funds for the future school and community center! People here are so eager to be supportive of the work of the Freedom Summer Project. I had plenty of people here and several others had coffees afterwards too. Altogether we raised $8,000! I have arranged to speak at churches to get their support and several friends said they would ask their clubs and organizations to contribute, so more checks will be coming.

You will be surprised to learn I even contacted your father and shamed him into giving donations from him and his firm. So that brings the total to $10,000 this time.

I hope this restores your faith in those of us up here in the North. I think our horror about the missing young men—Schwerner, Chaney, and Goodman—inspires us to support your work. I do wish the FBI would find them.

The rest of the letter was full of family and local tidbits of information. With tremendous pride in my mom, I went to join everyone at the table to share the good news.

I was anxious to get word to Mac about the amount collected, so I asked Elizabeth to accompany me to the school after dinner so I could call Ruleville from the phone there. We chatted about the class on the way over. Elizabeth told me a discouraging statistic: Mississippi is the only state that has no compulsory education law. *That explains a lot,* I thought to myself.

15

Ideas will not save us, he thought. Not right or wrong, or peace or retribution. Our stories are all we have. The only thing that can ever save us is to learn each other's stories. From beginning to end.
—Karen Fisher, *A Sudden Country*

Harry met with Brenda, Tom, and me in the morning to go over the territory to be covered the rest of the week. He said we were finally making better progress in signing up people to be part of the Mississippi Freedom Democratic Party. We were surprised when he told us that Bob Moses 'original goal was four hundred thousand signatures. That objective had been cut down to one hundred thousand, and we were still short of meeting it. That's why all the staff members and volunteers were working toward that mark, no matter what their other responsibilities were.

Harry folded the county map we'd been studying and told us that Ruleville had had its precinct meeting on Friday night, and it had been big success. Evidently, there had been a lot of protocol and parliamentary procedure to learn about as well as the process of precinct voting.

Harry stuffed some reports in his brief case and explained, "Yeah, Mac said it was a crazy night. Exciting, though. COFO and SNCC have carefully studied what is necessary to be absolutely legitimate when we go to Atlantic City at the end of August. Those at the precinct meetings are learning about drawing up resolutions and everything. They're also preparing for the state convention in Jackson from August 6 through August 9. We'll be sending three youth delegates and a chaperone from every Freedom School. After all, we're trying to grow future leaders."

I held my breath. "Who'll be going from here?" I asked.

Harry reached in his briefcase and pulled out a sheet of paper. "Cornelius, Anabel, and Thelma," he read. "And, Lenore, you'll need to go with them."

My heart skipped a beat. "Great! I'd love that."

"All the arrangements have been made. You'll find out everything you need to know tomorrow when we meet with Mac. I'll pick you up at nine tomorrow morning."

I tried to suppress a grin. "I'll be ready." I could hardly believe I was going to be part of such a historic event. Plus, I already knew that Jane would be there. We had so much to catch up on. Then another good thought hit me. *Maybe Luke is going too.*

During a blistering hot morning of walking through a community near Mystic Springs, we managed to sign up several people for the Mississippi Freedom Democratic Party and two were even willing to try to register to vote. It was definitely a successful morning. Afterward, Harry dropped me off at the school to meet Lynn. We'd agreed to try having lunch in the park again. I really hoped Jenny would be there, but she wasn't, so I decided to fill Lynn in on my plan.

"We need a new building for our school for lots of reasons. You see how crowded it is and how you have to squeeze your kindergarten in. But the ultimate plan is to keep Freedom Schools going after this summer and to add a community center. Schools don't start here until after the harvest season, remember?"

Lynn jumped in. "That makes sense. We can manage now, but it's definitely crowded. And if the school is to keep going, a nice new building would be so much better."

"Mac and Pastor Hendricks learned the school that was just torn down was on what's called Section 16 land, which is supposed to be held in trust for a school."

"Oh, I've heard of Section 16 Land," Lynn replied. "That's from the days when they first set up a town. That was a very smart idea."

I nodded. "It's possible that this land, Section 16, could be used for the new school building and community center. It's within the Negro community. But the problem is that it's up to the white school board, whose president is Mr. Williamson. Right now, he's saying no for no reason other than exercising white power."

Lynn watched my face.

I smiled at her and plunged ahead. "Mr. Williamson has one daughter, Jenny, who happens to be an Alpha Chi."

Lynn's mouth formed an *O*, but she managed to withhold any comments.

"So," I continued, "I'm hoping when you meet her and become friends, you can get her to convince her father to let SNCC have that property."

She started to nod then frowned. "Yeah, but I don't see why Mr. Williamson won't let SNCC have the property? They're certainly not going to build a white school there if it's in the Negro community."

"Exactly," I agreed. "The problem is Mr. Williamson, like many of the whites here, is a racist. But maybe Jenny could help convince him that by building an alternative school there, the Negroes are less likely to push for integrating schools. He might buy that. You know how sometimes daughters can get their fathers to agree to something they might not ordinarily have considered?"

This time, Lynn did the nodding. "So I'm a pawn in the plan to try to get Mr. Williamson to release the land."

I squirmed a little. "Well, uh...you know...I mean, I knew you'd want to meet a sorority sister, so it seemed like a good idea."

Lynn laughed. "That's okay. I understand. I know I talk a lot. My whole family does. But that doesn't mean I'm stupid."

A guilty feeling washed over me. "I don't think you're stupid, Lynn. I'm sorry. It's just that it's so important that we do every single thing we can to help the students here get ahead. They have such an uphill battle." I sighed and confessed, "I thought you were our best chance."

I stayed quiet and hoped for the best as we found an empty picnic table and sat down. Lynn and I pulled our sandwiches and drinks from our bags. Lynn held up her Dr. Pepper toward mine. "A toast," she said, "to the success of our school project." We clinked our bottles together, and that was that.

As we ate lunch under the shade of an oak tree, Lynn told me about her family and herself. As she shared her story, she became more three-dimensional and real to me, and I came to appreciate her as an individual. *If only Negroes and whites could do this,* I thought to myself, *sit together and learn about each other. Maybe then we could build a bridge toward ending racism.*

As we approached the school, Lynn said, "Don't worry about a thing. Whenever I do meet Jenny Williamson, I'll know exactly what to say. You should know, though, that sorority sisters from different schools don't have the same kind of relationship that sisters from the same school have. Even so, I'll lean on that connection. And in the meantime, these picnics are fun," she said with a wink as we entered the school.

~~~

We found Anitra and Elizabeth sitting at the backroom table relaxing before their afternoon responsibilities. Anitra began telling us about Barbara Jean Nave, Miss Mississippi 1963, who was from Jackson.

Anitra explained that because the Naves were curious about Freedom Summer, they invited a few of the white SNCC workers over in order to learn more about it, evidently hoping they could use their influence to keep a lid on things. But someone must've identified a SNCC car in front of their house because that night, the intimidation started. People loitered in front of their house, yelling and cursing at them. Their longtime friends ignored them and gave them dirty looks. They got constant threats. Barbara Jean's dad got kicked out of his office and his business started to fail. Word around Jackson was that they were planning to leave town.

After moving a pile of papers, I sat at the table too. "That's terrible. All that for meeting with white members of SNCC?"

"Right," agreed Anitra. "All they were doing was asking for information. That's how deep the hatred is of what we're trying to do."

Anitra pushed the weekly report of incidents across the table to me. I picked it up and read:

McComb: Two bombs were thrown at the home of a local civil rights leader.

Mileston: SNCC car burned outside a home housing volunteers.

Itta Bena: Voter registration house broken into during night. Front porch supports broken, leaving badly sagging roof. Door half torn off. All windows broken.

Meridian: Mount Moriah Baptist Church burned to the ground.

There were many more incidents, but I slid the report back across the table. I felt as if we were living in a war zone. And I guess we were—all of us: Jane, Luke, Silas, the Johnsons, all the people I had come to know and care about. How could our country have come to this?

Thinking back on what I'd learned teaching our students their history, it suddenly wasn't so surprising that our nation had come to this. It had been ingrained in our culture since the first slaves arrived in 1619. Now we had a chance to change and go in a new direction.

SNCC was a grassroots organization working for change in Negro communities, trying to get citizens registered to vote. But we white people needed to change too, and no one seemed to be talking about that. How could the situation for Negroes possibly change until other things changed? Until whites stopped throwing bombs, beating people, and burning buildings? Until white people stopped forbidding Negroes from building schools in their own neighborhoods and preventing them from voting?

Mac had mentioned once that a group of twenty-five white Freedom Summer volunteers were assigned the job of trying to connect with other Mississippi whites. They had gone to an area that was more liberal than most. Even so, the results were of no consequence. The understanding that the volunteers came away with was that white Mississippians felt they couldn't speak out against the system. There were exceptions, of course, but it didn't matter whether it was the churches, people in leadership roles in the community, or high-ranking officials from colleges or universities. According to the volunteers' findings, whites did not dare challenge the status quo. Some felt they would lose their friends and the white community would shun them. Others were afraid it would affect their jobs. And they all indicated that it would be pointless anyway because, ultimately, it wouldn't change a thing.

When I got in the car to start our afternoon of canvassing, a shadow of doubt followed me. Harry glanced over at me as he drove. "What're you frowning about over there, Lenore?"

"Just thinking about the attitudes of whites. It's so discouraging."

"Now don't go lumping all whites together. There's lots of whites in the Movement who are owning up and standing up—and paying the price."

"I guess so," I said with a deep sigh. "I remember meeting Reverend Ed King at the training, and his face was still bandaged from a beating he'd received a few weeks before."

"Yeah, and there's Charles Morgan, a white attorney from Birmingham, Alabama, who spoke out publicly the day after the bombing of the Sixteenth Street Baptist Church when those four little girls got killed. He dared to accuse white power of being responsible for the bombing and the deaths. Because of that, his business suffered and he and his family received death threats. Eventually, he and his wife felt they had to move away."

I looked at Harry and, as I often did, wondered how he could keep on with the work of the Movement so steadfastly. "There's some, I'm sure, like Joan Baez and Pete Seeger. I know they raise money for the Movement."

"And there's us," Brenda chimed in from the back seat. I joined in as the rest of the group chuckled.

As Harry pulled into the rutted drive up to a small wooden shack, the mailbox noted that it was the home of Jacob and Mary Washington. Chickens pecked the ground around the home, and a tan-and-white hound dog barely looked up from his spot in the shade under the porch. A battered pickup truck looked like it didn't have many miles left on it.

Despite the 101-degree heat, Mary Washington was on her knees in the garden, and her husband was working on a fence around back. Tom and Harry headed toward Mr. Washington while Brenda and I introduced ourselves to his wife. She greeted us but only gave us a fleeting glance before returning to her gardening. Brenda commented on the heat and remarked at how nice the garden looked. We knelt in a nearby row and started to pull weeds around the bean plants.

"Have you always lived around here?" I asked.

"My husband and I been workin' this land for 'bout fifteen years now."

I hoped our casual conversation would put her at ease, and eventually, it did. Everyone responded to Brenda's open, friendly manner. She talked to strangers as if they were good friends, and soon they felt that way. I'd learned a lot from her.

"We'd like to talk to you about the Mississippi Freedom Democratic Party," Brenda finally said after we'd continued our small talk for a while.

Mrs. Washington beamed. "Oh, I know all about that." She reached into the pocket of the apron she was wearing and pulled out a folded copy of *The Freedom Story*. "Jacob and me, we ready to sign up. We was going to do that the next time we went to town."

The low spirits that had shadowed me all day suddenly lightened.

Brenda signed her up while I kept pulling weeds. I pictured the expressions on former students' faces when I told them about this and the role they'd played in it.

~~~

Dinner table conversation at the Johnson house had become even more interesting as the summer wore on. Since I wasn't in the classroom anymore, Anabel would bring me up to date by describing Freedom School activities from her viewpoint. She especially loved anything involving drama. She reported that they'd done some role-playing in preparation for understanding what the state convention would be like. She had us all laughing by recapping the arguments between counties and did a perfect impersonation of Mrs. Hamer insisting that her resolution be passed.

After dinner, unless we were working a neighborhood, Elizabeth and I enjoyed watching the news and sitcoms with the Johnsons. Mr. Johnson often made a wry comment that showcased his dry sense of humor.

Anabel liked to have us watch her favorite show, *Mr. Novak,* on NBC, about a high school teacher and his students. She enjoyed making remarks about the white students' behavior, the way they talked back, how the girls flipped their long hair, and the boys' arrogance. She was in the middle of one of her critiques when the words *NEWS BULLETIN* flashed across the screen. That announcement usually meant some bad news. This time, it seemed to suck the air right out of the room.

The news was brisk and brutal. "Today, the bodies of Mickey Schwerner, James Chaney, and Andrew Goodman—the three missing civil rights workers—have been found."

We sat in stunned silence for moments, bound together by our tears. Three young men I had known had been buried in an earthen dam after being shot. Three I had known were now dead for working against the injustices toward Black Americans, killed for being on the side of good against evil.

We had long known in our hearts that they were dead, but we'd been able to tuck the thought away in far corner of our minds. But that was no longer possible. They had been found. Murdered.

Now I had to face it. No more could I believe what the SNCC vision statement said: "courage displaces fear, love transforms hate,...justice for all overthrows injustice." There really were people in Mississippi whose hate

178

was so strong that if you were working with SNCC or COFO or any of the others, you were a target.

I was a target!

16

This new leadership must come and will come increasingly from those elements of our diverse citizenry who for too long have been excluded—from Blacks and from recent immigrants who are now winning their spurs as able and visionary men and women capable of meeting any challenge.

—Mississippi Governor William Winter, Speech, Leadership Florida, Orlando, Florida, March 24, 1990

Mrs. Johnson blotted her face with her apron as Elizabeth and I swiped tears from our cheeks. Mr. Johnson gripped the arms of the chair tightly. The program returned to *Mr. Novak* and the antics of the students on TV. Serene and Anabel giggled along with the canned laughter, but Mr. and Mrs. Johnson remained staring silently at the television screen. Elizabeth and I sat with them. We didn't know what else to do.

I finally got the courage to say what I was feeling. "I am so sorry we live in a world where this would happen. I can hardly believe someone we knew has been murdered like that. I...I feel..." I stopped myself midsentence, unable to find the right words.

Mrs. Johnson nodded. "We're so sorry too. It's a terrible thing, killing those boys."

"That's our world, young ladies," Mr. Johnson muttered, keeping his eyes on the TV. "Know how many bodies those feds have pulled outta swamps since they started looking for those three? Eight. Eight Black boys. That's our world. And they wouldn't even have been out there looking 'cept two of those SNCC boys was white. That's the whole of it, right there." He sat back, his hands still clinging to the arms of the chair.

Elizabeth and I shared glance. While the Johnsons did not condemn us for being white, we felt the burden of it in that moment. We had taught the students about slavery, the Black codes, and Jim Crow. But what carried those, what made them continue, was the white culture. And we were part of that.

I saw in Elizabeth's face the resolve that burned in my heart. The narrative had to change, and we were here working toward that change. I no longer believed that good always triumphed over evil, but I still knew the good was worth fighting for. We were here. That was our first step.

~~~

I had another restless night, and from the sounds of her tossing and turning, Elizabeth did too. The faces of Mickey, James, and Andy—and of Rita Schwerner when she told us they were missing—stayed near the surface of my mind.

Elizabeth and I walked to school in silence. I greeted some of the students who were there early that morning and briefly answered their questions: "Yes, I knew the three." "No, I don't know any more than what was on the news." "Yes, they were found in an earth dam on a farm near Philadelphia." "No, I am not leaving to go home."

When Elizabeth and Anitra began their class, I made my way to the back room to meet Harry, Tom, and Brenda. Harry looked over the incident report and slapped it down on the table. "Let's head over to Ruleville and see what Mac wants us to be doing," he said.

~~~

At Ruleville, the volunteers sitting under the tree were unusually quiet. There was muted conversation but no guitars and no easy laughter.

Harry commented casually, "This crowd's having a day off. They all got out of jail yesterday. Been up at Drew."

Luke had told me about Drew. It was a small town near Ruleville and was considered the hardest town to crack. Supposedly, the Andrews Plantation southwest of Drew was where Emmett Till had been taken and beaten. None of the voter registration volunteers really wanted to work in Drew.

I was glad to see Luke sitting on a bench reading. He looked up and closed his book.

"Were you arrested?" I asked as I walked up to him, the words tasting bitter in my mouth.

He nodded and shrugged. "Just spent one night at the county prison farm."

"Oh, Luke, how awful!" I sat down on the bench beside him. "What happened?"

Luke shook his head as he scratched insect bites all along his arm. "It was something, for sure. We'd been working Drew for a few evenings. The pastor there didn't dare let us hold a meeting in the church, so we met in the churchyard. A few of the Drew kids joined us as well as a few women. The men were standing around across the street, not daring to be part of our meeting. Sheriff Hollowell had let the local police know we were out there just canvassing, but they were out there anyway. Even so, they didn't keep the whites from driving by, yelling curses at us, spitting toward us, and making threats.

"The whole time, we're singing freedom songs and all while Mac is urging the men to join us. Then Mac started taunting the men, calling them boys not men, saying they had to stand up to Mr. Charlie. Nothing happened that first night, but the second evening, the sheriff told us the deacon withdrew permission for us to be in the churchyard, so Mac just moved us over to a vacant lot.

Luke chuckled. "You can't stop Mac, and that's the truth. Well, it wasn't long before a police car rolled up with this old, white lady in back. The chief said she owned the lot and wanted us off her land or he'd arrest us for trespassing."

"Oh my God! They just won't quit, will they?"

"That old lady, I actually felt sorry for her. She looked so bewildered, like she didn't understand what was happening. Anyway, of course Mac wasn't about to leave, so we were all arrested. The girls went to the jail in Indianola, and the rest of us went to the prison farm."

I had to ask. "Was it awful?"

"It was really bad—filthy, dirty, smelly, full of bugs and rats, and hot as hell. Really bad. But Mac and a few others had been in a block building jail in Drew the night before. That was pretty scary too. If anyone had thrown a bomb in there, they would've been trapped."

"Did the COFO lawyers get you out on bail?"

"Right. Word went out to COFO and SNCC places across the country and someone went to the Rexall drugstore where there's a Western

Union and picked up all the money orders that were sent in. It was $4,500!" He snorted as he added, "All we wanted when we got out was a shower!"

"Oh, Luke, I hate that you had to go through that. I'm guessing you heard about Mickey, Andy, and James?"

"Yeah." Luke bit his bottom lip and was silent for a moment. "But we needed to have them found. For Rita and their parents."

"Do you know when the funerals will be?"

"Soon. The word is that since they can't be buried together in Mississippi, James will be buried in Meridian, and Andy and Mickey will be sent back to New York."

Luke slumped down, his shoulders sagging. I wanted—needed—to hold him close, to pull the sadness from him. But I could only lay my hand on his for a moment. We sat together, silently, feeling the warmth of each other.

Mac would be there soon, so we didn't have much time left. I took a deep breath and told Luke, "I'm going with the Freedom School kids to the state convention in Jackson tomorrow. Will you be going?"

Luke leaned forward, his arms resting on his thighs, head lowered. "I was supposed to go, but now we're staying back to go to James's funeral. I might get there for the last day or two, though. Have to wait and see."

Disappointment was becoming too close a companion. I wanted to shake it like an old rag and throw it away.

Mac drove up just then and had us all come together. Like the others, he must've taken the time to shower and change. His eyes were hidden behind his usual sunglasses, but when he took them off, the strain and fatigue showed. Even so, once he started talking about the convention, what to expect, and what arrangements had been made, his upbeat manner returned.

Harry and I would take three students to Jackson. Harry and Cornelius would camp out at COFO headquarters, while Thelma, Anabel, and I would stay at the Summers Hotel, one of the two Black hotels. My spirits lifted when I thought about having a real shower, even if the bathroom was down the hall.

I had to laugh at myself. Two months earlier, if someone had said that in the space of five minutes my emotions would cover such a range, I never would've believed it. I had gone from grief over the brutal murders of Andy, James, and Mickey to frustration over not being able to spend time with a Black boy I liked to excitement about taking a shower. I wondered

183

how life would be back in the other world after this summer.

Before I came to Mississippi, I lived in the real world and the Deep South was the other world. Now all that had changed. Mississippi had become real to me, but it was so much more than the excitement of connecting with students, feeling the warmth of a family circle, the thrill of singing freedom songs, and the host of possibilities that the future held. It was also the world of a Luke who was the sum of generations of hurt and of knowing people who'd been harassed, jailed, beaten, and murdered for no other reason than their race. Mississippi could never become "other" to me again.

While Harry made plans with Mac, Luke and I stole away to the car, which was hidden from view behind a pickup truck. We had a short time of privacy, a gift, but knowing Harry would be arriving any moment, we sat slightly apart.

I touched Luke's cheek. "I know it'll be hard going to the funeral."

He nodded but had no words.

"I'll be thinking of you." I squeezed his hand tightly.

He cleared his throat and straightened up. "I'll be glad when it's over." He gazed out the window as if his eyes were not seeing what was in front of him but some shadowy something in his mind. "It's hell for Black men here. We expect to die young: me, Mac, Roscoe Jones in Meridian, Harry. We're on the brink of making a life, but as leaders in SNCC, we're targets. And Mr. Charlie loves his target practice."

Now I had no words. How could I respond to that? But it was the truth, the bitter, heartbreaking truth.

Luke straightened up, pulled his happy-go-lucky self from deep inside, and smiled at me. "Don't worry. Anyway, if I can get away and meet you down in Jackson on Saturday or Sunday at the convention, we'll have us a great time."

I saw Harry approaching. I took Luke's hand for the last time. "I'll be looking for you. Stay safe," I added as he got out of the car.

Harry scowled at Luke as they passed each other.

~~~

Early the next morning, Cornelius, Thelma, and Anabel were practically bouncing with excitement as we loaded the car for the convention. I was excited myself. I hadn't been particularly interested in the

184

political process until I came to Mississippi but being in on the grassroots level was fascinating. I loved hearing about the enthusiasm at the precinct and county meetings. At this point, each of the five congressional districts had elected delegates, and they'd all be convening at the Masonic Temple on Lynch Street in Jackson with almost two thousand of us supporters cheering them on.

I was most excited about seeing Jane, though. Since I'd only found out I was going two days earlier, I hadn't been able to let her know. I knew from her last letter that she'd also be staying at the Summers Hotel, so I couldn't wait to surprise her.

Harry answered hundreds of questions all the way down to Jackson. He told us that Joseph Rauh had arrived there the night before. Rauh was important to the Mississippi Freedom Democratic Party since he was the attorney presenting the group's request to be seated as the delegates from Mississippi to the Democratic Party's credentials committee. He was also chief counsel for the United Auto Workers and a friend and ally of Senator Hubert Humphrey.

It seemed to me that the procedure was being organized in the most professional manner possible. With Joseph Rauh and Fannie Lou Hamer behind this drive, how could it possibly fail? But then I imagined hearing Luke say, "That's thinking like a white person, girl. If the white power doesn't want the Mississippi Freedom Democratic Party delegation to be seated, they're not going to be seated."

We got to Jackson just in time to drop off our things at the hotel then rush to the Prince Hall Masonic Temple on Lynch Street in the center of the Black community. Excitement and energy crackled in the air as men in white shirts and dress slacks, women in their Sunday best, and excited teenagers waved posters and pressed their way through the entrance.

I put a hand on Thelma and Anabel's shoulders. "You both stay glued to me." Turning to Harry and Cornelius, I added, "Don't you dare let us get separated in this crowd, or I'll never find you again."

Harry chuckled. "Yeah, 'cause all Black people look alike."

I gave him a dirty look and marched on with the girls.

Anabel tugged on my arm. "Lenore, you're the one who won't be hard to find in this crowd!" she said with a giggle as she raised her eyebrows and glanced at the sea of Black faces in the auditorium.

With students as observers, we were assigned to sit in the very back of the room. Heading that way, I looked for Jane and there she was. She, too, was easy to find.

We introduced our groups and barely had time for another word when Aaron Henry, the NAACP leader from Mississippi, called the meeting to order.

Harry whispered, "He's got a drugstore up in Clarksdale and heads the local NAACP. Been real active in the Movement."

Mr. Henry presided over the hundreds of delegates with about a thousand of us spectators in attendance. He assured us that the rules of the Democratic Party would be strictly followed so that everything that was done would be acceptable at the Democratic National Convention later in the month. The whole purpose of having precincts, county delegates, and this state convention was to unseat the all-white Mississippi delegation at the Democratic National Convention with a legally mixed delegation and to present the Mississippi Freedom Democratic Party as an authentic entity.

Anabel, Thelma, and Cornelius sat on the edge of their seats, eyes shining with excitement to be part of this incredible moment in history. I felt the same way. Jane and I with our expressions exchanged whole silent conversation starting with Jane's, "I told you you'd be glad we came to Mississippi," and my soundless responding, "Yeah. Yeah, you're right. Wait 'til I tell you the rest."

Ella Baker, the organizing force behind SNCC, came to the podium for the keynote address. Above her, across the top of the stage, was a banner, "FREEDOM DEMOCRATIC PARTY." When I saw that sign, I felt a sense of pride in the work of the Freedom Summer Project.

Ms. Baker's talk was powerful. She outlined clearly what a real democratic platform was. When she said the Mississippi Freedom Democratic Party was open to all, the crowd burst into applause. She said even the plantation owner's son was welcome if he ascribed to the Mississippi Freedom Democratic Party's principles. She reminded us that being seated as delegates at the national convention was only one part of the struggle. She also talked about the importance of education and gave voice to a plan for a better future. I probably wasn't the only one in attendance who clapped until their hands were sore.

All the delegates sprang up, marching around the auditorium, county signs and flags held high, singing and waving to the crowd. Cornelius, Thelma, and Anabel jumped to their feet, belting out the songs and waving their American flags. They called excitedly to Sunflower County's representatives as they marched by. It was an exhilarating time, singing

"Ain't Gonna Let Nobody Turn Me Round" and "We Shall Not Be Moved" with its many, many verses.

Attorney Rauh spoke next. He was very confident that the Mississippi Freedom Democratic Party would get seated at the Democratic National Convention. Listening to him, no one in the audience doubted that we would pass the credentials committee's criteria.

But Harry had painted a different picture on the way down. "Bob Moses doesn't think it's possible," Harry had told us. "The thing is, President Johnson is afraid he'll lose the Southern vote if he allows the Mississippi Freedom Democratic Party to be seated. There's all kinds of behind-the-scenes politics going on."

The work of the state convention continued. Lawrence Guyot, a SNCC field secretary, was elected state chairman, and Mrs. Hamer was named vice chairman. There were sixty-eight delegates: four whites and sixty-four Negroes. I prayed they would be the delegates seated at the Democratic National Convention in a few weeks.

It was a thrilling day, an exhausting day, and a historic day. The students talked excitedly all the way back to our hotel. The next day, the students from the Freedom Schools would meet to develop their own platform and learn to make resolutions just as the adults were doing. Jane and I would have time to visit then. Now it was time for a shower.

~~~

Since Anabel, Thelma, and I were together in one room and Jane was sharing hers with three other SNCC workers, Jane and I sat in the hallway to visit. We talked for hours. I loved telling her about the Freedom School, Mrs. Parker and her stories, Mrs. Johnson's mothering, and Mr. Johnson's teasing. I needed her sympathetic hug when I told her about Rose taking her name off the voting list and about me and Elizabeth being stopped by the police. Jane brought me up to date on how hard she was working on voter registration. We laughed together about Lynn, and she also confided in me about her new boyfriend, a white volunteer she'd met in Hattiesburg.

When we finally said goodnight, I collapsed, exhausted, on the too-soft bed. In spite of all the stressful things in my Mississippi life, I felt content. Talking through everything with Jane tied all the loose strands of my life into a tidy bundle—like wheat after harvest—so they no longer overwhelmed me. That's what having a close friend does, I guess.

In the morning, buses took us to the Masonic Temple again. The students struggled with their own policy platform planning, so Jane and I went back and forth between the delegates' side and the youth side. It was hard to say which group was more impassioned. Shouts of dissention, cheers, and bursts of applause carried the work on both sides.

After lunch, Jane and I slid down to sit on the sidewalk with our backs against the brick of the Masonic Temple. We still had a lot to talk about, but we sat quietly, feeling the heat vibrate off the concrete. I looked at my watch and announced, "James Chaney's funeral is going on right now. I kind of wish we could've gone to honor him."

"Mm-hmm," Jane murmured. "But I can't imagine being at a funeral for someone we knew, someone our age, who was *murdered*."

"But it wasn't only those three! There were eight other bodies pulled from the swamps while they were looking for James, Mickey, and Andy." I opened my purse and pulled out a folded scrap of paper. "I wrote down their names because I think we need to know them. The first two were," unfolding the paper, I read, "Henry Hezekiah Dee and Charles Eddie Moore from Alcorn University, who were working on voter registration. Then Herbert Oarsby, a fourteen-year-old who was wearing a CORE T-shirt. The five other bodies haven't been identified. Eight more, and that's only in the Delta."

Jane slid her arm around my shoulder and squeezed. At last, the tears started to slide down my face, and I was finally able to weep with my friend.

~~~

The next morning, Harry and I delivered our charges to the Youth Convention and assured them we would be there when they finished that afternoon. When Harry left to meet with some SNCC staffers, I joined Jane in the back of the main auditorium. It was fascinating to watch the delegates struggle back and forth with parliamentary procedure, trying to get certain resolutions ratified, and all the other work that goes into getting ready for the Democratic National Convention. As interesting as that was, I kept turning my head toward the entrance.

"Stop it," admonished Jane. "If he gets here, he'll find you."

I gave her the kind of look she usually gave me and tried to pay attention to what was happening on the dais.

Then he was finally there, easing into the seat next to me that I'd held empty with my purse. He nodded a greeting to Jane and me.

He was neatly dressed, but he looked as if he hadn't slept, the fatigue marking his face and causing his shoulders to droop.

"How was it?" I whispered. "How are you?"

He slumped back and drew in a deep breath. "It was a beautiful service 'til we got to Dave Dennis's eulogy. That was brutal. Don't want to talk about it yet."

As we watched the proceedings before us, Luke relaxed slightly in his seat. "How's all this going?"

"It's been great, very exciting," I murmured back. "Mac was elected as one of the delegates."

He smiled and peeked at his watch. "I have Silas's car. Want to go somewhere private?"

The flush on my face wouldn't let me deny the heat that rose through my body. I didn't need to give an answer.

"I'll get the car and meet you at the corner in ten minutes," he said as he rose and headed out.

Jane put a restraining hand on my arm. "Lenore, think! Are you sure you want to do this?"

"I can't help it. It's not fair! If Luke was white, no one would care."

"But he's not white. Lenore, think about the consequences! Think!"

I looked at Jane and sadly shook my head.

"All right," she said. "Then we'll both leave at the same time so it won't be so obvious. I'll go check in on the youth work. Meet me there when you get back, and we'll come back in here together."

I bit my lip, holding back tears as I nodded. Having a close friend is a blessing.

What was probably only ten minutes passed like an eternity. When we finally drove away, Luke said, "Where shall we go?"

I grinned. "COFO headquarters?"

Luke's chuckle started deep in the back of his throat. "I don't think so."

"But where else can we go? Luke, I'm scared. Just driving through town like this is dangerous."

Luke slapped his hand against the steering wheel. "I know, damn it! You think I haven't thought about it? But Lenore, when else will we ever have a chance to be together? When?"

We drove a few blocks past small, shotgun houses and pulled to a stop by an empty lot with a little shade. Luke switched off the ignition. "We're in the Black part of town, so we should be safer here."

I slid close to him. I could feel my heart beating faster. "After I go back to school you could come north. We could find a way up there."

"Sure *then*. But this is now. We have a chance *now*, girl. Do you want to take that chance or not?"

"I want to, but I'm afraid. I don't want to be the cause of something awful happening to you, Luke."

He took my hand in his. "That's only if someone sees us. You have a room at the hotel. No one is there now. We could go there, Lenore. We'd be safe."

Luke gazed at me for a moment. His expressive eyes that had told me so much of his anger and pain now spoke a different language—a language I found hard to resist. He leaned in, cupped my face in his hands, and began with a soft and gentle kiss.

Our kisses became deeper as his hand began caressing me. With every ounce of strength I had, I pulled away. "I...I can't Luke. I want to, but I can't. Not yet."

Luke leaned back against the car door and looked at me, shaking his head. "You're killing me, girl. You are killing me."

Tears burned in my eyes. "That's exactly what I'm trying to avoid, Luke."

17

I don't want to have to go to another memorial. I'm tired of funerals! I'm tired of it!

—Dave Dennis, CORE's Mississippi project director, eulogy at James Chaney's funeral

The first few miles heading home from the state convention, Thelma, Anabel, and Cornelius talked incessantly about all they'd seen and done, but soon they drifted into the deep sleep possible for teenagers. After that, the ride back to Mystic Springs was a lot quieter than the ride down to Jackson.

Harry glanced my way. "So what did you think, Lenore? How was it?"

"It was a phenomenal look at history in the making! I'm so glad I could be part of it."

We drove in silence for many miles. I wished I could doze off, but I was still keyed up from the trip. "Harry, do you think we'll ever get that lot to build the new building?"

He shrugged. "No reason not to. The white school board just needed to flex their muscles for a while to remind us of our place. There's no way they would build anything there in the Black community. We'll get it sometime."

"My mom has been working hard to raise money for it."

"That's great! And we'll get more from SNCC and COFO places across the country. 'Course, right now they're sending support for bail money. A lot of volunteers have ended up in jail this summer."

"I was so glad that policeman didn't arrest Elizabeth and me. I really don't want to experience that."

"It's no fun, for sure. 'Course if the law came along now and saw the two of us together, you know what the result might be."

Harry's comment—and the truth of it—brought me back to thoughts of Luke, so the silence drove a wedge between us again. It had rained in the Delta during the early morning hours, and the low-hanging fog still nestled over the cotton fields. Gazing at it now, I thought of the play *Brigadoon* about a Scottish town that only appears out of the mist every hundred years. Fiona from Brigadoon and a young man from present day meet and fall in love and manage to bridge that seemingly insurmountable gap. I wondered if Luke and I would be as lucky.

~~~

Back at the Johnsons' house, Elizabeth and I sat up late talking quietly on our bed. I shared with her the excitement of the past few days. The retelling made it sound like the atmosphere at a college football game, but everyone knew it was no game. We knew the future of Negroes in Mississippi depended on what happened in that special place.

Elizabeth told me about how the classes had gone. Anitra had continued with a little more of Langston Hughes's work before getting into James Baldwin's writing. I could see how having a Negro teacher discussing those writings could be more meaningful than a white person doing so, especially when that white person was just learning herself.

I knew the group from Mystic Springs had gone to James's funeral, so after Elizabeth got me caught up on the events at school while I was away, I asked her about it.

Elizabeth looked down at her lap. "Lenore, it was heartbreaking but important to see that so many people came to honor him. We all marched down to First Union Missionary Baptist Church, which was already packed with mourners when we arrived. I saw his mother with his three sisters and nine-year-old brother, Ben. Roscoe Jones told us that Ben, even at that age, had actually gone with James to some CORE activities.

"What really hurt was seeing Ben. He looked like a deer caught in the headlights, in shock and disbelief. Then, during the service, he just sobbed and sobbed against his mother. Even through Mrs. Chaney's black veil, you could still see the strength in her. I'm telling you, Lenore, you couldn't have kept from weeping for them."

Elizabeth's eyes filled with tears. After a minute, she continued. "The most emotional moment was Dave Dennis's eulogy. He started with some notes but then tossed them aside and poured out his heart. He told everyone to stop bowing down, to hold their heads up. I'll never forget his last words. He slammed his fist on the lectern and shouted to us as if the words were torn from his very soul: 'We've got to stand up!' And then he stormed out. It was the most powerful funeral you could ever imagine, honestly. I'll never forget it—ever."

We sat quietly for a few moments. I thought about the way Luke had looked when he got to Jackson after attending the funeral, how he seemed like a tightly wound spring. I could understand that very well now.

Elizabeth sat up straighter, moving on from funeral memories.

"Well," she said, plumping her pillow. "Let's get some sleep."

I turned out the light, but sleep eluded me. My mind was filled with images of a nine-year-old boy weeping for the brother he would never see again.

~~~

Meeting with Harry, Brenda, and Tom the next morning in our SNCC backroom office was another reminder of how desperately we needed more room. I had to remove box of kindergarten supplies from a chair before I could even sit down. Piles of teaching materials were stacked on every surface. Our voter registration maps and summaries were mixed up in the shuffle, and Harry was grousing about finding the incident report he'd set down five minutes earlier. We cleared a spot and got to work.

Harry rummaged through his briefcase then began to plan our week. "The Democratic National Convention begins August 24. We need at least a hundred thousand members when the Mississippi Freedom Democratic Party goes before the credentials committee. The hard part is finding anyone at home since people are at work during the day. Early in the mornings won't work, so we'll just have to work really hard in the evenings and on weekends. Across the state, everyone—all the SNCC staffers and summer volunteers—will be working on this."

He unrolled a map of our territory. "We'll put the emphasis on getting people signed up for the Mississippi Freedom Democratic Party, then later we can try to get people registered to vote. By the way, Lenore, good job with the school paper. That's helped a lot."

I smiled. "I'll let the kids know. They'll be proud."

Harry nodded. He bent over the map and traced our target areas with his finger. We had already covered a large part of the Negro community, but there were still pockets we'd missed, plus a large amount in the rural outskirts.

Lynn walked in as Harry and I were telling the others about the convention. It was unusual to see her there so early in the day.

"Hi! Good morning, everyone. I hope you slept well. I bet you were tired after the convention. Very exciting. I would've loved to have been there."

Harry gestured toward a large storage box. "Clear a space and have a seat. Lenore and I were filling the others in on it."

"Great! Thanks." She sat down and smiled at everyone then whispered to me. "When you're through, can we talk for a few minutes?"

Harry and I gave a quick but enthusiastic summary of the convention. Once the others had left, Lynn faced me and patted my arm. "I want you to know that everything is under control."

"What's under control?"

"The lot. You know, the lot for the school. I did it exactly the way you wanted."

I was surprised to hear that. "Tell me what happened!" I asked eagerly.

"I talked to Jenny and told her how to convince her father to let SNCC have the lot."

My mouth actually dropped open before I could speak. "You talked to Jenny Williamson? About the lot? How did you meet her?"

She clapped her hands together like an excited child. "It was easy. You mentioned that she worked at the insurance company, so I went down there and introduced myself. She was so excited to meet a sorority sister. We went out for lunch and talked and talked. I told her about the lot and told her what to say to her father."

I shook my head in amazement. "That's great! What did you tell her to say?"

"Just those things you mentioned. You know, like by giving us the lot, he'd look like a hero in the national press, and by allowing us to build a school and community center there, it would keep the Negroes away from the white school, the town park, and other places. Plus, it would keep Pastor Hendricks and Mac from bothering him about it."

"So what was her reaction?" I held my breath.

Lynn laughed and nodded. "Oh, your guess was right. She said she had her father wrapped around her little finger, and she thought it would be fun to work on him to do something he didn't want to do. She was glad to do a favor for a sorority sister."

I gave her a quick hug. "Lynn, that's terrific! I'm really proud of you and grateful. Let's hope it works."

"I think it will," Lynn replied as she stood to leave. "And by the way," she paused at the door, "Jenny invited you and me to the club next Saturday for lunch and a swim."

I opened my mouth to protest, but she scooted out the door before I could respond.

~~~

During our afternoon canvassing, Brenda and I got a few additional signatures for the Mississippi Freedom Democratic Party. That always made for a good day. Later when we stopped by the school to turn in our paperwork, we peeked at the kindergarten class in session. Lynn was on the floor reading to fifteen little kids. They were sitting quietly, absolutely transfixed on Lynn. As she read, she was overflowing with enthusiasm and...well...perkiness that she made the story come alive for them. I had to admit that she'd found her niche. Perhaps perkiness has a place, after all.

~~~

It was slower going for the rest of us. Jane's letters detailing the events from southern Mississippi and Harry's sharing the incident reports made me despair of any progress we were making. Not every incident was violent, but, even so, they managed to suppress Negroes in some way. Jane's latest letter told of Sandra Adickes, a teacher in a Freedom School, who expected the Civil Rights Act had opened up public spaces such as libraries. She and five of her teenage students went to the formerly whites-only library in Hattiesburg so the students could get library cards. After the librarian's rudeness failed to discourage them and get them to leave, the police came and closed the library. A few days later, the library was closed indefinitely. *We all had thought the passage of the Civil Rights Act would immediately open up segregated spaces,* I thought, *but that hasn't been what happened at all.*

Harry's weekly incident report almost always included at least one church burning, several arrests for traffic violations, a number of beatings, Molotov cocktails thrown, and on and on. The reports were so depressing. I wasn't writing home as much as I had been because I couldn't find upbeat things to write about, not that I had any free time to write letters. We were working all day and evening in the final push to meet our goal of a hundred thousand Mississippi Freedom Democratic Party members.

Harry didn't cut us any slack. "This is 'lay by' time in the Delta," he announced one morning. "The cotton's been tended to and they now have to wait until picking time. That's good news for us because more people will be home during the day. We'll go back to all the people who said no the first time. Now that they've learned more about it, they might be ready to sign."

It might've been 'lay by' time, but it certainly wasn't 'laid-back' time. The temperature was as hot as a blast furnace and working so closely together didn't help. Tempers were short, and the days were long. Whenever we stopped by other SNCC headquarters, it was exactly the same.

Difficulties were inevitable. Before the Freedom Summer Project, there had been only a handful of whites associated with SNCC. Now the organization was inundated with whites, and those whites were moving in on a lot of the tasks that the Negroes had formerly done. Besides that, the coverage of the Freedom Summer Project in national magazines and newspapers focused on the white students doing things that the Negroes had been working on for years. There were bound to be resentments, and there were. Plenty.

One day, a white volunteer at one of the other headquarters pulled me aside. I guess she needed someone to vent to. "Honestly, I'm so annoyed that I feel like quitting and going home," she began. "I'm a college graduate. I know how to write essays and such. But if I correct any of the things like press releases or articles the Negroes in this office write, you'd think I'd committed treason! They look down on me because I haven't been jailed or beaten like they have. I didn't know that was a prerequisite for the job!"

There was so much caught up in what she said. I, too, had felt the undercurrent of disdain from Negroes since I hadn't had the same experiences because my whiteness had kept me protected and I didn't know what it was like to always have to be on guard, to never feel safe. I had learned a lot about that from Luke, and that had helped me understand, but I'd never experienced it firsthand.

There was another part of what she said that I'd also become more aware of. I was sure she tried to be tactful when she made her corrections to things the Negro staffers had written; however, there was a thin line that the white volunteers often crossed. Whites tend to take control of meetings, to assert their opinions as the correct ones, and to come across as more knowledgeable. I've come to realize, though, that when we get down to the very basics, there's something in our makeup that can make Negroes feel like the outsider. *Why?* I often wondered. *Where does this come from?*

I listened to that white volunteer with sympathy and encouragement. But I could hardly wait to leave so I no longer had to deal with her problems. I had enough of my own.

The differences weren't only between the Negroes and whites. There were disagreements among the Negroes about how to proceed with the Movement. As soon as the Civil Rights Act had been signed, there were those who wanted to test it, to try integrating lunch counters, libraries, pools, and so on. Silas McGhee, and now his brother Jake, were determined to integrate the movie theater. On the other side were those who believed all efforts should be put toward voter registration and getting people signed up for the Mississippi Freedom Democratic Party.

When we had business at other headquarters like Indianola and Greenwood, I noticed a subtle but growing dissatisfaction with the philosophy of nonviolence. One of the strongest opponents of it was Stokely Carmichael, which didn't surprise me. I remembered his passionate disagreements about nonviolence with Reverend Jim Lawson during training in Ohio.

One of the volunteers in Greenwood told me about an incident on August 4, the day the bodies of James Chaney, Andrew Goodman, and Mickey Schwerner had been found. A rally had been organized, but a lot of Negroes were hesitant to participate. As Stokely ranted and raved that they didn't have any "race pride," he became more and more agitated.

The volunteer added, "I heard him myself when he said SNCC wouldn't stick with nonviolence forever. Later, there was a big debate about bringing guns here to headquarters. But then Bob Moses talked to Stokely, and that was the last I heard about it. Anyway, John Lewis is the head of

SNCC, and I don't believe he'd allow it. He's been for nonviolence all along."

This kind of talk made me very uncomfortable. Ever since the bodies of Mickey, James, and Andy had been found—and especially since James's funeral—I'd noticed that the Negroes were more restless, more on edge, angrier.

Dave Dennis's eulogy at James's funeral had even stirred up people who'd been staunch supporters of nonviolence. Anitra had told me more about it. "He kept making the point that we shouldn't take it anymore," she said. "That we should stand up against white supremacy and injustice. At one point, he said, 'If you go home and sit down and take it, God damn your souls!' And at the end of his talk, he was crying out to us to do something. It almost felt like a call to arms. We all wanted to storm out with him."

I know exactly how those words must have fallen on the wounded hearts at the funeral. I know how they felt on mine.

I tried to understand where everyone was coming from with their varying viewpoints. There was an unrest—an agitation—brewing throughout the summer, and it was getting stronger and stronger, like the rumbling inside a volcano before it erupts. And this uneasiness was on all layers: among the Negroes, between whites and Negroes, and among the whites. We were all so tired, so very tired. It was a fatigue that went beyond simply needing more rest. It was a soul-aching need, a longing for something that was just beyond our reach. Something had to happen, and we were pinning our hopes on the success of the delegates being seated at the Democratic National Convention.

~~~

One scorching hot afternoon as Harry, Brenda, Tom, and I drove back from Greenwood, Harry began telling us about the work down in Meridian. "That's where Mickey and James were working. Philadelphia, where the three were jailed, is about an hour north. You've met Roscoe Jones. He's in Meridian too. Mickey and Rita started the big library there.

"But what's kind of interesting, even ironic," he continued, warming to his subject, "is that only a few miles away from where the bodies were found, the Neshoba County Fair is going on right now. It's one of the biggest events in Mississippi."

"I've heard of it," said Tom, "but I thought it was a regular county fair."

Harry chuckled. "No, it's not a regular county fair at all. It's advertised as the biggest house party. It lasts all week and people come from all over and camp or stay in cabins. Lots of families use it for their annual family reunions. There's dancing every night at the pavilion and then a community sing-along the rest of the night. 'Course, I don't really know what it's like because we aren't allowed there, except to work."

Brenda nodded. "So it's really a political rally?"

"Exactly," said Harry. "Traditionally, the governor gives the opening speech and politicians from all the local and state offices are there, stumping and trying to win voters. This really old guy, J.B. Hillman, has been chairman of it forever. On the news the other day, he assured all the good white folks that they wouldn't let the business of finding those bodies interfere in any way with the Neshoba County Fair." Harry scowled as his hands clutched the steering wheel.

I felt like muttering a curse myself. I'd heard Governor George Wallace of Alabama was going to be speaking at the fair. That told me what kind of event it would be.

I leaned my head back on the car seat and remembered an evening when Mr. Johnson had been in a good mood. I could tell because that's when he'd find ways to tease Elizabeth or me. When an advertisement for the Neshoba County Fair came on the news, he pointed to the television and said, "Now there's somethin' y'all shouldn't miss. If'n you had a car, you could go over there. Maybe I should take off work and carry y'all there in my pickup, hmm?" I loved to hear his chuckle.

"Sure," said Serene. "You could be their chauffeur."

I had politely smiled then, but the image of Mr. Johnson chauffeuring us around because we were white wounded my heart and soul. We'd gotten so used to being treated like family with the Johnsons, but every so often, some little remark or action nailed the difference between us. Mrs. Johnson acted like a mother to us, seeing that we ate well and got enough sleep and watching over our coming and goings. Anabel and Serene were like little sisters to me. And Mr. Johnson had become so dear to me with his courage and his funny comments and observations.

Yet, we were not family. We were worlds apart. We whites thought we'd eased our way into the Black culture in Mississippi by learning from the Johnsons, Mrs. Parker, Mrs. Logan, Mrs. Dawson, Pastor Hendricks, and so many others. We found bridges between us and crossed them, feeling we were all part of the same race—the human race. But then something would happen or some words would be spoken, and it was as if a flood had come and destroyed those bridges. And then, once again, we were on separate shores.

~~~

By the time we got back to Mystic Springs, I'd put those thoughts behind me. We had work to do, and that's what was important. Lynn was finishing up with her kindergartners when we pulled up. They were bouncing up and down around her, wanting a last hug goodbye. It was like seeing fifteen little Lynn all at once. I don't know how she managed it, but it made me smile.

We were unloading our new supplies into the office when Lynn came in. She greeted us all then put her hand on my arm. "I have some bad news, Lenore," she said. My heart sank. *No lot for us*, I thought.

"I got a note from Jenny. Her parents made her withdraw the invitation for lunch and a swim at the club. They're afraid that her association with us—with anyone who is connected to SNCC—will cause problems for their family. I'm so sorry, Lenore."

I almost laughed out loud. "Lynn, there is no way I would've gone to that club! You left before I could say that the other day."

Lynn looked bewildered. "But...but Jenny and I are sorority sisters. We had such a good time at lunch. I can't believe her parents have forbidden her from having anything to do with me."

I gave her a sympathetic hug. "That was to be expected, I'm afraid."

"In her note she said her mom thinks we've come down here to ruin their way of life, that we think we're better than they are. Her mom told her we're all Communists!" Lynn put her hands on her hips. "That's ridiculous! We're here to help the Negroes get on an equal footing, which is only right."

When I nodded in agreement, Lynn's perplexed expression changed. She smiled and added, "Well, Jenny was really mad at her parents for saying she can't have any contact with me—a sorority sister! She said she would get back at her father for that. She thinks she knows how to manipulate him into giving SNCC the lot." Lynn giggled. "I think Mac and Pastor Hendricks can count on it now."

18

I've looked at life from both sides now
From win and lose and still somehow
It's life's illusions I recall
I really don't know life at all.
—Joni Mitchell, "Both Sides Now"

Harry, Brenda, Tom, and I huddled around the table in the school's SNCC office, studying the map of our territory. Harry sat back and rubbed his hands over his face as if trying to erase the fatigue. That wouldn't help, though. We'd been working on getting people signed up for the Mississippi Freedom Democratic Party twelve to fourteen hours a day, not counting extra time needed for planning. House by house, we'd been covering all the Black sections of Mystic Springs and its outlying areas, plus expanding into the little towns and countryside nearby that didn't have a SNCC presence.

Tom stood up and stretched. "How close are we getting to our goal of a hundred thousand?"

Harry shrugged. "If I had to guess, I'd say we're close to sixty thousand, but we've only got about a week to go. When I've talked to other SNCC staff members around the state, they tell me more about the harassment that they're getting from whites."

I'd been remembering that too. It made me think of another incident Jane had mentioned in her last letter. Five voter registration workers on their way back from a morning of canvassing were attacked after two men in a pickup tried to run them off the road. Jane knew the two white volunteers, Larry and Dave, but she didn't know the two Negro girls with them or fifty-one-year-old Rabbi Arthur Lelyveld.

The girls weren't beaten, but the rabbi sustained many severe bruises and cuts, Dave needed seven stitches in his head, and Larry's arm was broken. The five workers reported the beatings to the police and FBI the next morning. I later found out that one man was actually arrested, but his trial ended up as a farce. He got a $500 fine and a ninety-day suspended sentence.

"I wonder if it'll ever come out publicly about all the beatings and murders and other incidents," pondered Brenda. "I can hardly believe the level of violence that threatens us all, simply for trying to get Negroes registered to vote."

Harry looked up from a paper he was studying. "Whenever there's progress for Negroes, there's an escalation of violence by whites. It's the whites' reaction to the signing of the Civil Rights Act. They think the best way to stay in power is to keep Negroes uneducated and segregated.

"But, anyway, on a more positive note, here's the list of those going to the Democratic National Convention. Besides the sixty-eight delegates, we'll have busloads of volunteers to hold the signs and demonstrate on the boardwalk. I've got you down, Lenore, and you'll share a room with your friend, right?"

"Right. Jane Carson."

"Brenda and Tom, you'll be staying here and continuing with the registration process. It'll be an important week. But for now, let's go get a lot more people signed up for the Mississippi Freedom Democratic Party."

I felt like we were football players getting a pep talk at halftime so we could take the field and win the game. But this was so much more important than a game.

~~~

At dinner that evening, Anabel gave her usual report about the school day. "We talked all 'bout what integration means. Started out we had two sides. One was s'posed to say what was good about it and the other what was bad. I got assigned the bad side."

Mrs. Johnson paused while passing another biscuit to Elizabeth. "What did you say?" she asked.

"Well, I had to think hard because I really think it would be good, but I said it would be bad because the white students would be mean to us. Earl said the white teachers would be harder on us. Thelma said in places

202

like big cities, Negroes would have to leave their neighborhood schools and ride buses a long distance to the white schools. You know, stuff like that."

I wished I'd been there for that discussion. "What were the reasons some said integration would be good?" I had to ask.

"Oh, that was easy. They just said we'd finally get as good an education as the whites, with new books and no secondhand stuff like desks and uniforms. Plus, we'd get extra stuff like art and music."

Elizabeth set down the biscuit she was buttering. "It was a great discussion, but I think most of the students feel that integration will never happen. One important thing they discussed was that they really don't know whites and the whites don't know them. They agreed that through integration, both groups might get to know each other better, which is a plus for both Negroes and whites. The bottom line, though, is that they don't expect it to become a reality."

Mr. Johnson nodded. "Sure nothin' I'll see in my lifetime."

"Do you think integration would be a good thing, Mr. Johnson?" I prodded.

He was quiet for a moment, carefully choosing his words. "Well, Lenore, I'll tell you true. I don't want integration really, but what I want is for kids to get an equal education. If'n they don't get education as good as whites, they won't get the jobs, and then they can't make a livin' for their families, y'see?"

Elizabeth said, "But don't you think integration would do that?"

He gave a slight shrug. "It might do it, but at what cost? We got strong teachers in our colored schools, teachers who look out for our chillun, who prepare them for dealing with the white world. Who's goin' to do that in those white schools, huh?"

Serene and Anabel looked from their dad to Elizabeth and back again. Serene frowned and complained, "I don't want to go to school with white kids. They're mean."

"Lenore and I are white," Elizabeth pointed out. "We're not mean, are we?"

"Nooo," Serene said slowly.

"Do you know any white kids your age?"

Serene shook her head.

Elizabeth continued, "If you did, you'd learn that there are lots of nice white kids. There's good and bad in every race. I bet there's even some mean Negroes in Mystic Springs."

Now Serene nodded her head. "There sure is. That Jake, he mean as a snake!"

The conversation made me think more deeply about integration. "Mr. Johnson, I see your point about equality being the main issue rather than integration. But that reminds me of something I learned in a course last semester.

"The discussion was about whether separate could ever be equal, and the sociologists and psychologists said no, it couldn't. They based it on a study that two Negro psychologists, Kenneth and Mamie Clark, conducted in the 1940s. It was called the Doll Study because they had two dolls that were exactly the same, except one was Negro and one was white. The Clarks asked all these Negro children about which was the prettier doll, which was the better doll, things like that. The children's responses showed that segregated Negro children felt inferior to whites. It was used as the most convincing argument in the Supreme Court's decision in *Brown v. the Board of Education,* which said that schools had to integrate because the study showed that separate was *not* equal."

Mrs. Johnson's eyes flashed with an anger I'd never seen in her before. She slowly set down her fork and said, "My chillun ain't inferior to nobody!...Nobody!"

I quickly reached over and put my hand on her arm. "Oh no, that's not what I was saying. Anabel and Serene are amazing, wonderful girls. We are so proud of both of them. No, the study didn't show that Negro children *were* inferior. It showed that segregation made Negro children *feel* inferior. So the sociologists and psychologists thought the study showed segregation wasn't successful and that we *need* integration to make things equal. I only brought it up to see what Mr. Johnson thought. That's all."

Mrs. Johnson quietly picked up her fork and began eating, but her eyes would not meet mine.

Mr. Johnson glanced at his wife before responding. "I jus' want my girls, and all young Negroes, to have ever' chance, ever' opportunity to become whatever they want to be. That mean havin' the same chances and opportunities as white chillun. If that mean goin' to integrated schools, that's fine." He looked around the table at each of us. "I only want the best for 'em. That's the whole of it, right there."

For a few moments, the only sound was the clinking of silverware against plates and the steady whirring of the fan. Finally, I couldn't stand it any longer. "Mr. and Mrs. Johnson, I am so sorry that my words sounded like I was saying anything against your daughters," I blurted out. Then I turned to Anabel and Serene. "I have come to love you two as if you were my own sisters. You are *not* inferior to anyone. I hope you believe that."

The two girls nodded, and Serene smiled at me. "I know for sure I'm better than that ol' Jake."

We all laughed, and the ice was broken over a dark place I never wanted us to go to again. Mrs. Johnson blew out a long breath as if she'd been holding it in. She looked at me and held out the plate of biscuits.

"Want the last one?" she asked me.

"I'll take it," Elizabeth said as she snatched it up.

And we all laughed together, like family.

~~~

In the morning, I walked with Elizabeth when she went to start school. As usual, I was early, the first one in our SNCC office. I used that time to work on our weekly newspaper or organize my tutoring work.

Harry walked in carrying his scuffed-up, tan briefcase. As he started stuffing reports in it, he looked over at me. "I'm headed to Ruleville to see Mac. Wanna come along?"

I blinked in surprise. Going to Ruleville meant maybe seeing Luke. I knew Harry didn't approve of me and Luke being together, but I figured he'd given up doing anything about it. "Sure. I'm ready when you are."

Riding along that stretch of miles, I leaned back, closed my eyes, and relaxed to the hum of the tires on the road. It was a nice change from walking house to house under the unforgiving sun.

Harry broke into my reverie. "You know, there was quite an incident last night at a mass meeting in Indianola."

I opened my eyes and turned toward him. "What happened?"

"I don't know the details. Hope to get them from Mac today. I do know it involved Tiny, though."

"Tiny, that Negro policeman I've heard about? The one who killed two Negroes?"

"He's the one. You've probably never seen him, but he is one scary dude: huge, dumb, and violent."

"Oh my God! How did he get to be a policeman?"

"How do you think? They needed him. If a white policeman kills a colored person, someone might say something. But if a Negro policeman kills another Negro person, no one will care or say a word."

The truth of that was infuriating, so I changed the subject. "Having a mass meeting at Indianola was brave, wasn't it? Beside it being the county seat, I remember Mac telling us at training that it's the birthplace of the White Citizens' Council."

"Yeah," Harry said as he pulled into Mrs. Hamer's yard. "Mac only expected a few people, but there was terrific turnout."

I was disappointed to see no one was congregating under the pecan tree.

Harry unfolded himself from the car. "Let's see what we can find out."

Mac greeted us at the door. "Harry, let's sit outside. They're using all the office space to work on flyers. Lenore, why don't you go on in and give them a hand." He brushed past me with a stack of papers in his hands.

As soon as I walked in, Luke jumped up from the table. "This is a nice surprise," he said. He pulled up a chair for me. We tried to act casually, but it wasn't easy. Inside, I was feeling a warmth, a sense of excitement, all the things you read about in novels. I took a deep breath to calm myself as Luke introduced me to the volunteers putting together flyers for the next mass meeting.

As I began folding the papers, I said, "Luke, Harry told me about the Indianola meeting. What happened?"

"Oh my God, girl, you should've been there! It was an amazing evening for lots of reasons. First of all, it was Indianola, right? Dangerous place to make a stand. We'd put out the word about the mass meeting, really not expecting more than a few folks to dare to come. A bunch of kids arrived early at the Negro Baptist School. We had Rabbi Al Levine, our chaplain, there too. Have you met him?"

I shook my head.

"Great guy. He's been in the Movement a long time. Went on an early Freedom Ride in '61. Anyway, he was there, looking things over. He went to the police chief and worked it out that especially with the kids inside, we didn't want any trouble. The chief agreed to keep police on the outside only. I was back at the Baptist School, and by then, more and more people were showing up. First it was the kids, then women, then people of all ages came, both men and women. By the time we were ready to start, it was packed, no seats left. People were lined up all along the wall."

"That's great!" I exclaimed, caught up in his excitement.

Luke laughed as he said, "That's just the beginning. Mac arrived, and, Lord, you should've seen the look on his face! We were singing freedom songs by then, and I swear there were tears in Mac's eyes as he came forward.

"But before he got started, a low murmur swept through the crowd. You know, like a shiver of fear. I didn't know what was happening until the horde of people separated, and I could hear whispers near me. It was Tiny, pushing his way to the middle. He's enormous and looks like he's a bit on the slow side, if you know what I mean," Luke said as he tapped his finger on the side of his head. "And he had his hand on the gun in his holster."

Picturing the scene, I felt a chill of fear myself. "What happened next?"

"Rabbi Levine got to Tiny before Mac did and explained nice and calm that Tiny had to leave because the police chief had promised there'd be no cops inside the building. But Tiny just said, real loud, 'I'm stayin'.'

"So Mac went back to the front of the room and told everyone that this was church property and the police chief had promised no police would enter. Then Mac asked the crowd if they wanted Tiny there or not. Said it was up to them.

"Someone shouted, 'Go! Go!' and soon everyone was chanting it and stomping their feet."

"Wow!"

"So then, Mac charged back to this guy who's twice his size, pointed to the door, and said, 'Go!' Tiny looked at him for a minute then pulled out his gun and growled, 'I could kill you.' When someone screamed, Tiny pointed the gun right at Rabbi Levine. It was a dangerous moment, but I guess the scream alerted the police outside 'cause a bunch of 'em came in and made Tiny leave. What a moment! We stood up to a threat and won! And to top it all off, the police helped us!"

I sat back, not realizing that I'd been holding my breath. "I would've been scared to death! But what a fantastic evening, the large crowd in a place like Indianola, the police doing right, and that awful Tiny not being allowed to intimidate all of you."

"But wait, it gets better. The police chief drove the rabbi to the police station so he could report it to the FBI. But all the people in that room that night...Lenore, I'm telling you, for the first time they didn't feel powerless. They felt strong." Luke's eyes burned with excitement. "Hope was born in that room. Hope. That's what we've been preaching, and there it was."

I had to put my hand on Luke's arm; I had to touch him. "Wow. That's all I can say. Wow."

"Then let's get these flyers folded," growled one of the volunteers.

Luke and I folded flyer after flyer until Mac came in to tell me that Harry was ready to go back to Mystic Springs. As I walked past Mac on my way out, he said, "I meet with Mr. Williamson about the lot again tomorrow. Keep your fingers crossed. Maybe he's changed his mind."

I smiled at him. "That wouldn't surprise me at all."

~~~

Harry and I stopped at several homes out in the country on our way back to Mystic Springs. We did pretty well at getting some signatures for the Mississippi Freedom Democratic Party. I'd learned a lot from Harry—as well as Brenda—about how to approach people. Harry had such an easy, relaxed way about him as if he'd stopped by for a casual visit with a friend. I'd come a long way from the stiff, formal, white girl I'd been when I first arrived on this red clay soil, this land of mosquitoes and heat and violence.

"A penny for your thoughts," Harry said as we drove the last mile into Mystic Springs.

I sighed. "Just thinking about how different it is down here."

"Are you sorry you came?"

"No, not at all!" I answered quickly. "It's really opened my eyes, and I've learned so much. I do wonder what I'll think when I get back to school in September. I might have trouble believing all this was real."

Harry looked over at me. "Yeah, I get that. If you'd come down for vacation with a white classmate from Mississippi, you'd have had a very different summer. You would've been in a home with air-conditioning and indoor plumbing. You'd be goin' to the pool, playin' tennis, spendin' days at the lake, goin' to parties. You'd think Mississippi is a lovely state, and you would've had a fun, relaxing summer."

I nodded. "And I would've seen the 'colored' and 'white' signs and thought they were terrible, but I never would've understood."

"So," he glanced sideways at me, "you think you understand what it is to be a colored person here in Mississippi?"

Harry pulled up in front of the school and turned off the ignition as I answered. "I've learned a lot about what it is to be a Negro, but at the same time, I've also learned that I will never—could never—really know.

You carry the blood of your ancestors—their history and their pain—within you in some unfathomable way. I believe that no white person can ever reach that and can never truly know what it means to be a Negro in America."

As Harry looked over at me, a grim smile flickered across his face. Then he nodded and opened the car door.

~~~

We finished our Mississippi Freedom Democratic Party work just in time for dinner with the Johnsons. I hesitated for a moment at the back door as I recalled the previous evening's conversation. I took a deep breath and went in.

Mrs. Johnson was fanning herself with a dish towel as she stood by the stove. "Come in, sugar. Dinner's almost ready. I made your favorite, red beans and rice."

I gave her a hug. "Thank you. I...I still feel bad that you thought I was saying something negative about your girls last night. I'm so sorry about that."

"Now don't you worry your pretty little head about that. It's all okay." She moved to the table and sat down, patting the place next to her.

When I sat, she took my hands in hers. "I know it's different for you down here, Lenore. Here, a mama has to fight ever' day for her chillun, to keep them safe, to keep them from thinkin' they nobody. It's hard. It's *so* hard. But I know you didn't mean anythin' hurtful. It's behind us now. We got to let go of the things behind us or we'd have too much of a load to carry." She pushed herself up and turned back to the stove.

I sat a moment longer, thinking about what she'd said. I hoped I would remember it. There was wisdom in her words.

Dinnertime held many laughs that evening. Anabel acted out the way Earl had leaned so far back in his chair that he fell over. We also learned that Thelma had insisted they start and end class with her leading the singing of freedom songs. Everyone sat in awe as I shared what I'd learned about the meeting in Indianola. Mr. Johnson knew a lot about Tiny and shared some stories with us. They all ended with Tiny being the laughingstock. It always amazed me that whatever happened in the Delta on any given day, either Mr. or Mrs. Johnson knew about it by suppertime. Beyond that, Mr. Johnson had a way of summing up and making sense of events in just a few words then ending with, "And that's the whole of it." In another month when I'd head back to the "safe, safe North," I would miss hearing those words. I would miss being part of the Johnson family.

I had to laugh as I found myself thinking, *And that's the whole of it.*

~~~

We were getting down to the last few days before the buses would carry us to Atlantic City. Every SNCC staffer and volunteer was working frantically to get as many names as possible signed up for the Mississippi Freedom Democratic Party.

Brenda tallied up our successes from the day before. "That's fourteen more," she said. We hadn't exactly worked "from can't to can't," the old slavery expression for dawn to dark fieldwork, but we'd been working long hours. Getting fourteen more folks to sign up was an excellent achievement. I didn't know how there could possibly be anyone left in Sunflower County to sign up, but we were certainly going to hunt for them in the next few days.

Our Saturday morning started with canvassing as usual, trying to cover a few more country roads. Harry didn't like dividing us up into twos, although that was the most practical way. I liked being paired with Brenda, but Harry wasn't comfortable having two white girls going off by themselves with stretches of road between houses. But if one of us was paired with Tom, leaving the other with Harry, a white girl with a Black man was equally dangerous. I could now see why Harry didn't like it when Anitra and I had switched jobs. So the four of us stuck together, kicking through dusty fields to speak with sharecroppers in one-hundred-degree heat. By this time, though, at least we all knew to bring canteens of water.

When we got back to the school late in the afternoon, we were really drooping like a wilted daisy. We always enjoyed checking on the kindergartners. This time, Lynn had them parading around the room holding up paper replicas of candles they'd made and singing "This Little Light of Mine."

"Who's got a light?" Lynn called.

Fifteen kindergartners jumped up and down, shouting, "I do! I do!"

"And what are you gonna do?"

"Shine!" They broke out in giggles.

I closed my eyes and said a silent prayer that they always would.

Suddenly, the precious moment was interrupted by the sound of a car slowing down and coming to a stop then footsteps hurrying toward the building. It caused the hair on the back of my neck to rise. We hurried to the school door and sighed when we saw Mac and Pasture Hendricks rushing toward us. Seeing their grins, I knew exactly what their news would be.

Mac waved a paper high in the air. "We got it!" he hollered. "We got the lot!"

Lynn rushed to the doorway of the school and clapped her hands at the announcement. She and I exchanged a glance, a secret message between us as special as any sorority sisters' ritual.

Pastor Hendricks and Mac led us into the back office and sat at the table. "We couldn't have been more surprised at how the meeting went," Mac began. "Mr. Williamson obviously had been thinking it over and had come to a decision."

"What did he say?" asked Harry.

"Well, of course, he wants something out of it. He wants us to let the national media know what a grand thing it is that the board of education has so *generously* given us the lot. And he doesn't want us to mention that it's Section 16 land in the Negro community where they wouldn't ever build anything anyway. I don't care. I just want that lot, and I want to start building!"

Pastor Hendricks nodded. "Have any of y'all been by there lately? They've torn down the old school, and the lot is all cleared off. We managed to salvage a few things before the demolition began—a few blackboards and some tables, but not much."

Mac's eyes shone with excitement. "We can start construction almost immediately. There's a need for this kind of all-purpose building all over, so the COFO network around the country had architects draw up basic plans for such a building. It's pretty much a prefab building, so we'll start the application process for permits and everything. We did suggest to Mr. Williamson that he tell folks around town about letting us move ahead with the plans before the news media gets wind of it." Both men chuckled. "I don't think he likes us very much."

Harry smiled. "Well, what about getting—"

The ring of the phone startled everyone. Harry answered it quickly then paused a moment, listening. "Uh-huh.... Oh my God! Wait, here's Mac." He handed the receiver over as he announced, "Silas has been shot in the head!"

19

For the newsmen of the world who sought them out, the cause of the Freedom Democrats was the number one story of the convention....It was a controversy which could rip open the convention.
—United States Information Service, *1964 The Conventions*

After waiting for hours the night before, we had learned only that Silas was in the hospital and was expected to live. Harry sent us home to try to get some sleep.

It wasn't until the next morning that Harry gave us the details. "Silas was lucky," he said. "The bullet went through his cheek near his temple and knocked out some teeth. He's been taken to Jackson for surgery to remove the bullet. It's still in his throat, but Derryle says he'll be okay." Silas had taken some volunteers who'd been released from jail, down to Lula's Cafe. He was waiting in the car for the rain to let up some. Someone said he was resting his head against the steering wheel when a car crept by and the passenger shot him up close."

"Did anyone get a tag number?" Brenda asked.

Harry shook his head again. "No one wants to be a witness ever since Louis Allen was killed for speaking to the FBI about Herbert Lee's death. But a couple people did tell SNCC staffers they thought it might've been Byron De La Beck with, the guy who killed Medgar Evers. He lives there in Greenwood now. Who knows?"

"Yeah, or it could've been the same people who beat up Silas last week," I said. "We don't know about that either."

"Well, what I *do* know is that when the volunteers heard the shot, they rushed out and opened the car door, and Silas just fell out, bleeding so much that two of the guys took off their shirts to stop the bleeding. They got him in another car and rushed him to the hospital. When they got there, the hospital folks wouldn't let the guys in because they were shirtless. That's why it took so long to get details—typical harassment."

"So is the FBI investigating it?" Brenda asked.

"The police finally came after about thirty minutes, took some pictures of the car, asked a few questions." Harry shrugged. "The FBI is supposed to look at it this morning. As I said, the usual....A lot of our people gathered at Lula's last night. Derryle said it looked like a riot might start."

"What happened?" I asked. I wanted all the details.

"Jesse Harrison was there. He's a SNCC staff guy who came down from the Atlanta office. Anyway, Derryle said people were bringing out guns, but Jesse defused the situation and got it all worked out. It could've been much worse, with people killed and all that."

I shifted in my seat uncomfortably, imagining how dangerous the night had been. "Well," Harry sighed, "let's go register some voters."

We rode to our first area in unaccustomed silence. I thought about what had just happened. We'd heard that a friend had been brutally shot. Then we simply put it aside and went on with our day. That was the way things were done down here. And yet, with each shooting, each bombing, each jailing, and each beating, there had to be anger. What was happening to that anger? Was it relieved when shared with a close friend? Did it get released with hard work or by being prayed away? Was it held inside until it exploded? Or was it just taken in and allowed to wear down a person's soul until they didn't have anything left to react with?

Harry parked the car by a sharecropper's shack. As I got out, I stuck a friendly smile on my face. But the anger was still inside me.

~~~

On Wednesday morning, August 19, Tom drove Harry and me to Greenwood to catch the bus for Atlantic City. I sat quietly in the back seat as we rode past fields of white cotton, called "Mississippi snow." Now I saw why because it did look like fields of snow, gentle against the rising sun. There was so much about Mississippi that was misleading. It was like an attractive lady who was lovely to look at but who held dark secrets inside. *Which one was real?* I wondered. *Or were they both?*

The thought of participating in the Democratic National Convention had never crossed my mind before, but if it was anything like the state convention, I knew it would be a boisterous, exciting time, and I was ready. Besides the excitement of being part of it, Jane was coming from the Hattiesburg area. Mac and Mrs. Hamer were both delegates from Sunflower County, and as far as I knew, Luke was still on the list of attendees. Plus, I was going to a safer place.

Another reason I was looking forward to the convention was that Mom would be coming down from New York to see me. I'd be glad to see her again, but I was a little apprehensive about where our conversation would take us. As my mom, she could read me pretty easily, but there were some things I wasn't looking forward to sharing yet. I did hope she and Mac could finally meet in person, though, especially since from the money she'd raised and some additional funding, there was almost enough money to pay for the new school building and community center.

Tom's voice intruded into my thoughts. "Harry, what does the Mississippi Freedom Democratic Party have to do to convince the credentials committee that they should be seated as the real delegates from Mississippi?"

"Huh...well, we sure have worked hard on it, but now I think it depends on two important things: First, we state the fact that the all-white Mississippi Democratic delegation excludes Negroes completely, and therefore, it doesn't represent 42 percent of the state's population, which is illegal. Second, we need to make it absolutely clear that the MFDP is prepared to support President Johnson and the Democratic Party's platform, but the all-white delegation isn't."

Tom nodded. "That sounds pretty persuasive to me."

I leaned forward to join the conversation. "So how will the convention decide which group of delegates is the official one?" I asked.

"First the MFDP will present its request to be seated to the credentials committee. If that fails, the hope is to bring it to the floor of the whole convention through a minority vote. Our delegation doesn't only include Blacks but a few whites too. We would've liked more, and we tried to reach that community, but we couldn't stir any interest. Even so, having some whites will help. We're hopeful. It's an exciting time."

When we arrived in Greenwood, the convoy of buses and cars was already forming. Despite a lot of bustle and activity, we all got sorted out with the delegates in one bus and the supporters in the rest. Jane had saved me a seat. I looked for Luke but couldn't find him in the crowd. I hadn't seen Mac or Mrs. Hamer either, so I thought that perhaps the Ruleville group was in one of the cars.

The air fizzed with excitement. I loved the carnival feeling of people laughing, hugging, and calling out to each other. There was a spirit of optimism, something I hadn't felt much this summer. Optimism was one of those things you didn't know you were missing until you found it again, like reuniting with a childhood friend who had moved away.

Jane offered me a piece of Juicy Fruit gum, and we immediately picked up where we'd left off, jumping into conversation, questions, catching up, and, of course, laughing. I didn't even notice when the buses rumbled away, beginning our long, twenty-hour trip North.

From what we'd learned at the state convention and what we were hearing from conversations around us, Jane and I understood the optimism. When the Mississippi Freedom Democratic Party had originally been formed, it was mainly symbolic, to give Negroes experience with the voting process. However, with the support it was receiving from other states, the leaders of the Movement began to believe that unseating the regular Mississippi delegation was a real possibility. Another major goal was to bring the issue of racism in America to the national television audience.

Jane and I had a lot of time to catch up on everything, including how her summer romance with another volunteer was progressing, the surprising results of Lynn's arrival in Mystic Springs, news about classmates from Barnard, and a myriad of other topics.

Finally, Jane lowered her voice and asked, "So what are we going to do about you and Luke?"

"What do you mean?" I flushed as I lowered my eyes away from her probing gaze.

"You know what I mean. I know you really like him, but you said you never have a chance to be alone with him. Are you two planning to get together now that you're away from Mississippi?"

We were whispering now, our heads close together. "I don't know. We'll have to see. Maybe he and I can find some time alone in our hotel room."

"Oh, Lenore. Are you sure about this?"

I looked at her and shrugged. I was so unsure about everything that had happened this summer. I didn't know if I wanted to change direction and get my degree in education instead of social work. I didn't know if I wanted to stay in Mississippi for another year as some other volunteers were doing. I didn't know if I wanted to move to Mississippi as soon as I graduated. And, while I knew I liked Luke a lot, I didn't know if I was ready to take things to a deeper level with him.

Jane pressed my hand. "Be careful. Make sure he has protection."

"Jane!" Her words were making me face something I had avoided dealing with.

She raised her eyebrows, gave my hand another squeeze, and sat back in her seat.

~~~

Once we arrived in Atlantic City, we stopped at the Gem Hotel to let the delegates leave their luggage then at the other hotels for the rest of us. Soon, though, we reached our important destination, the Convention Hall at the Boardwalk where it all would happen.

The scene along the boardwalk in Atlantic City was chaotic to say the least, with people milling about in all directions, hot dog and saltwater taffy vendors calling out their specialties, the background drone of a thousand conversations, shouts, and laughter. I couldn't help but notice the sight of Negroes and whites mingling together so casually, which was something I hadn't seen all summer.

We supporters weren't allowed inside the convention hall, of course, so we clustered in groups outside, sharing our expectations of the days ahead. We thought we understood the background politics: Lyndon Johnson had become president when John Kennedy was assassinated less than a year before, and now Johnson wanted to become president in his own right. His concern was that if the Black delegates of the Mississippi Freedom Democratic Party got seated, he would lose the Southern vote, and he could not afford to let that happen. Johnson let Hubert Humphrey know that if he stopped the Mississippi Freedom Democratic Party, Johnson would reward him by naming him as his vice president. Humphrey immediately gave Walter Mondale the task, and they headed to Atlantic City.

On Saturday, August 22, the credentials committee began hearing speeches, including those of Revered Ed King, Martin Luther King Jr., Aaron Henry, Rita Schwerner, and others. But none was more powerful than the one Fannie Lou Hamer delivered.

Mrs. Hamer had stirred up fear in the hearts of many of us that summer, and evidently, that was true even of President Johnson. When he learned she was about to speak before the televised audience, he arranged an impromptu press conference for the same time period, knowing the TV stations would pull away from her to cover him.

As she sat at a table and pulled the microphone closer, a hush came over the crowd. She was dynamic as she introduced herself and told her story. It would've been impossible for an audience not to have been moved listening to her simple testimony.

President Johnson was shrewd to try to keep it from America, but his efforts failed. Even though the television coverage did indeed turn to the president's press conference while Mrs. Hamer spoke, the TV cameras continued to roll at the convention hall. The essence of her message was played for the country on the news broadcast that evening. I'll never forget her concluding remarks:

"All of this is on account of we want to register to become first-class citizens. And if the Freedom Democratic Party is not seated now, I question America. Is this America, the land of the free and the home of the brave, where we have to sleep with our telephones off the hooks because our lives be threatened daily because we want to live as decent human beings in America? Thank you." (from *Freedom Summer* video, PBS American Experience)

She wiped the perspiration from her face with her handkerchief, pushed herself up, and, putting her white purse over her arm, left the table.

After listening to all the testimony given to the credentials committee, we moved away from the loudspeakers set up for us outside and joined the masses forming along the Boardwalk. Groups, some from Washington D.C. and other states, built up our numbers into a well-organized assemblage. We took turns kneeling and praying, marching, and sitting quietly in rows with our signs speaking for us: "Freedom Delegation Now;" "Mississippi Freedom Democratic Party Supports LBJ;" and "We Shall Overcome."

I was parading behind Jane trying to hold high a "Freedom Now" sign. My arms ached from carrying it, but we would soon alternate with those who were sitting. When someone joined the line right behind me, the shiver that ran up my spine told me it was Luke. I smiled to myself and kept walking.

I felt his hand on the small of my back. "Hey, girl. Keep up the pace. No slacking off." And then his irresistible chuckle that made me smile.

Without turning, I said, "It's about time you got here instead of loafing around."

"Not loafing at all. That's impossible when you're with Mac and Mrs. Hamer." He laughed again.

We spent another ten minutes walking the oval pattern before we had a chance to sit down. Luke put his hand on my back and whispered, "Keep going until we get to the back of the group."

We settled on the ground, our backs against the wall, before I could really turn and look at him. He dipped his sign in front of his face and gestured for me to do the same. As soon as I did, he leaned over and gently kissed me. I'd been waiting for that moment. I eased into the kiss, reaching up with my free hand to touch his face. Suddenly, I opened my eyes wide, started to push him away, and look around. Then I remembered that we weren't in Mississippi anymore. We kissed again, still shielded by our signs.

"Luke, we still need to be careful. Anyone could report us to Mrs. Hamer."

"Yeah, I know. But most of these people don't know us. Besides, Mrs. Hamer has much more important stuff to be thinking about."

We settled into our easy pattern of conversation, catching up with each other and talking about the convention, feeling each other's warmth as we snuggled together. Before I knew it, it was time for us to march again.

With the formal plea made to the credentials committee, we just had to wait for a verdict. Supporters of the Mississippi Freedom Democratic Party were organized to maintain an around-the-clock vigil outside the convention walls. Luke went with Harry and Marcus, while Jane grabbed me. We all headed back to our respective hotels to get some rest before our assigned times. Between the long trip and marching, I was exhausted.

~~~

The next day, in spite of the crowds, Luke and I moved toward each other with an invisible magnetic pull. I smiled at him as he gave my hand a squeeze, something we wouldn't have dared do in Mississippi.

The day wore on slowly as we alternated again between parading and sitting. The mood of the Mississippi Freedom Democratic Party supporters remained hopeful, and conversations around us were full of speculation about what the day would bring. Jane was given the afternoon off to rest; Luke and I were given the evening. Because of that, the day seemed even longer. Luke and I worked out a plan to meet back at my hotel room when our shift ended. Since Jane and I had been given different break times, our room would be empty.

After lunch, the latest information from the convention hall filtered out to us. Walter Mondale had come up with a compromise: Of our sixty-eight delegates, Hubert Humphrey would select two to be seated "at large." However, they would not be able to vote. Humphrey chose Aaron Henry and Reverend Ed King, one of the four whites. The other side of the compromise was that the regular Mississippi delegation would have to swear loyalty to the party's nominee and platform.

After hearing the news, I saw Mrs. Hamer and Mac returning to the convention hall. With Mac scowling and Mrs. Hamer looking down at the ground, their expressions told me they were not happy. By evening, it was clear that the Mississippi Freedom Democratic Party would not accept the negotiation.

As the end of our shift finally approached, I glanced at my watch for the hundredth time. Luke and I exchanged a look and headed off through the crowd in different directions to avoid suspicion. Trembling, I unlocked the door to the room Jane and I shared, knowing Luke would knock a few minutes later. My breath quickened, and the room was so strangely quiet that the silence roared in my ears. Thoughts, emotions, Jane's advice, and Mrs. Hamer's voice saying, "There will be consequences!" surged through my mind. I felt conflicted, wanting what I should not want. But after a short knock on the door, Luke was there, right in front of me.

A flush rose from my chest up to my face. Butterflies stirred in my stomach. A storm of both fear and excitement raged inside me. When Luke entered the room, I looked at him with desperation. "Luke, what are we going to do?"

"This is what we're going to do, girl," he said as he pulled me close and kissed me, gently at first then stronger and deeper. I reached over and locked the door.

Before we had to leave, we plumped the pillows up and leaned against the headboard, snuggling and talking as we tried to imagine what the future held for us.

"When I came to Mississippi this summer, I thought my path was pretty clear. I'd enjoyed my other summer experiences working with the kids from New York's Lower East Side, so going into social work seemed like a good plan. But now, I don't know. I feel such a passion for what we've been doing, I just—"

"Yeah, girl," Luke said with that mischievous chuckle, "I'm feeling that passion too."

"Luke!" I gave him a flirtatious smack on the arm. "I'm serious! You know what I mean."

Luke's expression became thoughtful as he replied, "I've seen that in you. In fact, I've seen it in almost all the volunteers, and I wonder how any of you can go back to your life before. So yeah, I get it."

I looked into those brown eyes that carried such emotion about the things in his life. I knew I was a part of that too. "I care for you so much, Luke, but the more I care, the more scared I become."

Luke's fingers trailed gently across my cheek then tucked a strand of hair behind my ear. "I know, girl-of-mine, but like I said in the beginning, we'll have to be very, very careful. We can't ignore what we feel. I care for you too, but I've got to keep working in Mississippi, and you've got your plans, right?"

Part of me wanted him to ask me to stay. I dreaded the long separation. "I want to keep working in Mystic Springs or wherever, but I think it's better to go back to school and get my degree. Then I can come back."

"To work getting the Black folks registered to vote?"

"No. I want to teach." Saying it out loud cemented it more firmly in my mind.

Luke kissed me. "You'll be a great teacher, Lenore."

"I want to teach the Negro kids. I want them to learn about Negro history, to feel comfortable asking questions, and to learn the truth about things. I want to—"

He hugged me tight. "You want to change the world. I know, girl. So do I. That's why we got to keep working."

That night, as Luke and I returned to the boardwalk, the Mississippi Freedom Democratic Party crowd seemed more discouraged, which was in stark contrast to what I was feeling. Inside, I was quivering with a newfound joy that I tried to keep to myself as we joined a candlelight march in memoriam of Andy, Mickey, and James.

Mac looked like he had the weight of the world on his shoulders. He gave me a tired smile as I caught up with him.

"My mom is coming down for a few hours tomorrow," I told him. "I'm meeting her at eleven at the diner down on the next corner. I'd love for you to meet her if you're available, but I know how busy you are."

He laughed. "If you see me walking around out here, grab me. I'd like to meet her. We really appreciate all the support she's given us."

"She told me on the phone yesterday that she was bringing some more checks."

"Wonderful! I needed to hear some good news." He turned away as someone else asked him a question.

As I rejoined the vigil group, I knelt next to Luke. When I was near him, I was so aware of his body and his beautiful, strong yet gentle hands. *I need to stop thinking about that!* I admonished myself. I could also sense the strength he held within himself, his mind, and his actions working for change. What had been a blossoming summer romance had become so much more. At the hotel, our talk included words about the future, seeing each other in the uncertain time to come, words about his coming to the North and my returning to Mississippi. But in the back of my mind, I wondered how we could, if we would dare.

When Jane and I returned to our room in the early morning hours after our turn at the vigil, she didn't ask me about my time with Luke, and I didn't mention it. I wasn't ready to tell her. Sometimes it's that way, even with best friends.

~~~

Pushing through the diner door at exactly eleven in the morning, I was glad to see my mom was already there. Her welcoming hug felt good; it was a memory of my normal, safe life.

After ordering, she opened her purse. "I brought more donations," she said with a smile as she handed me a fat envelope. "Everyone I talk to is very interested in the Freedom Project. But, then again, I'm very selective about whom I talk to."

Mom paused discreetly while the waitress brought us our drinks, coffee for my mom and a Coke for me. As soon she left, Mom leaned forward with a familiar expression on her face. "Now, tell me all about it: the work, the people, any romances, everything."

I looked at my mother. She had changed since she and Dad had divorced. She'd become more relaxed and seemed stronger. I was so proud of what she had done for our future school. "I don't even know where to start," I said. "It's been quite a summer, but it's the kind of experience that can't exactly be explained, Mom. It's like what people who have been through a war say, you know?"

"Did it feel like a war, hon?"

As I nodded, I felt tears wanting to come to my eyes, but I forced them back. This was my mom, the woman who'd dried so many of my tears, but this wasn't the time or place. "I've learned so much about the world that I didn't know—like how cruel people can be to each other simply because of their skin color. And I've learned how strong people can be to stand up for what is right and moral."

"I'm so proud of you, Lenore. Of course, I worried about you going down there, but I'm really glad you had this experience. It'll help you as you go forward with your career."

"Well, that's another thing, Mom. I've been thinking that maybe I should go into teaching instead of social work." I held my breath.

Mom sat back, her eyes wide. "But what about child welfare work? Your summer jobs and your courses in college were all geared in that direction. You're about to start your senior year. Why would you change your mind at this point?"

"Social work seemed like a good thing to do, mostly since I like working with kids. But I'd be doing that with teaching too, and I loved what I was doing at the Freedom School and the way the kids responded. What we taught was so important."

Mom tilted her head, puzzled. "I don't understand, Lenore. If you like teaching so much that you're willing to change your career path, then why in the world did you switch to doing the voter registration work?"

"Because," I sighed, "because it was the right thing to do. I told you in my letter about Anitra. She was trained and certified as a teacher already. She could do so much more for and with the kids than I could."

Mom gave me one of her looks, like she knew there was more than I was telling her. "And was that the *only* reason?"

"It just seemed right. Anyway, what do you think about me becoming a teacher?"

She leaned back and gazed at me a moment before answering. "I think you'll do well at whatever you want to do, Lenore. Only you can make that decision. You would be a wonderful teacher. Are you thinking about high school level or what?"

"Probably high school. But I need to give it some more thought." I paused briefly then said, "There's something else. I...uh...I want to go back to Mississippi after I graduate. I want to teach down there."

"Really?" Mom said with surprise, her eyebrows knitted close together. "Why? Why would you ever want to set foot down there after this summer?"

We paused again while the waitress placed our plates in front of us and asked, "Can I get you anything else?"

We shook our heads. Picking up my fork, I said, "I guess it grows on a person. I met so many wonderful people. And I can't help it, but I care about Mississippi and what happens there."

"Lenore, I'm not happy about your plans at all. I can't think of any reason for you to go back to such a violent, difficult place. I want you to get through the summer safely and come home again. And what's this business you wrote about staying longer and going directly back to school? Why won't you come home first? Is there a guy? Is it that Luke you mentioned occasionally?"

I set my fork back down. It was a now-or-never kind of moment. "Yes, there is a guy. Yes, it's Luke. And, Mom, he's a Negro."

~~~

When I got back to the Mississippi Freedom Democratic Party group, I was exhausted. The conversation with my mom had taken a lot of emotional energy. I knew she was disappointed with my decisions and with me, and I hated that feeling. I had hoped she'd understand once I explained what Mississippi had come to mean to me, but she just didn't get it. I knew she wouldn't like the fact that I had a Negro boyfriend, but I hadn't expected how adamantly she had objected. I guess I was disappointed in her too.

I didn't see Luke, but Jane was sitting in the back. I hurried to join her and slid down with my back against the wall. She patted my arm and asked, "How'd it go?"

I sighed deeply. "About like I expected. Not good. At least I won't need to discuss it again until I go back just before fall semester starts in three weeks. I'm too tired to talk about it now. What's new here?"

"Also not looking good. The credentials committee's report came out." She pulled a folded paper from her purse. "Here's a copy of it. It's what we expected, though. They propose that only the two at-large delegates are seated without a vote and that the regular Democratic Party delegates are seated after taking the loyalty oath. It will be voted on this evening. There's a lot of lobbying going on, but no one here is happy."

By nightfall, the scene at the convention was less like a carnival and more like a three-ring circus. In one ring, all but three of the regular, white Mississippi delegates had left rather than sign the loyalty oath. A presidential aide was carefully guarding the remaining three. In the second ring, outside the convention hall, we supporters remained in heated discussions. Some leaders were urging the delegates to sign the compromise, while others were telling them to reject it.

The third and final ring was the most newsworthy. Knowing that the regular delegates had abandoned their seats, the delegates from the Mississippi Freedom Democratic Party simply went inside and settled into those empty chairs. This, of course, was unacceptable.

That night the newscast showed the sergeant at arms dragging those treated as second-class citizens from the building. We heard that those orders came from the president, but at that point, we believed anything, no matter how preposterous it might seem. It was crushing to think how far we'd come and at such great risk, only to be treated that way. Yet, there was some consolation in knowing that America was seeing on the national news how Negroes were really being treated.

~~~

224

On Wednesday, our delegates met at Union Temple Baptist Church with the main leaders of the Movement. However, nothing was resolved. Those in favor of accepting the compromise pressed on. Those opposed, resisted. I could've told them to give up trying to change Mrs. Hamer's mind. It didn't matter what President Johnson wanted, or Dr. King, or anyone. She knew the right thing to do, and her body and soul had the scars of standing up for it. We'd heard she had undergone another beating just weeks earlier, so there was no way she'd give in to a weakened agreement at this point. She would rather go home with nothing than take an empty trophy of tokenism. She remained my heroine.

When the meetings ended and everyone was back at the convention hall, the MFDP delegates intended to go back inside and sit in the empty seats from Mississippi, but those chairs had been physically removed from the floor. However, three lone chairs remained for the delegates holding out from the regular Mississippi Democratic Party. They sat surrounded by men in suits who looked much like members of the FBI, with obvious gun bulges under their jackets.

Even so, the rejected delegates of the MFDP were not deterred. They simply marched in and stood in the empty spots where the chairs had been removed, claiming their places with their firm, upright posture. They gazed defiantly around the room, meeting the eyes of anyone glancing their way.

Our attempt at showing that the 42 percent of Mississippians who were Negro deserved a say in the presidential nomination came down to that moment. Sixty-eight courageous individuals were left officially and literally without a seat at the Democratic National Convention. All the work of the summer, the mass meetings, the traipsing from house to house and field to field, all the words of explanation—all of it—had come to this disappointing end. The goal for all of us—to get the Mississippi Freedom Democratic Party delegates seated—was left unattained.

On the last evening, as LBJ and Hubert Humphrey stood in victory and fireworks lit up the sky over the boardwalk, the group from Mississippi held hands and sang freedom songs. Mrs. Hamer led us in "This Little Light of Mine." As the last note of the song faded into the night air, I wondered about the light we'd been trying to make shine.

After this, the media attention on the plight of Negroes from the South would be gone. Many of the white student volunteers were leaving from the convention to go back to their other lives. I wondered what the SNCC and COFO staffers and other grassroots workers would do now.

There were shared tears and hugs. There were words of commiseration—angry words and sad words—and even attempts at understanding. Those who had arrived wrapped in a blanket of community began to feel some loose threads starting to unravel.

After that, there was nothing left to do but go back to Mississippi.

20

Hear my cry, O God;
listen to my prayer.
From the ends of the earth I call to you,
I call as my heart grows faint;
lead me to the rock that is higher than I.
For you have been my refuge,
a strong tower against the foe.
I long to dwell in your tent forever
and take refuge in the shelter of your wings.

—Psalm 61:1–4

The mood on the bus ride back was so different from the ride up; it had switched from hopefully optimistic to utterly dejected. Our efforts to build a party that would represent almost half the state's population and would be represented by delegates at the national convention had failed. *We* had failed.

The couple across the aisle from Jane and me spent the first two hours going over how everything had played out, incident by incident. "We just didn't get it," the man said. "Didn't understand about all the backroom politicking. Didn't know how to do all that lobbying."

The woman shook her head. "But now we know. We'll know what to do next time."

Harry turned from two rows in front of us. "In the meantime, we've got to keep working, keep getting people registered to vote."

"That's right," agreed his seatmate. "That's right, brother. Keeping on working, that's what we got to do."

I looked around at all the SNCC and COFO staff members and volunteers on the bus. They wore their discouragement and fatigue like a heavy blanket, with their shoulders slumped and voices hoarse. But I was aware of something I had seen over and over. The Negroes of Mississippi could be beaten down, again and again, yet they kept getting up, trying once more to change the system. Their sense of failure was very real now, but I was sure that at the next mass meeting they would sing the freedom songs with the same belief in the words as they always had. I had no doubt that Harry, Mac, Mrs. Hamer, and the others would still be out urging people to try to register to vote, and now, many would actually have the courage to do so.

The lesson about perseverance was one I hoped I'd remember. As I'd become more and more involved in the voter registration work over the summer, I learned so much about the value of perseverance. When I had first arrived in Mississippi, I was ready to help Negroes with *their* work of registration. However, I had grown to where I was now determined to help in *our* work of getting Negroes registered. It was a special connection with that part of Luke that had seemed so distant before.

We were headed back to Mississippi, but it would be different. Last week's dignified delegates would go back to being sharecroppers and maids. Many of the summer volunteers had gone straight home from Atlantic City. Jane and the volunteers from Mystic Springs would be leaving in a week.

Jane whispered. "Why are you staying longer than the rest of us? Do you think it'll be any easier to say goodbye later?"

I shook my head, dreading that goodbye. "I'm going to miss the Johnsons so much and Harry and Brenda, all of them."

"And Lynn?" Jane asked with a smirk.

"Oh my God, Jane. I'll even miss Lynn!" We laughed, and that felt good. I was so glad that there would be someone back at school I could talk to about this summer. How could we expect anyone else to understand?

Jane nudged me. "You didn't answer me. Why are you staying longer?"

"To get to see more of Luke, of course, but it's also important to me to see them break ground for the school. And, honestly, it's so I won't have to spend much time with my parents grilling me about my latest decisions."

Jane nodded with understanding. "Tell me more about your visit with your mom."

"Well," I began, now ready to talk to Jane about it, "she was almost okay with my switching to teaching. Everything went pretty well until I told her I wanted to move to Mississippi after I graduated. I could tell she didn't like that idea. Then she asked if it was because of a guy."

"Did you tell her about Luke?"

I nodded. "I figured I'd have to tell her sometime. She couldn't speak for a minute. I think she was really shocked. Even in the North, interracial relationships are not acceptable. Then she started in with all the reasons it wouldn't work, like even if it led to a serious relationship and marriage, then we'd have trouble finding a place to live; we wouldn't be accepted by Negroes or whites; our children would be bullied and ostracized; we might not be able to get certain jobs, and on and on. She actually had tears in her eyes. It wasn't anything I didn't already know, so I just sat quietly."

Jane patted my hand. "She needs time to think about it. She'll come around."

"I hope so. I know my dad will never accept it. If he could've stopped me from coming down this summer, he would have. And this summer has meant so much. I..." A lump started in my throat like I knew it would. "Sorry. I don't want to talk about it now."

Jane and I leaned back in our seats and closed our eyes. After a while, I heard the soft purring of her gentle snore, but sleep evaded me. It wasn't only thoughts of Luke that kept me awake, although that was certainly a big part of it. I also felt as though I'd aged years since I'd gone to the first workshop in Oxford, Ohio. This summer's experience had taken my life and turned it upside down.

As I sat on the bus surrounded by dispirited people, I started to question what kind of progress we could make working for change in the Jim Crow South. They would keep trying, though—I knew that much—so I would keep on trying too.

Jane stirred awake as we pulled into a rest stop. We washed up as best we could, bought some Cokes and sandwiches, and settled back in our seats. As the bus drove on into the darkness of the night and the conversations became more muffled around us, so did mine and Jane's.

"Ready to talk about Luke?" Jane whispered.

"Yeah," I said. I knew it was time. "We really talked things over this time. We needed that time alone, just the two of us, without having to keep looking over our shoulders. Jane, it's such a mess. I know we care about each other, but—"

"But what?" Jane nudged me on.

"But we're not quite ready to commit in a public way, you know?" My heart was so full but devoid of words.

"No, actually, I'm not sure what you mean," Jane replied.

My voice trembled as I started counting the reasons on my fingers. "Well, besides the fact that my father will probably disown me, interracial relationships are against the law in Mississippi, so our lives would be in constant danger. Plus, I'll be back at school this year and long-distance relationships are hard to sustain." I sighed. "Everything is against us. We still want to try to see each other whenever possible in the next year. We'll write and phone, of course. But we're just going to have to see how it goes and keep our determination to be able to be together."

Jane gave me one of her knowing looks. "And exactly how *are* things now?"

I grinned at her and actually blushed. "Being able to have that private time together back at our hotel was the best thing that could've happened." That was all I needed to say.

At the morning rest stop, we bought more Cokes and muffins for breakfast. Those around us seemed less disheartened in the dawning light in spite of not having a good night's sleep. The couple next to us was talking about the support the Mississippi Freedom Democratic Party had gotten from so many people.

They turned to include us in their conversation. "Where are y'all from?" the woman asked.

"We're both from New York. We've been down working for the Freedom Summer Project," I answered.

"That was a wonderful project." She reached across the aisle and patted my arm. "Thank you both for doing that. I met a number of volunteers outside the convention hall and so many others from all over."

Her husband spoke up. "We met people from several northern states and lots from Washington, DC. Some folks gave us money for the expenses of our work. It cost a lot to come up here."

I hadn't really thought about that. "How do SNCC and COFO get enough money for things like this?"

"Oh, we couldn't do it without help from famous people like Harry

Belafonte, Joan Baez, and Pete Seeger, people like that. Lordy, they've given so much."

Jane leaned around me and chimed in, "I know Harry Belafonte's contributions have been put toward a lot of bail money this summer."

"For sure, girls. For sure. Y'all spend any time in jail?"

Jane shared her experience of being in jail for a few hours while waiting for bail money to be arranged. I had nothing to share, and I was glad about that.

"Jailing can be pretty scary," the man said. "Right now, I'm worried about our neighbors in Greenwood, the McGhees. Their boy Silas was shot, you know."

I nodded. "Yeah, I know Silas and how he's been trying to desegregate that movie theater."

"Well, Jake, the younger one, was arrested a couple of times right after that for some phony traffic charges. When their mama went to the police station to pay Jake's fine, the policeman wouldn't let her see him or do anything. Finally, he shoved her hard, and she reacted and punched him a good one."

"Oh my God!" Jane and I exclaimed at the same time.

"That policeman went for his gun, but the two COFO workers there held his hand down until another officer came and calmed him down. They handcuffed that poor woman and entered a warrant for her arrest." He let out a deep breath. "I don't know where it will end for that family."

We were quiet for a moment, then I asked, "What do you think the effects will be from the MFDP delegates not being seated at the convention?"

"Hard to tell this soon," the woman said. "I think we'll work even harder to get everyone signed up to vote in November. That's more important now than ever."

"There's going to be some bad fallout," her husband added. "Now Stokely Carmichael can rant that even Democrats are racist. Gives more fuel to the fire. He's wanting to make it less and less of a nonviolent movement and have fewer whites involved. And after this convention, he'll find more folks who are thinking like him."

The man sitting in front of our new friends turned to face us. "You white folks will be going back North, taking the media with you, and we'll be back where we started. No wonder we're thinking nonviolence hasn't worked."

Defensive thoughts reared up in my mind, but I said, "Don't you think all the people who have registered to vote will make a difference?"

"Ha!" he scoffed. "It's one thing to register and another to actually dare to vote." He turned back around, ending our conversation.

I looked at Jane, feeling confused by the man's animosity toward us. She shrugged. We watched the scenery of farms passing by and slowly drifted back to sleep.

~~~

Later, Jane and I said our goodbyes when I got off the bus in Greenwood and she continued on the bus heading farther South.

Harry and I entered the building that housed the Greenwood SNCC office on the second floor. Tom would be there soon to pick us up and take us back to Mystic Springs. Harry and I greeted Mr. Berns, the building's owner who had dared to rent to SNCC. He was a World War II vet whose photography shop occupied the first floor. Upstairs, the Greenwood office was a lot quieter with the volunteers gone. Harry and I were surprised when we walked in and saw the SNCC staffers packing up the office.

"What's going on?" Harry asked, gesturing to all the boxes.

"You haven't heard?" Levon Brown sighed as he sat down. "Two days ago, three of us—me, Lawrence Guyot, and Sam Block—were working up here when there was a big commotion coming from downstairs, shouting and banging noises. It was the Klan wanting to attack us. Mr. Berns tried to warn us and stop them, but they were charging up the steps."

Sam picked up the story. "We took off out the window, ran up to the roof, then jumped onto the roof next door. We got across four buildings that way, all the way to Broadway, then into those woods over there." He pointed out the window. "Just barely made our escape. Anyway, result is Mr. Berns can't rent this space to us anymore, so we're closing down our operations here."

"Where'll you go?" I asked.

"Temporarily, we'll be living and working out of Hattie Miller's place. She has a beauty shop here. We'll try to find a regular office to set up in by the fall."

Hearing Tom's footsteps on the stairs was a welcome sound. "Ready?" he asked as he entered the room.

I, for one, was more than ready to get back to Mystic Springs.

On the drive back, Tom wanted to hear our firsthand accounts of the convention. Our telling of it reflected our different roles this summer as Harry, a SNCC staffer, was able to report on more of the backroom dealings. I, as a volunteer, told about what went on outside on the boardwalk. Our stories showed what a complex event the convention had been.

Tom brought us up to date on Mystic Springs. The volunteers had made their plans to leave; Elizabeth would depart on Sunday, and he, Brenda, and Lynn would head out on Monday.

His big news, though, was that plans had been made for breaking ground on the new building for the school and community center. After church on Sunday, Reverend Hendricks would lead us down to the lot for that event. I smiled to myself. I was sure that Mr. Williamson probably would've given the lot to us eventually, but I believed Lynn's talking with Jenny had something to do with it, and that gave me great pleasure.

21

"There is no real ending. It's just the place where you stop the story."
      —Frank Herbert interview, February 3, 1969

The next few days in Mystic Springs seemed like a whirlwind of activity. Elizabeth was busy packing and trying to finish up the summer's responsibilities. Brenda, Tom, and Lynn were doing the same. I would soon be the only summer volunteer left in Mystic Springs. The idea left me strangely unsettled. The night before, Elizabeth had asked me why I was remaining. Earlier, the main reason was that I wanted to stay where I could see Luke, but I had to admit there was another reason now. I didn't want to have to defend my change of plans to my parents. They didn't mind that I was going into teaching. That's where the approval ended. If I went directly back to school, I could avoid that discussion for a little while.

After I told Mom about my plans to return to Mississippi, both she and Dad had fired off strongly worded letters expressing their disapproval. My mother had obviously not told my father about Luke, though. That would result in an explosion I wanted to put off for as long as I could. Needless to say, the attraction of returning to the "safe, safe North" was losing some of its appeal.

~~~

Before I knew it, it was Sunday and time to go to church with the Johnsons. Elizabeth and I started out with them, our hats on straight, purses neatly in our gloved hands. Anitra and Brenda caught up with us in the next block, and soon Lynn and Mrs. Akers joined the procession. Mrs. Johnson led the way, the mother hen with all her chicks behind her.

Even with the excitement of the groundbreaking ahead of him, Reverend Hendricks felt no compulsion to rush through the service. He asked for as many "hallelujahs" as usual after the hymns we enthusiastically sang. He preached the Word from Genesis and Romans, showing that God was always thinking of us, and when others in the congregation called out, "Amen, brother," and "Preach it," something inside me silently agreed.

When the service was over, Reverend Hendricks led us forth toward the empty lot. I was not at all surprised when someone started singing freedom songs. We sang as we marched on, more and more of the Black community joining us along the way.

We shall not, we shall not be moved,
We shall not, we shall not be moved,
Just like a tree that's planted by the water,
We shall not be moved.
We're fighting for our rights and
We shall not be moved.
We're fighting for our rights and
We shall not be moved.

I loved that song with its many verses, but one verse especially spoke to me. We were singing it as we arrived at the lot.

Black and white together,
We shall not be moved.
Black and white together,
We shall not be moved.
Just like a tree that's planted by the water,
We shall not be moved.

I smiled at Lynn. I did believe that finally getting this lot for SNCC was an effort of Black and white together, but a certain part of that effort was a silent secret between Lynn and me.

At the groundbreaking ceremony, Reverend Hendricks reminded us of all the effort that had gone into getting the property and how special the old Lee Junior High School had been for many of those present.

Additionally, he emphasized how important it would be in the future as a school and community center, which was so desperately needed. He gave thanks for all those involved, even Mr. Williamson and his white school board. I appreciated the tribute he gave to my mother. After a symbolic shovel of dirt was dug, he released us all to our Sunday dinners, and the group broke up following a round of applause, laughter, and goodbyes. I saw Lynn on the edge of the crowd with several little girls clinging to her, all of them with tears moistening their cheeks.

Elizabeth touched my shoulder. "I need to be going," she said. "Derryle's coming to take me to the airport in Jackson. It's a long way back to Massachusetts," she said with a small laugh, "in more ways than one."

We walked back to the Johnsons' house and talked about future plans. She had a teaching job waiting for her near where her parents lived.

"Do you think you might ever want to come back here and teach?" I asked.

She was silent for a minute before she finally replied, "No, I don't think so. I loved what we were doing here. And I know if I'd stayed much longer, I would've wanted to stay forever. But I need to separate myself because life down here is too much, you know? It's too hard, too painful, too...too brutal. Yet, at the same time, the people here are so strong and courageous and beautiful. If I came back, it would wring the life out of me. I want to have something of myself left for myself. I couldn't do that down here. I know that sounds selfish, but..."

It surprised me to hear that coming from her. She'd nailed my feelings and struggles exactly. "No. No, I understand. And you're exactly right. Maybe after this last year at Barnard, I'll change my mind about coming back. Or maybe things will change down here, or—"

"Or maybe pigs will fly, Lenore!" We both laughed as we mounted the steps to the Johnsons' porch.

I'd always hated goodbyes: waving to grandparents as they drove away, leaving friends to go off to college, saying goodbye to college friends at the start of summer vacation. There's something about an ending—no matter how temporary—that's always stirred my emotions. I wanted to avoid it, but I stood with the Johnson family as Elizabeth hugged us all, wiped the tears from her eyes, and settled into Derryle's station wagon. As we turned to go back inside, Mr. Johnson gently patted my shoulder. His kindness made it even harder to hold back my tears. The summer was ending, but I wasn't ready.

That night, with Elizabeth gone, it felt strange having the bed all to myself. Our room was so very quiet, which made time for thoughts to dance around in my head. Thoughts about Luke, about how our lives might be connected, and about the career direction I might take. At Barnard in the spring, I hadn't looked past this summer. Now I realized that my final year of college would be a time of decisions. That was a scary thought. I wasn't sure I would know what to do. There wasn't a clear path in front of me. I simply wanted to follow my emotions, and yet, where would that lead me?

~~~

The next morning, I made my way to the school where Brenda, Tom, and Lynn were meeting Derryle to take them to Jackson. From there, they would scatter to points all across the country. Lynn had been unusually quiet that morning. As the others climbed into the car, she turned to me, threw her arms around me, and hugged me tight. "Oh, Lenore! I'm going to miss you so much! I'll never forget you and this wonderful summer! Your friendship has meant so much to me!" She pulled back and handed me a scrap of paper. "Here's my address. Let's be pen pals, okay?" After one last hug, she also got into the trusty old station wagon.

As I waved goodbye, I was struck with the surprising realization of how much I had come to like and admire Lynn. *Hmm,* I thought to myself. *That's another lesson I learned this summer: How you shouldn't judge a book by its cover because you might feel very differently about someone after you get to know them.*

Anitra went into the classroom, and I greeted Earl and Jimmy as they sauntered up the steps before class was about to start. Then I joined Harry in the back room. "Well, it's just you and me," I said. "What do you have in mind for today?"

We drove far out in the country, past field after field of white cotton. "We'll start out here and work our way toward town," Harry said, stopping at a tiny shack near the road. As we visited with the owners, they were anxious to hear all about the convention in Atlantic City. They regretted that they hadn't signed up before then and readily put their names down as members of the Mississippi Freedom Democratic Party. After a few such stops, there was no doubt in my mind that the Negroes of Mississippi were ready for political action. *It'll be interesting to see how the upcoming election plays out.*

Late that afternoon, we were a few miles outside Mystic Springs when an old blue pickup passed us then made a quick U-turn and pulled up behind us, coming closer and closer. Harry sped up a little but so did the truck. I kept looking back. "Harry, be careful. What do you think they're going to do?"

"We'll be okay. Hang on."

When the truck's grill hit the back of Harry's car, the jolt almost lifted me off the seat. Harry stomped down on the gas pedal, both of his hands tightly gripping the steering wheel.

The next bump was delivered with even more intensity, so I was thankful we were almost back in town. When the truck pulled up beside us. I could barely hear what the boys were shouting, but I didn't need to in order to get the message. The look of pure hatred on the face of a total stranger still made no sense to me.

They swerved toward us, but Harry had the foresight to hit the brakes, and suddenly, we were behind them. They raced off, leaving us in a spray of dust and gravel. Harry pulled over, stopped the car, and exhaled deeply. "You okay?"

After I managed a weak smile and nodded, he pulled the car back onto the road and we drove into town without saying another word.

Back at the office, Harry called the headquarters in Greenwood to report the incident. After he finished, he took one look at me and sat me down on a chair. "You look as white as a sheet!" he remarked, stifling a chuckle. "Forget about it. They were just a couple of yahoos. They can't stand to see a Black man with a white girl. Until you leave, we should probably stay in the Negro community here in Mystic Springs."

We worked on paperwork for a while then planned our route for the next day. When school was over, Anitra stuck her head in the back room. "There were several ideas for your last issue of the paper, Lenore, but the class settled on interviewing you and Harry about the convention. Want to do that tomorrow?"

"Sounds good," said Harry. "Let us know a good time."

"Will do," Anitra agreed, then she disappeared back into the schoolroom to tidy up for the day.

Harry pulled two Cokes from the refrigerator. I'd become more used to the steaming Mississippi heat but still couldn't resist rolling the cold Coke bottle over my face. We sat back and talked about several individuals who might be ready to register, like Mr. Thomas, Sadie's grandfather.

Just then, I heard Anitra scream from the other room before the *whoosh* sound registered. Seconds later, our window exploded inward. *A gunshot?* I wondered as shards of glass cascaded over us, and Harry pushed me to the ground. Splinters from the floor scratched my face, but I tried to press myself even closer to the floorboards. Then a bottle crashed beside me and sent flames streaking around the room. They hissed at us as sheets of papers—weeks of schoolwork and months of registration reports—burst into flames that jumped from pile to pile. Crouching low, Harry tried to smother them, but the heat and smoke curled around us. I choked, unable to breathe. I started to stand up to get away from the searing flames nearby.

"C'mon, girl," Anitra hollered as she jerked me up, and we headed for the door. I gasped for breath and looked back for Harry. *Where is he?*

"Harry, you fool, come on!" Anitra screamed. "You can't save anything."

As we rushed into the open yard, I gasped and gulped in the fresh, clean air. Mrs. Logan appeared from out of nowhere and comforted us, saying, "You're all right, girls. You're safe now."

~~~

Mrs. Johnson, Anabel, and Serene pushed through the throng that had assembled near the school. When they found me, Mrs. Johnson wrapped me in her arms repeating, "Oh, my girl, my poor, poor baby!" She kissed my forehead, and Anabel and Serene rubbed smudges of soot off my arms.

People were scurrying around, shouting. I was shivering, even though I wasn't really cold. "What happened?" I asked.

"Molotov cocktails," Mrs. Dawson answered. "They threw the first one in the front door of the school then two more in the back."

"Harry...Where's Harry?" I cried. The swarm of people blocked my view of the building, but the smoke hovered above them, a blot against the bright blue sky.

"They've taken him to the hospital in Ruleville," someone said.

I put my hand to my mouth. "But what happened?" I was so confused. "Wasn't he right behind us?" I looked at Anitra for an answer, but there was none.

"I think he was trying to save some supplies or something," Mrs. Dawson said. "Someone went in and dragged him out."

Sirens finally sounded as the town's fire truck pulled up. The firemen jumped out and stood with their hands on their hips as one of them checked out the damage. "Looks like y'all got it under control with your hoses," he called out. "We'll leave you to it then." With that, he climbed back on the truck and they took off down the street.

"Humph," Mrs. Johnson grumbled. "Let's get you home."

We were sitting at the kitchen table drinking iced tea when Mac and Reverend Hendricks arrived. I still felt like I was in a tunnel. Voices echoed around me, but I kept hearing the window breaking, which sounded like a gunshot.

Mac pulled out a chair and sat facing me. "Well, I'm glad you and Anitra are okay."

"But Harry?" I asked. "What happened? Is he going to be all right?"

"He should've left and not worried about any of the stuff. But he did, and he stayed a little too long. He's suffering from smoke inhalation, and he's got a concussion from hitting the edge of the table or something when he collapsed. Thank God someone darted in to pull him out."

Mrs. Johnson handed Reverend Hendricks a glass of tea, and he nodded his thanks. "They said he needs to stay in the hospital for observation for the next twenty-four hours, but they expect that he'll be okay. We're all prayin' for him."

I swiped the tears from my cheeks. "Can I see him? Would you take me to the hospital?"

"Best let him rest for now. I'll take you over tomorrow," said Reverend Hendricks.

"Do you know who did it?" I asked.

"No, and we probably never will. Now that James, Mickey, and Andy's bodies were found, the FBI isn't very interested in anything else. A lot of them are leaving. In Hattiesburg, they've gone from sixteen agents to four. Anyway, we've reported it. That's all we can do."

I was afraid to ask, but I needed to know. "How bad was the damage?"

"Fast work on the neighbors' part saved a lot. In the schoolroom, there's only a charring in the middle of the floor. The flames were worse in the back room because of all the papers in the office."

My shoulders sagged. "Why? Why would they do that?"

Mac and Reverend Hendricks exchanged a glance. "After talking to Harry about what happened earlier, we think it was their knee-jerk reaction to seeing a Black man and a young white woman together."

"What? You mean...because Harry and I...but," I couldn't speak through the lump in my throat, "we were only driving back from canvassing. We..." I wanted to say that it wasn't as if Luke and I had been together, but I couldn't. I couldn't go there. What if it *had* been Luke? But it wasn't Luke. It had happened to Harry. Either way, it was still my fault. How could I live with that? How could I live with myself if something happened to Luke because we were together? There were no answers, only tears.

"Lenore, the rest of the volunteers have gone. Your work here is done." Mac's voice was gentle, but I knew the brutal truth that was coming next. He stood and put his hand on my shoulder.

"Freedom Summer is over. It's time for you to go home."

EPILOGUE

"I shall be telling this with a sigh
Somewhere ages and ages hence:
Two roads diverged in a wood, and I—
I took the one less traveled by,
And that has made all the difference."
—Robert Frost, *The Road Not Taken*

Spring 2023
Jackson, Mississippi

We had worked so hard that long-ago summer, and one by one, almost 17,000 Black Mississippians tried to register to vote. Freedom Summer volunteers and members of SNCC and countless other organizations all prodded, encouraged, inspired, and supported them, and yet only 1,600 were actually able to register.

The price for our idealistic efforts was steep: That summer thirty-seven churches were burned or bombed as were the homes of thirty Black citizens. Our arrests were over a thousand, eighty of us were beaten, and four were critically wounded. Bob Moses had warned us there might be deaths, and there were. The world learned about the deaths of Andy Goodman, Mickey Schwerner, and James Chaney, but there was no mention of so many others, named and unnamed. However, there were good statistics too. Forty Freedom Schools were started, which reached over two thousand students. Those schools became the model for the Head Start Program. In addition, many years later, Mac told me that there were slow and important changes in the area of politics. After the work at the Democratic National Convention in 1964, Mississippi never again had

242

another all-white delegation. From then on, Blacks began to have an ever-increasing role in local and state politics.

By the end of Freedom Summer, those of us who forged on through the frustration, the heat, and the violence were tired and discouraged. Yet with the perspective of years, I have come to realize almost everyone who participated in that summer was changed in some way. There were those within SNCC, like Stokely Carmichael, who became more militant. But now with so many intervening years to look back at the effects, the impact we made was impressive. What we volunteers saw and learned and experienced that summer led us to find ways to make a difference in other people's lives. We became teachers, community organizers, counselors, activists, civil rights lawyers, and environmentalists—and our work has made this world a better place.

When I reminisce about Freedom Summer, I think about teaching and the eagerness of the students to learn. I remember the earnestness of Cornelius, the shyness of Thelma, and Josh's newfound joy in discovering the poetry of Langston Hughes. I think of the Johnsons, their courageous hospitality and their fierce pride, and Mrs. Parker with her stories and her grandmother's corn husk doll and the day her daughter helped her call me to say that she had finally voted. I wept with joy. I love to unpack those pleasant memories one by one from the trunk full of experiences from the summer that changed my life. The difficult, unpleasant, and violent memories are there too, and I think of them sometimes. Also there, as if wrapped in tissue paper on the bottom, is the memory I'm not sure I want to unwrap: Luke.

While I was finishing my last year at Barnard, Luke was in Mississippi working with SNCC. The end of Freedom Summer marked a turning point within SNCC. From the beginning, most members of the organization hadn't really wanted the northern whites to come down, and the tension that grew throughout the summer made many of them want to weed out any whites who remained in SNCC. As Stokely's influence grew, SNCC became more militant. In fact, in 1969, the group changed its name to the Student National Coordinating Committee because it no longer believed that nonviolence was working.

After that scare with the Molotov cocktail just because of being seen with Harry, I became more frightened than ever about endangering Luke's life. Even so, after graduation I came back down to Mississippi hoping things would change. But it wasn't meant to be. I was completely involved

243

in my teaching and making a life for myself in Jackson while Luke was very busy in the Delta. It simply became harder and harder for us to try to get together.

When Luke received his draft notice for Vietnam, I felt as if there was no hope for us. He went to Vietnam and lived thirteen months of hell. He managed to come home without being wounded, at least not with visible wounds, but nothing had changed in Mississippi. He was still treated as a second-class citizen.

Luke eventually went to Oakland and joined the Black Panthers. They were doing a lot of good, setting up breakfast programs, clinics, tutoring, and organizing Black neighborhoods. The work took over his life, and the more time he spent with the group, the more enraged he became not only with fighting racism but with the indifference of so many whites and white institutions. He became a bitter, angry person, and he came to see all whites as the root cause of the poor conditions for Black people— and I was white.

I can remember how I felt then. So...lost. When Freedom Summer ended, I'd made a plan. I'd finish school, move to Mississippi, start teaching Black kids, go with Luke until we could actually get married, fight racism, and make the world a better place. Instead, I was only offered a job in a white school with a few token Black students. I was disappointed and saw no future with Luke. Even so, for a time, I became estranged from my parents.

Reflecting on that time in 1964 not only reminds me of the importance of Freedom Summer but also of that long ago feeling I shared with Luke of working for a better world. That yearning is still within me. It makes me face the truth as I consider the state of our nation today. There is still so much work to be done.

The hardest part of that summer wasn't the fatigue, the lack of alone time, the unbearable heat and bugs, or any of the things I'd complained about. The hardest part was facing the truths, the realities that existed outside my safe cocoon.

I had inched my way toward those realities throughout that summer. I'd believed that the narrative of "all men are created equal" and "equal protection under the law" was possible for all Americans, but learning the individual stories and then the deeper narrative of Black Mississippians revealed to me a true history so potent it could not be ignored. We need to acknowledge that history so we can move on from it.

I had gone to Mississippi in 1964 thinking I was working to help "the other." But by peeling back layer by layer of naiveté that summer and in the years since, I have finally arrived at the central core.

The truth is, there is no "other."

READERS GUIDE

1.Do you think that Lenore in her naitivity was the norm for her time and place? What do you think is the norm today for a white girl in similar circumstances?

2. Discuss the tension between the whites and Blacks during training week in Ohio. What would the dynamics be if such a training session were set up today?

3 Freedom Schools were an important part of Freedom Summer. What are your observations about them? Are you aware that there are Freedom Schools in existence today?

4.What do you remember about first learning that three civil rights workers were murdered in Mississippi? Were you aware that there were eight other bodies pulled from the swamps? What does that say about that time and place?

5. How did you react to the developing relationship between Lenore and Luke? How would you have felt about it in 1964?

6. Who was your favorite character in the book? Why?

7. A number of leaders from the Movement have a place in the story. Which of them did you already know about?

8. The issue of voting rights is a central theme in *Layers of Truth*. How does that issue compare with today's state of affairs?

9. Do you think that the efforts of Freedom Summer made a difference?

246

10. If you had been a college student in 1964, would you have volunteered for Freedom Summer? Why or why not?

11. What role did music play in the Civil Rights Movement?

12. What surprised you in *Layers of Truth?* Why?